Penguin Book 14 003001.8
God is an Englishman

Donald Horne has spent many years examining
public affairs, notably as editor of the Sydney
Observer and, later, the *Bulletin*. He has
written a number of books including *The Permit,
Southern Exposure* (with David Beal), *The Education
of Young Donald,* and the highly successful and
provocative analysis of modern Australia,
The Lucky Country. He lives in Sydney but has
travelled a good deal through Asia and the Pacific,
Europe, Britain (where he lived for five years) and
in the United States.
He is married, with two children.

DONALD HORNE

GOD IS AN ENGLISHMAN

PENGUIN BOOKS

Penguin Books Ltd, Harmondsworth, Middlesex, England
Penguin Books Australia Ltd, Ringwood, Victoria, Australia

—

First published in Penguin Books 1969
Reprinted 1970

—

Copyright © Donald Horne 1969

—

Printed in Australia for Penguin Books Australia Ltd
at The Griffin Press, Adelaide
Set in Linotype Baskerville

CONTENTS

CONTENTS

PROLOGUE

Come to Britain

Some delay in the mails had meant that a number of my copies of the *Economist* had not arrived until just before we were leaving for England. Even if they had arrived sooner there would not have been enough spare time to read them: there were too many things to pack, too many farewells to make, and in any case I had gone on working until the night before we sailed from Sydney. However, I was in the habit of reading everything in the *Economist* – how the Smith's Potato Chips dividends were going as well as the balance of payments position – and as we sailed across the Great Australian Bight and then into the Indian Ocean it was what successive issues of the *Economist* had to say about the apparent failure of the recent devaluation of sterling that seemed to matter more than the news on the ship's radio of developments in China or the election of a new Australian Prime Minister. I had got into the habit of underlining sentences and sometimes whole paragraphs in the *Economist,* so that I could go over them again: I remember giving a double underline to *you can't get a quart out of a pint pot* and *you can't have your cake and eat it.* Obviously the future of Great Britain was soon to be decided. It was 1949.

Nothing signficantly new has been added to *la crise anglaise* since then, except the extension of its existence. It has become institutionalized: it is now part of the British way of life. Come to Britain and see the crisis. Those who were born during the devaluation of 1949 were starting their careers by the devaluation of 1967; they had spent the intervening eighteen years growing up in a nation that could never seem officially certain of itself for more than two years on end. This crisis is not likely to subside through any external event (except through a catastrophe, in which case it would explode rather than subside). The show of humility that became fashionable at the beginning of 1968 merely represented a heightening of crisis. It is a crisis of habit, in particular of affronted habits of self-esteem, and of tenacious habits of social value. It is almost entirely a crisis of the élites, not of the ordinary people (who still display remarkable patience), and it is likely to end only through sharp, painful change or in a slow breeding-out of the habits of the élites.

In either case the crisis can end only with a new definition of British society and of British history. This redefinition must be one in which there can be pride, but pride in those things that are still relevant to the age, not in the irrelevant or, even more to the point, in things that did not happen, or, if they did happen, were not unique to Britain. But as well as pride, perhaps there must also be a sense of historical shame and a recognition of the baseness in origin of some of those habits that still characterize the British.

That I am Australian has been useful in writing this book, but only in the sense that I have those advantages of part-involvement, part-detachment that are not so available to those who see things from the centre in London. The book is in no sense a contrast between Britain and Australia, a my-country-is-better-than-yours kind of thing. In fact while I was writing the book it occurred to me again and again not only how many of Australia's faults were connected with Australia's historical origin, but also how many of Australia's virtues were also the virtues of that provincial Britain, the aspirations of which Australians express more openly, sometimes giving themselves more native credit than they have earned.

In writing about one country there are implicit comparisons with others. Here and there I have made some of them explicit. To understand Britain better it can be illuminating to compare it in certain respects with Japan, or America, or Germany, or Sweden, or France, or Canada, or Holland. Or for that matter with Nigeria, or Cambodia, or Brazil. But the process must stop there. There is no final overall judgement on Britain in this book that compares it with the other 124 nations in the world. Such judgements are impossible. To criticize Britain in some particular way is not to say that other countries cannot be criticized in the same way; and to criticize Britain overall is not to rank it in relation to all the other countries. If you contrast them with the aspirations we have about the human race all nations are a mess.

In an account of a live and complex society that has not been simplified into history some of the tenses of verbs may later seem to be wrong and some of the sense of direction may later seem to be false. This book attempts to write about the *now* of British society, and how things got that way; there is a continual casting back into the past to explain how present situations arose. In a sense it is a historical study of Britain in the twentieth century, with a special emphasis on the last twenty years or so.

Although the style in which it is written is of a kind that might sometimes suggest otherwise, the book is not intended to be mainly argumentative or polemical; it is an attempt to establish points of observation and then to take from them a comprehensive look at the various kinds of British habits and institutions. In a sense it is a kind of Guide to Britain, some of it written from an unfamiliar point of view. In attempting to examine senses of similarity and difference in Britain, Part I establishes the observation posts and points of reference. Part II looks at the world from Britain, and looks back at

Britain from the world, sometimes casting its observations very generally, talking about the world as much as about Britain, since neither of them can yet be understood without the other. Part III concerns itself in detail and in turn with various aspects of élite life in Britain. That so much of the book is concerned with the élites rather than with the ordinary people of Britain is the main reason why so much of the book is so critical. It should be added that where it is sharpest in its criticisms the book may be concerned with beliefs that I once held myself.

Part I

LOOKING FOR BRITAIN

1. BRITAIN IS BEST

A lucky country

Britain is one of the fortunate countries. It has not suffered foreign invasion for nine hundred years. It has not had a revolution since the seventeenth century, or civil war since the eighteenth. It picked up its Empire without much trouble and although when it let the Empire go something between half a million and a million people died, only a few of them were British. In the Second World War Britain did not suffer the ravages of Germany, Poland, Russia, or Japan, nor the humiliations of the defeated nations of Western Europe. Its language is the mother tongue of four of the world's most prosperous nations, one of them the world's principal power, and its institutions have been imitated, if not always maintained, by twenty or so other countries. It is one of fewer than a dozen nations where democratic government has survived throughout the century: it has little racial violence; almost all of its peoples speak a common language; and, despite their divisions, they have formed such remarkably peaceful and stable relations with each other that tolerance and liberty are sometimes taken as uniquely British virtues. Britain is the eleventh most populous nation in the world, the third nuclear power, the greatest owner of overseas assets after the United States, the financier of a third of the world's trade, and the world's second biggest exporter; and, while it no longer leads the list in any significant statistic of production, it still has some good third, fourth, and fifth bests.

As a member of one of the world's dozen most prosperous nations, the average inhabitant of Britain spends on gambling and drink as much or more than most people in the world earn; he eats as well as anyone and more than most; he dies less often from road accidents than anyone in all but seven nations; his babies die less often than the babies in all but eight other nations; he reads more newspapers than anyone except the Swedes. So far as the statistics of higher education are concerned he belongs to the eleventh most educated nation in the world.

It is true that according to the estimates at present fashionable, Britain is only something more than half as prosperous as the United States, but if its prosperity is compared with that of nations of roughly equal size, it is twice as prosperous as Italy and eight times as prosperous as Nigeria. Compared with Japan, a nation of roughly similar geographical predicament, all Britain's prosperity indicators are at least twice as good, or at least one and a half times as good, or at least one and a quarter times as good as Japan's – except for book and newspaper production (only slightly better), infant mortality (a bit worse), and higher education (quantitatively, only half as good as Japan).

To the British, of course, it would seem insultingly irrelevant to compare what they see as their unsatisfactory lot with that of the peoples of Nigeria or Brazil, or even of Italy or Japan. The British problem is not a general failure but the particular failure to find consolation for the chagrins of fallen pride. To be third best at the production of synthetic rubber does not cheer up a nation which acquired its present habits when it was still used to the idea that it should be recognized as being best at anything it turned its hand to. The British have not been taught to be thankful for their great mercies. Old habits have inculcated such an effortless assumption of superiority that now, with their world supremacy collapsed, it can seem irrelevant to tell them that they should be thankful for what they have.

Following the myth that the British are a uniquely pragmatic people, some British intellectuals decry the whole idea that societies, like people, need some sense of orientation. But it would seem obvious enough from what the British now say about themselves that what gets on their nerves is that they no longer know who they are. A people once poised and assured have become socially awkward. They have not yet learned how to talk in a new way about their past, their present, and their future. Their traditional idea of their past is so irrelevant to their present that, except to those who are lost in nostalgia, it seems merely absurd; and there has not yet begun that critically important task of writing an interpretation of their past that would make their present and their future understandable and invigorating. Their future is now a blank, and their present a series of unlikely, disconnected events. It is as if they had been ordered both to break step and to mark time.

This has happened to a nation that more than almost any other threw up the misty shapes of an official sense of identity so thickly that it is still almost impossible to penetrate through its dark images to reality. The gradual realization of the irrelevance of these images has been like the slow and painful withdrawal of an addictive drug: it has not been replaced by a return to reality, but by confusion and pain, and, to some extent, by a reaching out for substitutes.

The result is a sense of emptiness: the hollow men of the day manufacture slogans, but the ordinary people find no interest in them; in all this rubbish the people cannot identify themselves for long with shifting, contradictory, and sometimes desperate expedients. The economy is seen to drift from one danger to the next, the trade unions to reaffirm old and irrelevant wisdoms, government officials to revolve like slow fans, merely stirring the air. The middle classes refurbish snobberies; the working classes are attacked as Admass dolts. Life goes on, of course. People grow up, marry, die, are happy or sad: things follow their patterns. But the result is so unbelievable that, according to a survey, nearly half the young people of Britain fantazise about emigration. To their ennui the old-fashioned look of Britain adds further incredibility. The vast plains of squalid streets and the dismal blacks and greys of the squashed-out provincial cities meshing into each other like clusters of blackheads are an affront to the dreams of the TV commercials, the bright disc jackets, the pop excitements that probably offer some of the main aspirations of young people in Britain. Even the weather is now old-fashioned. Before the cult of the sun shone through into their imagination the British managed to use their infinite capacity for fanciful make-believe to see virtues in their dismal weather, even attributing to it what they saw as their sense of moderation. Now it is hard to imagine that the balance of payments crisis can be solved in a country cursed with such a fitful summer and such a dark, dripping winter.

Britain was not alone in this problem of having to decide that it is not what it once seemed to be and that it is time it now seemed to be something else. But it was almost alone in the stubbornness with which it failed to make a real attempt at facing up to the task. The nations of 'Asia', for instance, with the collapse of European colonialism, had to redefine themselves as belonging to a geo-political concept that did not previously exist: and, as well as attempting to redefine themselves as living in their own neighbourhoods (a task that some of them, like India and Indonesia, evaded for a while, preferring a fictional globalism inherited from the colonial power), they have also had to strengthen, or even to create, their own nationalisms, and, with the foreigners gone, to provide new relations between the peoples of their own societies. Japan, its power and ambition blown up by the Americans, had to rethink itself as a peaceful nation, global only in trade. America itself, with much internal political violence, shocked itself out of its old isolationist dream to become the principal world power and now shocks itself into the beginnings of the realization that Negroes are Americans. The Netherlands, its colonies gone, built Europort. Germany had to cease being the ruthless conqueror of Europe and become a divided nation. As a result of the almost complete reshuffle of power that came from the disasters of the Second World War and, in the developed societies, as a result of the new potentials of the technological age, brutal to old wisdoms, almost every nation in the world has been forced to think of itself as something else. What nation has tried less hard to do this than Britain?

The envy of them all

It was in the eighteenth century that the British began to be proud of themselves in a global way. Since the Elizabethan Age there had been an English rhetoric of national pride, contained in the idea that England was the nation elected by God to carry out his new purposes, but in the eighteenth century there began that special type of boasting that saw the British as a nation divinely destined to the secular purpose of being supreme throughout the world. 'Rule, Britannia!' became the second national song, along with the new 'God Save the King', affirming that the very land mass of Britain had erupted out of the Atlantic as an act of divine will so that Britons could 'rule the waves'. The oceans belonged to *them*. Two centuries later Britannia was still to sit there on her sandbank on the back of a British penny, girt in shield, helmet, and trident, ready for battle against the French, to depart only in 1971 because the new decimal penny wasn't big enough to fit her in.

But in the eighteenth century there was a freshness in the idea that Britannia would do the ruling. Britannia was not an old widow, fat, dowdy, and worried about her declining percentages. She was an Athena, still good in bed. And behind eighteenth century British boasting there was not simply blind self-assurance but the lively, realistic anxiety of the newcomer. 'Great Britain' had been formed only with the incorporation of Scotland at the beginning of the century, but, although losing the old American colonies, the British were to seize so much of the world that Earth seemed a place they were allowed by God to plunder and manipulate to the power and advantage of their enterprise. By the third quarter of the century there was already talk of a 'British Empire' that could rival the Roman. The whole overseas world was a place where the British could have fun and make money. By the end of the century, when Ireland was added directly to the realm (through mass bribery of the Irish Parliament), the eighteenth century seemed to have been 'the English century'.

Commercial racketeering, military adventure, enterprise, a love of sailing and discovery, and hatred of the French prompted the acquisition of Empire, and the images of justification were at first simple: mainly that it was a self-evident truth that Britannia was best. Whatever her avarice demanded was rightly hers to grab. But while it was common enough in the eighteenth century for those British who were indifferent to conquest to attack as rogues the conquerors among their fellow countrymen, those British who enjoyed conquest usually sweetened their Might with some Right. Their particular Right was that in their aristocratic autocracy, corruption, and muddle they had begun to see themselves as uniquely solving the paradox of the tension between order and liberty; British institutions were seen as the paradigm of what political and judicial things should be. In 'Rule, Britannia!' as well as ruling the waves, Britons were declared to be not only great but free, 'the envy of them all'. It was in the combination of a belief in freedom and a belief in the uniquely good character of British institutions that self-righteousness and hypocrisy, the true *vices anglais*, began. Because Britain was believed to be 'free' there was later to develop the idea that even her imperialism was motivated by the impulses of freedom, and that her subject social classes or subject colonies were fortunate because their masters were free. Sustaining stiff-backed British high-handedness was the belief that Great Britain was the fountainhead of good institutions so that both in Britain and in its Empire many arbitrary acts were to be carried out in the name of freedom and many scandals were to be concealed in the name of good institutions. British *hauteur* retains to this day a feeling that institutions 'abroad' are in reality gimcrack. Part of Britain's present predicament is that the kind of British who got into the habit of believing such things cannot, in their honesty, still believe that Britain sets to the world an example of how it should run its affairs, yet they feel that it should still be doing so.

Another part of their difficulty lies in the relentless stubbornness of the concept of 'freedom' that developed in the eighteenth century. This was at first mainly a 'freedom' of nation and class – above all, a national freedom against threats from Europe and an aristocratic freedom against centralized absolutism. It was because of the outspokenness of the privileged, for example, that the novel, the newspaper, and the circulating library can be said to have been invented in eighteenth century Britain. But the rhetoric of 'freedom' in Britain in its aspirations for the future was limited and even reactionary compared with the rhetoric of progress in America, in France, and in some other continental countries. The British rejected most of the concepts of an equality of a human brotherhood. This aristocratic sense of freedom continued into the nineteenth century and still survives; it has been tempered by humanitarianism and meliorism, but, apart from the British democratic radical movements (now dead) and the underground mateships of working-class life, those who spoke up for freedom in Britain did not in their habits of thought really believe that men were brothers. Some of the most elegant spokesmen for British freedom have seen it as carefully contrived by regulation and privilege out of a brutish world; freedom is seen as a sense of predictability and tolerance protected from violence by the police.

In an attempt to evade Britain's real perplexities some of the British now try to write off British world power, as if it were merely a small aberration in the otherwise cosy life of Little England, sometimes even suggesting that the British won their Empire by some kind of amusing chance, as if at cards. The more honest of them might see British power extending for about two hundred years (from the gaining of India to its loss), but to cut it down to size they compare it with the Hapsburg monarchy, which lasted a bit longer, or the Ottoman Empire, which lasted more than twice as long, and then say: *Look, it wasn't much of an Empire after all!* The less honest confine British power to the fifty-five years between the defeat of Napoleon and the foundation of Bismarck's Germany, something you need hardly notice. This second concept evades the fact that the regular modern forms of British global self-righteousness began in the eighteenth century (although of earlier and different origin); that they have been running for so long is why they still matter. The habits of world arrogance run deeper in contemporary Britain than the habits of European arrogance run in contemporary Germany. But even those who admit that the corruption of habits of world power began in the eighteenth century are misleading if they compare this power with that of the Ottoman Turks or the Hapsburgs, because not only had Britain by the end of the eighteenth century acquired a widely spread *overseas* Empire different in kind from the contiguous land territories of the Turks and the

Austrians, and with settlements of its own people growing from colonies into nations; in a double triumph it was also in the eighteenth century that the industrial revolution began in Britain, further strengthening its self-righteousness and hypocrisy, giving it a world strength not previously imaginable, and extending imperialism to the homeland as the subject natives of Britain assembled in colonies of slums to feed the mills.

But important as the eighteenth century was to Britain, there were other parts of the eighteenth century idea that later vanished. These were the parts of it that gave a greater sense of modernity to eighteenth century Britain than has characterized most of twentieth century Britain: a liking for the non-traditional; a sense of enterprise, manifest in discovery and invention; a sense of *change*. In a century in which parts of the oligarchies saw life as something new and experimental, the aristocratic idea had more dash to it, something more than the mere insistence on antiquity and hierarchy into which it has now dismally collapsed. Eighteenth century Britain was not absorbed in that strange worship of the old that was later to turn it into a museum.

The Northern and the Southern Metaphors

It was the kind of changes the industrial revolution made to British images of Britain that first produced the ambivalence about what Britain *is* that still puzzles both foreigners and the British themselves. The industrial revolution changed Britain, but it did not change it enough. It came with the force of novelty – nobody had had an industrial revolution before – but it came with some of the weaknesses of novelty. It did not throw up enough strong new habits and forms. It enervated the aristocratic values of the period that preceded it: but it did not destroy them. It softened them; it turned them into effete travesties; but in this weakened and pernicious form they survived and even now continue to work much whimsical mischief.

Since some of the famous ideologists of the industrial revolution were Scotsmen and Northern English, and since the south of England was at first less affected by change, the ambivalence caused by the industrial revolution in Britain might be expressed, illuminatingly if not altogether accurately, in metaphors of the North and the South.

In the *Northern Metaphor* Britain is pragmatic, empirical, calculating, Puritan*, bourgeois, enterprising, adventurous, scientific, serious, and believes in struggle. Its sinful excess is a ruthless avarice, rationalized in the belief that the prime impulse in all human beings is a rational, calculating, economic self-interest.

In the *Southern Metaphor* Britain is romantic, illogical, muddled, divinely lucky, Anglican, aristocratic, traditional, frivolous, and believes in order and tradition. Its sinful excess is a ruthless pride, rationalized in the belief that men are born to serve.

In both metaphors it was assumed that *Britain is best*, but in the contest as to what Britain was best *at* it was, on the whole, the Southern Metaphor that won. Suffused by the ideologies of pride in world power (more attractive to aristocratic values), the ideology of the industrial revolution became muted: it continued to have an intellectual following and it made an enormous impression on some intellectuals 'abroad', but it did not prevail. The Southern Metaphor led the British to believe that their success was due not to their own efforts but to the whimsicalities of their superior nature. It was not for

* The emphasis on Protestantism can become so great that it is forgotten that the Renaissance, growing from developments in the Middle Ages, began in Catholic countries, then more civilized than the north, and that even modern financial institutions and expansionary commercialism were first Catholic until the Counter-Reformation broke them up.

what they did but for what they were that destiny had
rewarded them so lavishly.

In talking about themselves the British still become
confused between these two metaphors, speaking, for
instance, of their 'empiricism' when what they are really
talking about is their romanticism; or contrasting their
own 'pragmatism' (by which they mean dreamy muddle-
headedness) with the fanaticism of Western Europeans
(who can now be more pragmatic than the British).
Although the Northern Metaphor produced perhaps the
most rational defence of the motives of self-interest
known to European civilization, the Southern Metaphor,
while acknowledging self-interest, turned it into an
ideology of 'service'. Among the other English-speaking
nations the confusions became even greater. An American
would come to Britain and talk about 'freedom', to find
that the British did not know what he was talking about.

It was symptomatic of the Southern Metaphor that
there was both pride in bigness and whimsical pride in
smallness. The British could not – and still cannot –
imagine what size they are. In the period of the *pax
Britannica*, between the downfall of Napoleon and the
rise of Germany, when British power was at its most
complete, the idea began to develop that Britain, the
land of liberty, would not only teach other nations how
to live; she would also champion the smaller nations
against the great. Not much championing went on and
the century ended with Britain sending four hundred
thousand troops to conquer a small nation in South
Africa. But, in the manner of the Southern Metaphor,
there was some genuine idealism of 'smallness' and some
of the British sense of order and fairness meant that
when the Boers were beaten the British welcomed them
to London with placards greeting OUR FRIENDS THE
ENEMY. The cult of smallness, growing out of the
Southern Metaphor, meant that the British wanted to
eat their cake and say that they did not have it, to be

the greatest Empire the world had ever known, and a cosy little island. On the one hand, in the frenzies of late nineteenth century imperialism and nationalist jingoism, they put forward a racialist theory of the divine superiority of 'the British race'; on the other hand, they congratulated themselves on their English reserve. One thing its rulers liked about the Empire was its cosiness: it made the world a familiar place. Even the British lions, put up all over the world to celebrate power, had pussycats' faces.

The Imperial Metaphor

As the nineteenth century progressed the habits of power grew as hard as Portland stone. It was a century of genuine radicalism, of considerable desire for reform and of remarkable self-criticism but alongside these movements, sometimes feeding on them, the sense of self-righteousness became stronger and stronger, finally bursting out into the Imperial Metaphor. In the Imperial Metaphor Britain's self-interests were humanity's. By commanding power, Britain served the world: to fail to serve British interests was a dereliction of duty to mankind. To say 'British interests are eternal' was not to be boastful or selfish; it was merely as if God had said 'I am eternal'. The world came alive through the exhilaration of British world pride: and if the Chinese and Ottoman Empires were to collapse and Britain could pick up most of the pieces the world would then become an even bigger place. If British prestige was harmed, both Britain and the world would lose their history.

It was the lesson of the sporting fields, the public schools, the cadet forces, the Boy Scouts, the press, the pulpit, that British morality was the backbone of civilization. Britain's power and prestige, those invaluable assets of humanity, were based on the moral conduct and character of Englishmen. Even the liberal enemies of imperialism, who saw its corruption, were themselves corrupted by the *scope* of the imperial imagination: to them the morality of Britain was also becoming the motive force in world progress. It is this imperial obsession with the moral importance of Britain to the world that, still entrenched after the imperial power has gone, creates some of the present 'crises' and gives others an irrelevant moral tone, so that even a currency crisis becomes a matter of morality.

When they bellowed out 'Land of Hope and Glory', after boasting of how their Empire was going to increase *ad infinitum* the British thanked God for making them mighty and then asked him for more: on the other hand, in the same song, they boasted of themselves as the 'mother of the free'. It was by these means that they both enjoyed their power and took away the frank contemplation of its duplicities and harshness. They then congratulated themselves that they weren't really very interested in the details of their Empire: this, now produced as an example of their true goodness, was in fact the final expression of their arrogance.

The reality was that Britain was the first great world power. There may never again be a nation to equal the world power Britain seemed to hold in the nineteenth century. (Whether it 'really' held such power or not does not matter: it is the belief in its power that changes a people's concept of itself.) The Empires of the Chinese, the Indians, the Romans, and the Arabs looked like world Empires in that they extended to what then seemed the horizons of civilization; now, however, they seem only regional Empires, as the Empires of the Turks and the Hapsburgs were. At its height in the nineteenth century the British Navy *did* appear to command all the seas and to be the final arbiter of who went where. It appeared to affect events more significantly than a contemporary nuclear super-power because the Navy appeared to be a weapon that could be used; decisions in the imperial city affected events more *directly* in more countries of more different types in more different parts of the world than had ever happened before or (one hopes) will ever happen again; the British economy dominated world trade and, even to a greater extent, world finance. Britain now saw itself as out of the world, believing it could exist in splendid isolation, removed from the tyranny of history. When in 1897 the British assembled 165 of their warships at Spithead, letting off their guns ostensibly to salute their old Queen, they were really saluting their imperial selves.

It is true that by 1897 the forces that were to destroy British power already existed, but the British went on for another two generations as if their power had never been challenged. It was in the nineteenth century that British imperialism was institutionalized in its modern form in history texts, in the financial institution of the City, in the public schools, in the armed services, in the colonial and imperial services, and above all in a sense of self-justifying morality. All this lived on when power declined, perhaps becoming more rigid, still seeming 'real'. The pompous boasts of Empire, laced with eighteenth century concepts of good government and 'freedom', brayed out above the old juggernaut as, its faded garlands of victory still around the necks of its ceremonial pussycats, it lumbered on for another four decades, undismayed by the Great War, picking up more conquests from the defeated Germans and Turks, not finally halting until the Japanese knocked off its wheels in 1942, whereupon, for the next twenty years, it fell to bits. But it still left behind the habits that had at first engendered it. Young people in Britain who may scorn the old ways, or pay no attention to them, are nevertheless still affected by them. They grow up not realizing why they act as they do. The old sense of superiority survives, even among those who cannot believe in it, or have never seen its proof. The past is now evaded, or excused. But perhaps it is only a frank and painful contemplation of the past that can finally destroy it.

Five decades of fantasy

It is no special criticism of Britain to say that the 1920s and 1930s were a twilight period of illusion. The special power of Europe came to an end in these two decades, chasing old dreams. As in a dying universe, some stars exploded in flames and others shrivelled and went cold. Official Britain was one of the stars that shrivelled and went cold. Nothing new came out of the land of uniquely good government. In this dispirited time (when most of the men who now run Britain grew up), Britain still gyrated with pomp in old habits, held now more rigidly than ever, perhaps because the life was going out of them. Britain was the Heart of the World's Greatest Empire, the Workshop of the World, the World's Bank, the World's Oldest Democracy, the Mother of the Free, and so forth, but it provided no leadership.

With the First World War won, Britain had put down its shutters on Europe. Its power was something to be paraded in ancient ceremonies, or to shoot at natives abroad, but it was not to be risked in the affairs of Europe, or for any great cause. Stupefied in old ways, its gaze whimsically transfixed on itself, Britain let the years slip by. It was Britain's decision, or no one's, that Hitler should be checked, but Britain did not make any decision. In 1933, when Hitler withdrew Germany from the League of Nations, Britain, for the first time in twenty-two years, won the Davis Cup. Since they had failed to use their power responsibly in the 1930s, perhaps it was just that they should lose it in the 1940s and 1950s.

All the same their defence of their island, their provision of a base from which the Americans could attack, and their wartime rhetoric gave the British after the Second World War a prestige in Europe that they had never enjoyed before and that might have been used to some purpose by a more serious-minded people. They were hardly aware of their opportunity. The shutters went down again. Lost in a mixture of pride and self-pity, the

British went about their own affairs as if they were still the affairs of the world; they were not interested in the possibility that they might have led Western Europe into a new relationship with itself. Years later they twice begged on the doorstep to be let into an edifice of which they might have been the architect and principal builder.

No catastrophe knocked the rubbish out of Britain, as it blew away much that was old and repellent in the Western European nations. The war enervated Britain, but there was no new start. The old habits of self-importance remained, even if they were pursued with decreasing credibility, and the old institutions survived, as if skeletons could obtain new flesh to clothe themselves again. One self-delusion followed another, as if Britain were governed by a series of advertising copywriters who dashed off slogans for products that did not exist. The illusion that Britain had really become a Welfare State was followed by the illusion that the Empire had really been replaced by a Commonwealth. With the return of the Tories, the coronation of Elizabeth II and the ascent of Everest by Hillary there was the proclamation of a 'New Elizabethan Age'. During the Suez crisis, it was briefly 'Great Britain Again', trying to grab back 'our canal'. Then there were 'winds of change'. Then the British were told they had 'never had it so good'. Then they became 'Swinging Britain' until the 1967 devaluation produced the 'I'm Backing Britain' campaign and the Union Jack that had become an article of apparel also became an advertising gimmick. New words and slogans, new manufactured images, floated through the air, but none of them landed. On occasions such as the invasion of the Caribbean island of Anguilla history repeated itself as farce. Perhaps the most credible event of the 1960s was that Sir Francis Chichester sailed around the world by himself in a boat. It did not matter. But at least it was true.

In the last two decades intellectual fashions and other vogues have whizzed around, but nothing seems to stick.

New energies shoot out, clash with each other and expire. Among the nostalgia and bombast much that is good goes on in Britain: in some fields what goes on is better than ever. But it does not *seem* so. Energy and talent flame out, but then they seem to fall back into smoke. People play roles. But in what play? On what stage? Lost between worlds, they can find reality only in the excitements of the fashion and the entertainment businesses.

In their twin crises of deciding who they are going to be now, and how they are going to pay their bills, the British still rely on old habits. Yet it is a characteristic of states that the habits that most help their success also bring them down when the conditions for success change. The institutions and attitudes that made Britain's 'greatness' work are now the very reasons why Britain is so slow to change. It is not so much when they have lost power but when they cannot destroy their old habits and old institutions that nations are said to decay.

2. AVERAGE BRITS

A people with no name

A Bavarian or a Prussian is happy enough to say 'I am a German', just as a Breton or a Gascon will say 'I am a Frenchman'. Citizens of newly created nations quickly got used to saying 'I am an Indonesian' or 'I am a Pakistani' or 'I am a Ghanaian'. But while a Scot or a Welshman or a Northern Irishman might say 'I am British', it is more likely than not that a resident of the England region of the United Kingdom of Great Britain and Northern Ireland will say 'I am English'; and it is not unlikely that a Scot or a Welshman (knowing this English habit) will assert himself as Scottish or Welsh instead of 'British'. When it comes to finding a noun, instead of an adjective, for one single inhabitant of the United Kingdom there is no noun that is acceptable. Alone among the nations, the British cannot speak of themselves in the singular. While the plural 'the British' is accepted, even if some of the English do not care to use it, no one accepts 'a Briton' or 'a Britisher'; the one is archaic, the other is American: and although there can be an Englishman, a Scotsman, a Welshman, and an Irishman no one has attempted to float 'a Britishman'.

In the school texts that formed so many of the minds now supposed to be concerning themselves with Britain's present problems, 'Britain' and 'Great Britain' were mainly *geographical* expressions naming a large island to the west of continental Europe. In history texts 'Britain' was a Roman colony that disappeared. Proper history began when 'England' – named after the invading Angles – was created in the ninth century out of some barbaric chieftaincies in the south of the island. When the Welsh were conquered in the thirteenth century they became

part of this history, not having had a history before,
except as 'Ancient Britons', a kind of gallant but primitive aboriginal people; and when the political entity of
'Great Britain' was formed in the eighteenth century the
Scots emerged from whatever darkness they had lived in
and entered English history. It continued to be the case
that it was an *Englishman*'s word that was his bond and
an *Englishman*'s home that was his castle. It is true that
the Empire was 'British', not 'English', but 'Britishness'
was of a lower quality than 'Englishness', a bit ersatz,
something for popular consumption, its standard debased
for export use, something to keep the Scots or the
Canadians happy. It was 'England', not 'Britain', that
was the centrepiece of this great enterprise.

Fowler's *Modern English Usage* has been one of the
many instruments by which the particular quirks of
Southern England have been passed off on earnest people
everywhere who seek a correctness in their lives, and his
comments (in the first edition) on the word 'British'
tell one a great deal about Southern English snobbery:

How should an Englishman utter the words *Great Britain*
with the glow of emotion that for him goes for *England*? He
talks the *English* language: he has been taught *English* history as one tale from Alfred to George V; he has known in
his youth how many Frenchmen are a match for one *Englishman*; he has heard of the word of an *Englishman* & of *English*
fair play, scorns certain things as *un-English*, & aspires to be
an *English* gentleman; he knows that *England* expects every
man to do his duty. . . . Who speaks of a British gentleman,
British home life, British tailoring, or British writers, or con-
demns with an 'un-British'? On the other hand the British
matron, the British parent & the British public have an un-
enviable notoriety. The attempt to forbid thirty millions of
people the use of the only names that for them are in tune
with patriotic emotion, or to compel them to stop & think
whether they mean their country in a narrower or a wider
sense each time they name it, is doomed to failure. The most
that can be expected is that the provocative words should be

abstained from on the more provocative occasions, & that when Scots & others are likely to be within earshot Britain & British should be inserted as tokens, but no more, of what is really meant.

Before proceeding with the question of what words to use in describing the people who are the subject of this book, it might be noted that in this statement of Fowler's there is the public arrogance of the colonialist talking about the natives to fellow colonialists in the natives' presence; there is both the ineffable allusiveness of the private joke, shared only by a clique and a *de haut en bas* patronage towards lesser breeds, regarding *their* pride as absurd, but one's own pride as inviolate; and there is the ability to regard oneself, although dominant, as nevertheless a cuddly little thing, deserving justice. Humour is used as a veil for vanity so that if an outsider attacks the vanity it can be disclaimed and he can be made appear as that worst of outsiders, an outsider without a sense of humour – a position I have just put myself into by taking Fowler seriously.

As Australian government officials began to examine their own nation's relations with Britain in a spirit of independence that seemed to make sense of circumstance, they needed a new word when they talked among themselves about the inhabitants of the United Kingdom: 'the English' and 'the British' were both too full of old associations, as were traditional Australian derogatory slang words such as 'the Poms' or 'the Chooms'. The habit grew of referring to them as 'the Brits', a term that allowed one to start all over again, as if trying to characterize a newly discovered tribe. In this chapter we shall look for some of the characteristics of the Brits.

The fringe lands

In looking for the Brits one might first see them as a kind of association of separate nations in which the sense of separate nationality is stronger now that the benefits of union seem less. Within this association the fringe lands of Scotland, Wales, and Northern Ireland make up less than a fifth of the total population of the United Kingdom, yet they have sharply defined senses of identity, as separate from the English – or at least the Southern English – as they are from each other. I shall now consider them one by one.

The Welsh are divided from the English by feelings of class, language, race, history, religion, and region. Their folk self-consciousness is institutionally defined and they still show some of the apprehensive and resentful fears of a people dominated by an alien culture. As a *race* the Welsh see themselves as smaller than the English, darker, neater, more finely formed. As a *region* (only 136 miles long by 40 to 100 miles wide) the Welsh are conscious of themselves as a valley people, squeezed in by hills, with a sense of remote wilderness in their barren uplands and rugged coast. As a *language*, Welsh is the tongue of the sixteenth century Welsh translation of the Bible: they are a 'people of the Book'. As a *religious* group Welsh Wesleyanism distinguishes Wales from Anglican England, taking colour from song rather than ceremony, with a greater feeling of individual guilt and with a kind of hopeful, puritanical, mysterious tribalism. For *history*, they were a set of principalities and chieftaincies conquered by an English king in the thirteenth century whose upper classes later attached themselves to the English court so completely that only the ordinary people were left feeling that they were Welshmen. They have memories of the peasant world of the eighteenth and nineteenth centuries and of their great period at the end of the nineteenth century and beginning of the twentieth when their rural populism broke through into English politics and for a while seemed to threaten the old order. A sense of attitude to *class* is also common to them, apparently dividing them from the English. Their religion is the religion of the poor and outcast; their history is the history of peasants and workers; even their sense of their region and of their own persons is one of smallness: as Southern England is fundamentally divided by a social cult, Wales is fundamentally democratic. Two-thirds of its population is crammed into the industrialized south; and in the valleys made black by the industrial revolution Wales threw up one of the world's heroic proletarian cultures, comradely, turbulent, ruffianly, cynical even of the great battles in which it engaged against its bosses, living with the myth of a true hero: that the end of the struggle might be disaster. Perhaps this is the 'real' tradition of Wales, rather than the memory of little peasants in their green valleys.

Scotland, like Wales, is distinguished from England by region, religion, language, class, and history, but in different ways. Its rugged highlands are lumped together in the north, populated now mainly by memories; to the south there are under-peopled uplands; but it is in the lowlands stretching between these two configurations that most of the people live, spread out across one big plain rather than cut up into a lot of small valleys. There is little pleasant greenness in the Scottish geographical imagination; even the Lowlanders, if they think of their physical environment, are likely to think of steep falls of grey rock, mountain mists, a rugged wilderness. Even their towns can look as if they were cut out of grey rock. The Scots do not see themselves as a little people but as a flinty, rocklike people. Like Welsh Methodism the Puritanism of their religion distinguishes itself from Anglicanism, but Presbyterianism is a more self-important religion, formed as much from its struggles against the Catholics as against the English, its Calvinism making it more European than British. It is part of the Reformation, not, like Methodism, an eighteenth century afterthought. And although its congregations themselves appoint ruling elders and ministers by democratic election, the elected can soon become as authoritarian as those who receive their office by privilege. It is a national and parish religion rather than a folk and tribal one, and, when she is in Scotland, by one of those expediencies of power which the English conceal as amusing anomalies, the Anglican Queen is the head of it. The Scots' literature gives them a sense of cohesion, but, unlike Welsh, Gaelic is almost dead and they have to read their literature in English. Among those who do not adopt the Southern English accent, the granite-like Scotch accent, however, gives a sense of difference strangely respected by the English, who do not despise it as they despise the lilting softness of the Welsh. Like the Welsh, and unlike the Southern English, Scotch society in its general tone is democratic, but there is again a difference. Scots recognize their common humanity, they see themselves as all belonging to the one species, but their immediate rulers have been Scotsmen, not Englishmen, and a sense of authority is also part of their history. But the greatest difference between the Scots and the Welsh is that Scotland is a kingdom that was destroyed by the action of its rulers, who combined it with England in the eighteenth century out of economic calculation. It was a European state, playing a part in European history, and now, despite its different (and more democratic) education system, its different institutions and legal system, it is an English province, even if much of the detailed administration of government is devolved upon civil servants in Edinburgh. Yet a sovereign state of Scotland would sit at the United Nations between Senegal and Saudi Arabia, an old nation between two new states. Since destroyed nations freeze their national memories at the time of submission, their nationhood becomes a museum of old things, not relevant to a later age. The 'auld sang' of Scotland's nationhood is an echo of something sung a long time ago. Now it doesn't make sense. But without it what is a Scotsman? A Briton?

The Irish did not see themselves as part of the British nation, not even as a province of it, but as its colony; their uprisings against the British were anti-colonialist guerrilla wars. After most of the Irish broke away in the 1920s, establishing their own nation in the predominantly Catholic part of their island, there was left Northern Ireland, now run by the ascendant Protestants, descendants of English and Scottish settlers, and outnumbering the Catholics two to one. For them self-definition came to be expressed in terms of mutual fear, hatred, and bigotry, but they are nevertheless Irish, or more Irish than anything else, speaking like the Irish, charming like the Irish, adopting Irish ways but unable to *be* Irish, and at the same time unable to be truly English or Scottish, for all the pictures of the Queen they put up in their cottages or the going to the Kirk on Sundays. They are transfixed in the colonial settler's dilemma, being one thing while pretending to be another, unfulfilled in either. Constitutionally they live in a kind of federal relationship with Britain, with their own parliament handling local affairs and also sending representatives to the British Parliament; politically they live in a museum of old causes (held together by masonic and papist conspiracies), the main party division being between the Unionists who hold to union with Britain, and the Nationalists and Independents who support union with Ireland by boycotting the parliament to which they are elected; economically, since Belfast, the capital, was thrown up by Britain's industrial revolution their prosperity depends on British exports and there is a large permanent eddy of unemployment; emotionally the Northern Irish may be the only true 'British'. Without 'Britishness' they are simply Irishmen. Perhaps ecumenism may finally lead to a fusion of the two Irelands, although bitterness has become such a habit that it may be a long time before it is washed away by a generation bored with its irrelevance.

In their 'British' moods the Southern English do not allow significant difference to the folk of Wales, the lost kingdom of Scotland, and the federated colony of Northern Ireland, and they regard as absurd the nationalism of these three fringe nations, although Scottish nationalism at least may threaten the Union. But at other times they use widely accepted images of difference. In these moments the Welsh are a dark, dirty, lying, superstitious, untrustworthy, primitive people – the aboriginal natives. The Scots, whose energy and brains are believed to have done much to build English prosperity and Empire and to have produced much of the ideology of the Northern Metaphor, are given more respect – as a uniquely mean, calculating people. Very shrewd, the Scots. In the Highland Scots, however, whose predecessors the English partly destroyed because they were Catholics and supporters of a rival claimant to the throne, the English find romantic images of an aristocratic recklessness and simplicity that now seems to be missing from their own lives. In general the Irish are charming cheats, amusing but untrustworthy boasters, but so far as the Northern Irish are concerned, the English had forgotten, until the violence of 1969, that they still existed. When their excesses then brought them back into mind, patronizing indifference turned to scorn or embarrassment.

A provincial nation

When I first arrived in Britain there were still people who would call me a 'colonial', by which they meant not that most of the inhabitants of Australia and of the British Isles were of common origin but that Australians were a kind of by-product of the present generations of Britain. At first I would try to explain that Australians were derived not from *them* but from a history that they were also derived from. But this merely put me on the defensive as one of those long-winded bores who wanted to talk about himself. I began to attack. Yes, I would say, in a certain sense Australians were colonial. But was not England a nation that was largely *provincial*? This question usually managed to give sufficient offence to cause a change in subject.

Yet, given the peculiar relationship of Britain to its

metropolis and the countryside that immediately surrounds it, there would be a case for saying that Britain
is the world's most provincial nation, that because of
their location more of its people are condemned to a
sense of dowdy second-rateness (or its opposite, a hollow
boasting that nobody hears) than is usually characteristic
of a people. To live in England anywhere north of somewhere around Warwickshire is to be provincial, and
although a few escape its implications by social class or
education, a majority of Englishmen are born into this
second-rate condition with an overriding sense of being
nothing much at all. Normally the English regard even
the fringe lands more as provinces than as nationalities,
perhaps seeing freaks like Scottish Highlanders or Cor-
nishmen as something different, but seeing Belfast, Glas-
gow, and Cardiff primarily as examples of the one thing
– as cities that are *not London*, cities that seem to them
as dreary as Manchester or Birmingham, Leeds or Liver-
pool, Sheffield or Bradford.

The English do not see rural villages as provincial, or
ancient cathedral towns that happen to be in the provinces. Things that are rural or ancient are at the very
heart of Southern English snobberies, even if they occur
in the North. *Provincialism is to live in or near an industrial town to which the industrial revolution gave its
significant modern form.* It is because most English people
live in or near such towns and cities, stuck together in
great black lumps, that most English people are provincial.

The buildings in a provincial city are grimy with the
smoke of the factories that spawned them: to the sunless-
ness of winter there is added even in summer a haze of
filth. The heart of the city is empty. There is nothing
much to do in it at night: nowhere much to eat, nowhere
much to go. Empty streets. Empty buildings. There is no
pride of display in its architecture, no sense of distinctive
belongingness. With true British 'freedom', its buildings
were just run up anyhow: lumps of buildings pressed

against each other, but ignoring each other, like Londoners in their underground railway. The provincial rich do not live in the city, giving it life and self-importance. They are ashamed of the city. At night they leave the city to the poor who still inhabit its outer rind. The hangers-on of the rich live in the housing estates while the rich themselves prefer to live in rural villages where they can act as if they were country gentry, not belonging to the city. Their wives may do their shopping in London. Manchester, Britain's second largest conurbation, stretches for twenty miles, encompassing four million people, but most of them would deny that they belonged to Manchester. They would consider themselves as belonging to the suburb or town or village that is their postal address. It is as if the Japanese who crowd into the Kyoto-Osaka complex, of roughly the same size and population, tried to deny that this was where they lived. There is a difference, of course. Amid the muddle of modern Kyoto there are also the architectural relics of old Japan. There is nothing much of old England in Manchester and the British seemed to come to despise the new, as if modern architecture ended at the beginning of the nineteenth century and it did not matter much how one built anything after that.

It is the sense of not really belonging to anything very much that provides the heart of British provincialism and helps to distinguish Britain from most other nations. An American does not necessarily feel out of things if he does not live in Washington. In their own ways New York, Chicago, and San Francisco are rival world metropolises, representing other 'choices' of what an American might be: but beyond these world-famous centres there are dozens of other large towns that, to those who live in them, are towns of importance, with their own pride. Some are the centres of regional politics; some are centres of international industrial importance; some simply have a self-assured belief in themselves; they all have their own newspapers and special sense of community. And along with them are the 'small towns', providing yet another view of what American life might be. In the same way, to turn from the largest English-speaking nation to the smallest, a New Zealander does not feel deprived of significance by his special location within his islands: he might despise New Zealand altogether, looking 'overseas' (to Australia or Britain) for importance, but there is nothing necessarily second rate to him in living in one part of New Zealand rather than another: his nearest city or market town will seem to him to be an important part of New Zealand. In Germany, a Bavarian does not see Munich as a nothing-place, and even industrial cities such as Dusseldorf or Hamburg have their own feeling of significance. Until recently, Italy was notoriously satisfied with itself as a series of city states and even now Milan can seem as important as Rome. With France the contrast breaks down. There can be the same sense of a dowdy emptiness in life in an industrial provincial city as there is in Britain. But France, in population, is not almost all provincial cities piled next to each other. Unlike Britain, but like most other countries, France also maintained a strong peasantry, which provided a rival view of life to that of metropolitanism and, with the associated market towns, provided a challenge to its social strength.

Earlier, when the North industrialized, there was a struggle between North and South. Words like 'Manchester' and 'Birmingham' were not only names of cities: they were also the names of world schools of economics or philosophies of Empire – restless, revolutionary, modernizing philosophies that became world words. But London and its surrounding counties absorbed this vitality like a sponge, taking some of it and discarding the rest. The sons of provincial enterprise went to public schools and universities and came out of them looking backwards. In Manchester they still sometimes try to see their city as a centre of innovation, but when they quote their old boast that 'what Manchester thinks today the rest of the world thinks tomorrow' they are themselves now merely looking backwards. Who cares what Manchester thinks? It might now be more true to say that what Manchester thinks today Osaka thought several years ago.

The people of the provinces could not revolt, like colonies, against the indestructible vanity of London; nor, like faded nationalities, could they put on kilts or sing at eisteddfods; they could not even quite define their predicament or properly feel resentful about it. They were deprived of national recognition of their provincial style, which was dismissed by the Southern English as uppity unobligingness; and while the accents of the fringe lands of suppressed nationality were at least accepted as something in their own right, even if they were not always liked, the provincial accents were not lovable like a cockney's or the accents of the people of the few rural counties, but a kind of assertion of ignorance by those who couldn't be bothered to learn how to talk properly.

The best they could do with themselves was to proclaim their lack of affectation, their more democratic manners; or sometimes, in revolt against the sophistication of the metropolis, they might assert their philistinism, in the manner of the American small town; or they might proclaim their greater 'shrewdness'. But in the long twentieth century twilight of the radical Northern Metaphor, it did not matter much what the provinces did. As their once vigorous industries grew old and feeble in the 1930s they became to the metropolis 'the depressed areas', embarrassingly poor relations one must do something about when one got round to it. After the war their apparently ancient factories and cobwebbed markets were symbols of Britain's failure in international trade; they were compared with all those spanking new gadgets the Germans and the Japanese had contrived out of the rubble. Now that new enterprise is moving in the provinces there is again some interest in them as money-makers, but more new enterprise is moving around London, in South-East England, than in the provinces.

Nations usually have a belief that there is, somewhere in their society, a mysterious force that can regenerate them. Sometimes it is simply The People, whose inherent goodness will cleanse a nation. Sometimes it is The Peasantry, whose honest shrewdness will restore the state's health. Sometimes it is The Small Town, whose simplicity will make sense of sophisticated intricacy. Sometimes it is The Barbarian, whose crudeness will shock the effete. Sometimes it is The Great Leader, who will right wrongs and destroy the wicked. In one way or the other, all of these myths are held (if by different kinds of people) in the United States. It is doubtful if any of them are held by the Southern English élites. They prefer the myths of a static society in which each generation is born to repeat the style of the previous generation and in which change is usually a form of bad taste. Their earthly symbol of the good life is a peaceful rural village inhabited by businessmen living in converted cottages. Yet there is an older myth, the myth of John Bull, blunt, bold, unaffected, courageous, down-to-earth. John Bull was a country squire. But his image is also that of the *provincial*. He is almost forgotten now and there is no myth of regeneration from the provinces: but it may now be in the making. In the entertainment business provincial accents are in vogue; in breast-beating the virtues called for are those of the Northern Metaphor; 'abrasiveness' is sometimes praised (if only in theory) as against gentility. However, the most significant thing to have come out of the North so far may have been the Beatles. But now they live in London, with M.B.Es. granted to them by the principal Londoner.

Megalopolis

When a traveller is moving around London it breaks up into little things. It has more self-definition than Tokyo (which is all corners), but it does not offer any grand prospect – such as the dreaming spires of New York or the logicality of the Place de la Concorde – that can hold the attention with its familiarity so that the traveller knows he has arrived. The mind slips away from the edginess, the mini-grandeur of Trafalgar Square, feeling more reassured by the double-decker buses and the peculiar construction of the taxis. Even the magniloquence of the Mall, with Buckingham Palace at the end of it, is inhibited by its isolation, as if it were the one good room in the house, kept for best. It is along the Thames that the imagination can be most easily transfixed, not from any architectural pattern, but from a recognition of history in the ugly Norman Tower, in St Paul's Cathedral defeated in a squabbling skyline, in the florid Victorian Revival of the Houses of Parliament, in the looted 'Cleopatra's Needle', trophy of Empire, in Shackleton's South Pole ship, reminder of true adventure stories, in the old guzzling confidence of the Savoy Hotel, and in the fake dawn of the Festival Hall, erected during a Festival of Britain that proved a thanksgiving without a harvest. The other appeal to the imagination occurs when you walk away from the river and slip back among the great entertainment centres that are now London's other principal face, the world of titled stage stars, pop singers, clothing designers, celebrity authors, striptease joints, famous controversialists, psychedelic basements, expense account restaurants, and Princess Margaret. Celebrity London is, in its own field, at least more lively and 'real' than Pageantry London, but nostalgia still sits on this city. What it principally looks back to is not Roman London or Shakespeare's London or Sir Christopher Wren's London. It looks back to the days before yesterday – when at Westminster a man could dream of being a Viceroy of India or in the City a man could dream of cornering the world market in bananas. The last great successful event in the history of this nostalgic London was Goering's blitz.

Most of the people who live in London do not spend their days sitting in the House of Lords or their nights starring in a West End production. Although these ordinary Londoners have a recognition of the importance of being a Londoner, it is mostly a muted self-assurance, different from the sharp arrogance of the Parisian, because it has been challenged by their uncertainty of their relationship to other Londoners. There was a contempt for the manual worker, often accepted by the manual worker himself in a city that on the surface seemed to live in a white collar, if sometimes a smudged one. A truer symbol of London than the old cockney cheekiness became a desire to speak with a BBC accent. Attempts to ape upper-class manners led to a type of pretentious low-status rudeness, the use of lah-di-dahness to put other people in their place.

The word 'spiv' was much used for a while in London after the Second World War. For those who were not pleased with how things were going it was comforting to imagine that what was wrong with the world was that blackmarketeers and barrow boys had taken over. When top people in Britain fail to do their jobs properly they often like to imagine that it is not really their fault, that the real trouble is that 'the wrong people' have somehow been let in. Although the word went out of use, spivvery became smart. In their dress, their accent and their ways of life, some of the operators in the city's celebrity business successfully challenged its old, outwardly stiff conventions and were applauded for displaying London's new robustness. As well as the old style of Saville Row, with arrogant servitors cutting their dukes according to pattern, there was the new style of Carnaby Street, cheeky, fanciful, acting as if the old London did not exist, cutting it up and putting it together again in a funny way, just for a giggle. In British cinema and TV dramas the new stylists, with their open assertions of the old spivvery, suggest the underground vitality that lurked in 1930s Hollywood movies in the form of 'the gangster'. But go-getting has been going on in London throughout its history. London is a city of ambitions and deals. It has always been a sharp-witted, tricky place. So much power does not fall into the lap of a metropolis ungrabbed, and the exercise of power must always be accompanied by some cheating. When it was the centre of world power, London had to develop a master style in duplicity and self-interest. Now as the centre of mass culture in Britain, the place that produces the mass circulation newspapers, the radio and TV programmes, the ads and the general manufacturing of chic, it must constantly contrive assaults on the commonsense of its fellow countrymen. In other countries the burden of so many inevitable dishonesties usually gets shared around among several cities; but London, because it is the centre of almost everything, has accumulated a collectivity of dishonesty.

A megalopolis usually generates a vast amount of intellectual and cultural activity. London was slower to put its wares on the streets than most other Western European capitals, partly because of the furtiveness with which the upper-middle-class English preferred to treat their cities. It is now a 'creative centre' like other European capitals, even if success in the arts is still rewarded by a cottage in the country; but when it looks to the export of its intellectual, cultural, and entertainment artefacts its gaze is usually trans-oceanic rather than cross-channel. The West End thinks of Broadway. The publishing business thinks of New York. Although once a centre of Empire, London has not been a cosmopolitan city. Its concern was more with itself as a centre for English-speakers, who seemed to be 'the world'. Despite its enormous contributions, London is still made curiously blind by the fact that its principal admirers are provincials, colonials, East Coast Americans, who praise it as a world centre when they mean that it has different things to offer from their own home towns. Although not as parochial as Paris, London still rejects, not only from Europe, but even from other English-speaking nations – in particular, America – alternate world views of what life might be about. 'Reject' suggests a conscious awareness; perhaps it is more a matter of a genteel, muddled despair.

Even in the English-speaking world London still sometimes tries to save itself from the realization that it is only third best to Washington and New York, although still ahead of Chicago and San Francisco. It is content with the habit of extending its influence outward and seeing the world come to London. A surprisingly small part of the world in fact comes to London. Britain has fewer visitors than France or Spain (which have more than three times as many) or Austria, Germany, and Switzerland (which have twice as many). It comes sixth on the list, just ahead of Belgium and Yugoslavia.

To some of the 'true' Southern English, London itself seems to have some of the characteristics that Londoners find in the provincial cities. Even some Londoners do not see themselves as Londoners but as residents of one of the surrounding counties; even if they live right in London, it is with some detachment, as if they were just on a holiday. The preference for the out-of-date can make London itself seem a ghastly modern invention. In this regard the final snobbery is to despise all cities and towns, apart from a few small old cathedral settlements. To take this view is to despise most of Britain.

Explosions of religion

Another way of looking at Britain is to see its social landscape as something thrown up by the earthquakes and eruptions of earlier religious disturbances. There are not likely to be any more eruptions; but from the sixteenth to the nineteenth centuries the colouring of the relations of the British with Europe and with themselves was so often religious that one could rewrite modern British history as a history of religious struggle. This would be false, but it would give a view of events as they seemed to the participants. There was such an interplay between religious doctrine on the one hand and imperial, national, and social struggle on the other that they sometimes became inextricable. As it later became fashionable to put everything into economic terms, it was a fashion of the times to put things into religious terms so that matters initiated by secular impulse could also acquire a religious colouring. But the prevailing importance of religion as a way of discussing things also gave religion its own initiatives, which were none the less real because they also acquired a secular colouring.

If a man from Mars surveyed the religions of Britain as social organisms, without concerning himself with their peculiarly religious nature, after noting that they were more diverse than in any other European nation, he would find something like this:

In England the Church of England is the only church of antiquity. It occupies all the ancient ecclesiastical buildings. It crowns the Monarch and conducts the other religious ceremonies of state. It does most of the burying (a third of it burning) and most of the marrying. But while more than three-quarters of the population are baptized in this faith in its capacity as the state faith, only a tenth of them regularly go to its services, so that its active membership is not much greater than that of the Catholic Church, which is otherwise a minor church, something of a parvenu, housed in modern buildings, still somewhat furtive, largely lower-class, with most of its adherents of immigrant origin, rather vulgar and not really rich in history like the English Church. There is a greater sense of The People in the Catholic Church; but it is in the Methodist chapels in England, although they hold a smaller allegiance, that the goodness of The People is most celebrated. *In Scotland,* however, the Church of England is a minor cult, a negation of Scottishness in favour of the alien. The ancient and powerful church is the Presbyterian Church of Scotland, embodying the national consciousness. Its only rival is the Catholic Church, also strong, more assertive than in England, with almost three-quarters as many followers as the Church of Scotland. *In Wales* the principal church is again different, this time the Methodist Church, embodying the ideals of the Welsh Folk, with the Church of England the main alternative religion. *In Northern Ireland,* in terms of its following, the Catholic Church is strongest, expressing one ideal of what the Irish people are. The Presbyterian Church is almost as strong in numbers, expressing an alternative ideal of what the Northern Irish people are. The Church of England, third in strength, expresses an ideal not so much of what the Northern Irish are as of what they should be.

The Church of England was conceived out of a marriage of national politics and the spirit of religious change; but once the initial reforming was done it opposed dissent. Further change occurred outside the church, although sometimes seeping into it. It was as a national and a class church that it finally took on its distinctive character. In the quarrels with Spain and then with France in defence of the British Crown against Catholic claimants and their knavish European backers, foreigners and Catholicism became almost synonymous. When Catholics were suppressed in Britain it was sometimes because they were seen as European spies plotting the downfall of the Monarch and the alienation of the kingdom; even now Europe can sometimes seem a foreign place inhabited by Catholics. Respect for Catholicism is strongest in Britain as a kind of tourist attraction (drinking chianti, eating in the sun), but even here it is its exoticism that appeals as, on other occasions, it is its exoticism that repels. The English are even less aware of the Protestant traditions of Europe. When confronted with Protestant Europe, the Church of England (which sees itself as both Protestant and Catholic) becomes more Catholic than the Catholics. Both Lutheranism and Calvinism are not *real* religions, like Anglicanism: the churches that sprang from them are just jumped-up affairs that came out of the Reformation, not truly derived from Ancient History, as Anglicanism is.

As a social force within England the Church of England conducted itself with great disgrace. It became the expression not only of national pride but of the vanity of the top dogs of Britain. Its parsons and bishops became prime offenders in the class exclusiveness of the Southern Metaphor and they were drawn almost entirely from the ruling

classes. Using the Monarch as their instrument, the great
political oligarchs of England appointed the bishops from
among their own numbers, and the parsons were appointed directly by local oligarchs, again from their own
numbers and without reference to anybody else. Even
now most of the clerics of this church speak with the voice
and manners of privilege. Now that the financial rackets
of the Church have been dismantled or have withered
away, more of the voices and manners have been
acquired to conceal a more humble origin than used to be
the case. If they are to change, churches, like individuals,
must sometimes confess to their sins, and atone for them;
in the case of churches the confession may refer to matters
of history, with the atonement to be performed by the
descendants of that history. But there is no real sign that
the Church of England is sorry for the way it served the
interests of English inhumanity. It is true that parts of it
developed a conscience in the nineteenth century and that
this tradition still exists. But with true Southern Englishness much of its energies are still concerned with genteel
flapdoodle, and even in its questionings and breast-
tappings it usually ends up quietly congratulating itself
on being what it is.

The Catholic Church. Perhaps the most convincingly
ecumenical thing the Pope could do would be to fall on
his knees in St Peter's and make a general confession of all
the past sins of his church. (The heads of the other
churches should, of course, also be down on their knees
beside him.) But, because of his church's long suppression
and its continuing powerlessness in Britain, the Catholic
Cardinal of Westminster need not make a similar confession. Pockets of Catholicism survived the long Anglican
suppression, but it would be misleading to see a continuity
between the modern English Catholic Church and the
English Catholic Church of before the Reformation.
Catholicism in England can be more accurately thought
of as a sub-culture of Irish-English origin, in social form
sharing some of the solid fraternalism of Methodism. It is

a product of the struggle between England and Ireland, and a reminder of England's passing victory. 'God Bless Our Pope' was more important than, or as important as, 'God Save the Queen'. Much parish activity was spent in fund-raising to maintain the ghetto schools and many sermons were devoted to attacks on mixed marriages, to maintain the ghetto numbers. The priest was a man of the people, sharing their secular aspirations. Ecumenism is now making a difference to all this, but compared with countries like Australia or the United States, in which the minority Catholic pressure sometimes seemed a threat to the Protestant majority, Catholics in England carried on their fraternity with such outward modesty that they were hardly noticed, and their true character became greatly misrepresented, principally by the kind of Catholics who had attended a Catholic version of the public schools and spoke the language of the ascendancy, but mainly because its most literate lay figures have been converts: G. K. Chesterton saw Catholicism as a kind of endless hike through the Pyrenees in which the hearty Catholic marchers sang their jolly peasant songs and quaffed their wine; Graham Greene sometimes seemed to confuse Catholicism with a Protestantism between guilty parties; Evelyn Waugh confused it with Anglicanism – the Catholic was the true antique English gentleman and it seemed unlikely that the Pope was really an Italian.

The Presbyterians saw Anglican prelacy as almost as great a work of the devil as Roman papacy. Succeeding only in Scotland, in double encounters against both the Scottish Catholics and the English Anglicans, Presbyterianism formed a tough religion which, despite its greater democracy (or because of it), was also more puritan and more ready to attempt to control personal lives than Anglicanism, the latter being more concerned with state and social conformity than with individual peccadilloes; at the same time its Calvinism made it more European, less a thing in itself, with related movements in the Low Countries and in France.

The Methodists. The Independent Protestants were crushed in England until the reform movements of the eighteenth century, when expression was finally given to ideals, first expressed more than a hundred years before, that both Anglicanism and Presbyterianism were tyrannical church structures, that what mattered in Christianity was personal belief and that the only church structure needed was a loose association of independent chapels. But the Independents (now mainly become Methodists) did more than that: they expressed the revolt of that other England, the great mass of its people, that did not belong to, nor yet belongs to, the official face of the community. They were an expression of a searching for common humanity that can break through the surface and mock the English hierarchies. When Cromwell's victorious army sat down at Putney to decide how to build the New Jerusalem, they thought of how 'the poorest he that is in England hath a life to live as the greatest he'. The Methodist revival was one of the revolts of the poorest he against the greatest he. Its continued existence is one of those institutionalizations of fraternalism that save the ordinary people of England from the insults that come from above, and perhaps also by their quietism save the greatest he's from their reckoning.

One of the social functions of religion in Britain is to provide fraternities for the poorest he's. Perhaps now that the old controversies have gone, religious differences are most significant as expressions of differences in nationality and attitudes to class. Considered in this way, as social organisms, fraternities of working-class Catholics have more in common with fraternities of working-class Methodists than with some grand English gentleman who professes to be an Anglo-Catholic.

The Victorian Metaphor

What the four diverse religions of Britain are most likely to mean in practice, insofar as they affect people's conduct, is the one thing. Sometimes it is called Puritanism, sometimes the Nonconformist Conscience. These are unsatisfactory terms, since this thing permeates the Catholic and Anglican Churches as well as the other two: it also permeates the Catholic Church in Ireland. A better word, although it may give a somewhat false historical emphasis, is Victorianism, a force that spread beyond the British Isles to English-speaking peoples everywhere, that conflicted with other metaphors of what Britain was, and that was, in a sense, *the* British religion. Its painful transformation is one of the things that contemporary Britain is about.

Victorianism produced an overall slummocky quality in people's lives, a turning away from a sharp sense of form into a muddiness of style in housing, domestic artefacts and cooking, which took on a general middling, muddling quality. The aesthetic was a wicked denial of the serious: the true forms of art were the sentimental and the well-intentioned. There was a nervousness about delighting in the world of the senses, and at the same time a final avoidance of the intellect. In morality the worst offences were sexual or other ways of enjoying oneself. The tone was one of individual guilt and social horror. In morality there was an emphasis on not lying, but this produced hypocrisy rather than honesty since there was so little that could be discussed. Obedience, industriousness, and neatness were taken to be among the greatest virtues, even in their perverted or insane forms, but intelligence was distrusted as a kind of deviousness. The cautious and the conformist were best; to do what had been done before was safest. The heroic style was distrusted and sometimes taken even as an expression of criminality. Tradition became a conservative preference for the rules of old thumbs, and a sense of order became a sense of obedience, lacking aspiration. Humility, or its outward forms, was encouraged, leading to much clever use of humility as a way of attracting attention. Pride was not so much personal as conformist, an attempt to sink individuality into collectivity. One had to know one's place in society, and accept it as a self-evident truth that it was for society's good that it should be ordered hierarchically. This involved awkward and subdued personal relationships, in which people had to work out who they were in relation to each other. At the same time it was obligatory to be charitable to those of lower status, who were taken to be less fortunate than oneself: sometimes one might try to elevate their consciences or alleviate their lack of material prosperity; at other times to be thankful for one's own station in life was a sufficient act of charity. Although the senses were otherwise officially denied, a solid English comfort was admired, as much for its conformity and spiritual assurance as for its pleasure; it was a highly materialist world in which money went to the good, and in the house of the father of the founder of the Christian religion there were many Victorian mansions.

In generalizing about the Victorian Metaphor in this way one can isolate it and describe it, but it is recognized that this is not, of course, a description of the Victorian Age, in which there were many other forces. Nor should it be taken as being exactly the same as the earlier Puritanism, which was revolutionary rather than conservative. For that matter the Victorian Age should not be thought of on the whole as a Puritan Age, in the sense of sensual asceticism. The brothels and gin palaces boomed, the prostitutes swarmed in the streets. It became ascetic in public rhetoric, but only partly in practice. Most of the alleged libertinism of contemporary Britain is nothing much compared with what was available in Victorian London. It is also recognized that within a particular individual or institution the Victorian Metaphor might have contested with quite different forces. Its high solemnity, for instance, contested with the frivolity of the Southern Metaphor, perhaps thereby strengthening that strange sadness with which many of the English took their pleasures. Its emphasis on industriousness and some of the other northern virtues gave it similarities to the Northern Metaphor, but its hostility to enterprise put it in opposition. Its dislike of the heroic brought it into conflict with the Imperial Metaphor, giving imperialism that *fin de siècle* mixture of boastfulness and a sense of doom so marked in Kipling's 'Recessional': it was only because the British were 'good' (that is, unsexy, teetotal, hard-working philistines) that they had their Empire; if they started drinking or sleeping with the natives the Empire would go away.

The Victorian Metaphor enjoyed perhaps its greatest vogue as a way of describing Britain thirty to forty years after Victoria was dead. In the nineteenth century it faced opposition from other views, but, adding to itself bits of the other metaphors, it was not effectively challenged until the 1930s. King George V was made to appear its symbol, with his son its necessary anti-symbol. This was not an accurate description of the King, but it seemed credible of his public person that he was a true Victorian and that the Empire had been won by Boy Scouts. Compared with the hysteria of the more heroic European societies of the 1930s and their oppressive theatricality of style, there even seemed to be great human benefits in the very stodginess of British neo-Victorianism. But now the trains are running on time all over Western Europe.

A working-class nation

Visitors to Britain may stay there for several years without observing one of the central facts about the British people: that Britain (and even more, England) is one of the world's most working-class nations. Unless they are stupefied by travel literature, they do not have to be in London long to realize that London is not all Vanessa Redgrave, Her Majesty the Queen, and Sir Laurence Olivier. But they may never travel through the industrial agglomerations of the North; England outside London may seem the green and pleasant land of the picture post-cards, with picturesque villages and delightful market towns. Visitors do not even see much of London's working-class areas. Their main impression of Britain is of a lower-middle-class and middle-class country, a white-collar country whose main relief is the green pride of the countryside. Yet, of the prosperous industrial societies, Britain is not remarkable for its percentage of white-collar workers. In Australia, for instance, white-collar workers already outnumber manual workers and are increasing at three times their rate; but in England there are still twice as many manual workers as there are white-collar workers. Manual workers make up about two-thirds of the working population and the proportion of them is still growing.

I have mentioned Australia because, if statistically greater weight is given to larger cities than small, Australia comes out as the most urbanized nation in the world and Britain is second.* Both nations have the same exceptionally low rate of rural dwellers (only one in five) and in both of them a remarkable proportion of the population lives in the seven biggest cities (about 40 per cent in Britain's case, about 55 per cent in Australia's). But the Australian cities are strung out across a continent and the distance between the two of them that are farthest apart is as great as the distance from London to Istanbul; and, although only one in ten of the Australian work force is employed on the land (in Britain it is only one in twenty), there is nevertheless, because of the impact on the imagination of its vastness, and because of its great economic value as a source of export revenue, a *presence* of the land in Australia that offsets Australia's otherwise uniquely high suburbanism in the same way that, in other countries, the effects of town life are offset by the presence of a peasantry. In Britain the land itself is honorific merely as a picturesque form of antiquity – a kind of national plaything: there is no sense of *the soil*.

* By this standard of comparison Australia scores 68 per cent for urbanization and Britain 65.9 per cent. (The United States scores 42.3 per cent.)

And since there is no strong class of independent small-holders of the kind that diversifies social, political, and economic life and affects a nation's vision of itself, such as can be found in the United States as well as in France and the other nations of Europe, there is nothing to offset Britain's predominantly working-class nature. *The typical Brit is a manual worker living in a provincial town.* It is he who is Britain's 'backbone', but he doesn't get even the thanks of being recognized as the average Briton.

It can be illuminating to look at this Average Briton as if his predecessors were immigrants who settled parts of their own country. The same disasters in village and market-town life that threw nineteenth century emigrants out to the colonies threw the predecessors of the Average Briton into the industrial towns that grew up around the new factories. Sometimes one member of a family might emigrate to Canada looking for a living and his brother might emigrate to Manchester. Each of them found himself in a 'new', improvising society that was making itself up as it went along, crudely formed, without much idealism about it (except for what came from hymns in Methodist chapels or – for the Irish – from their priests). Such civic idealism as there was became concentrated on the pursuit of *money* – and he didn't have any money. Somewhere or other there were the Monarch and the Archbishop of Canterbury and all the other nobs; they had plenty of money, but they didn't seem to care much about *him*. The main consolations of the new existence were scepticism and comradeship; what happened didn't really matter, but if it did happen, it was best that it should happen in the company of a man's mates. But things proceeded more slowly in Manchester than they did in Canada as the Canadian cousin began to fulfil what still seemed mere dreams in Manchester, and by the time of the First World War, when their descendants met on the Western Front, they saw themselves as two different races. In Canada the masters' plans had gone wrong.

In the industrial colonies of Britain the masters also retreated, if more slowly, as the main degradations of the earlier rural life were blown away. The agitations of the poor inflamed the fears of some of the rich and revolted the conscience of some of the privileged. The beginnings of the modern suburban common man were born. When transferred to the factories, the child labour of the villages, traditional to their history, seemed so nakedly wrong that it was abolished and there began to be adopted among some manual workers the view, already obtaining in the other classes, that children were special kinds of person. The traditional British 'freedoms' to maintain danger and degradation in working conditions began to be challenged and what had been known before was discovered again – that society did not necessarily fall to pieces, nor prosperity decay, if the state sometimes told the master what to do or not to do – and it was learned that society could survive even if manual workers began to obtain higher wages or work fewer hours. Escaping into the cities from the immemorial chattel life of rural villages, the common people began at last, through the collectivity of the trade unions and the chapels, to establish a secular status for themselves as human beings. Jack sometimes could show more strength than his master. But as the British economy began to beat more slowly and the long economic crisis began to show its first symptoms in the early 1920s, unemployment stifled further change in the industrial colonies. Between 1921 and 1939 the average level of unemployment was 14 per cent. However, since the Second World War social welfare has been a concept hardly any British politician would dare challenge directly, and in wage gains manual workers have increased their purchasing power comparatively more than almost all other occupational groups.

They are moving into the suburban HP age, but with a curious emptiness and a continuing lack of human recognition that is a leftover from their earlier history. If the manual workers are now to be looked at not from their own level but from the viewpoint of higher status occupation groups, it might be more illuminating to change the metaphor and to regard the places where their predecessors lived in the industrial towns not as colonies but as 'the native quarters', and to see the earlier manual workers not as 'colonists' but as 'the natives', uprooted tribesmen piled into their hovels, a dirty, possibly dangerous people who, not understanding the civilization around them, had to be driven to perform their simple tasks, in their own interest, and in the interest of the greater good they unknowingly served. The inhabitants of the native quarters were sometimes seen as knowing nothing more of life and wanting nothing more than their simple lot: in that case their deference, whether real or assumed, was praised, as one praises the loyalty of a good dog; sometimes it was even transformed into a national characteristic on which the other classes prided themselves. At other times the inhabitants of the native quarters were seen as a seething scum, dull-witted savages envying what they could not understand; in that case society was to be protected from their ignorant rapacity. 'The natives' emerged from their quarters in books or plays as criminals or comics, or as the unconvincingly facelessly faithful. Whereas the literature of the other English-speaking countries partly created itself by discovering a credible humanity in manual workers, this was beyond the imagination of almost every writer in Britain. A literature of the lower-middle-class developed, but not of 'the workers'. This deprivation was not necessarily a matter of insensitivity but of a frozen incommunicability, so that even some of those who most spoke up for 'the workers' could not understand them, nor even feel comfortable in their company. Manual workers in Britain played something of the role of Negroes in America. Decent and humane people began to want to improve their lot, but still felt self-conscious in their presence or did not want to talk to them.

When a middle-class Australian speaks of 'Australians'

he has a composite picture in his mind that includes 'the workers'; when a Frenchman speaks of the French he includes in his mind the peasantry and the manual workers of France; but when an educated Briton speaks of 'the British people' he does not necessarily think of the majority of his fellow countrymen: he may still think only of himself and his own kind. There are not any acceptable words in which he can address most of his countrymen. This may be one of the reasons why British rhetoric continues to fail; its copy platforms and slogans evade the genuine aspirations and styles of most of the people, who are still usually addressed as if someone were talking not *to* them, but *about* them in their presence.

The principal cultural uses of the manual workers lay in their entertainment value. For a long time they could be laughed at without any inhibition, just as it used to be possible to make jokes about niggers without looking around to see if there was one in the room. Now scriptwriters have had to become more subtle and laugh merely at the *pretensions* of manual workers (that is to say, the attempts of manual workers to become like other people), although the traditional poking of fun at accents still gets plenty of laughs. But there is another trick now, and that is to get entertainment value out of manual workers as a whole by exaggerating the predicament of the section of them who are poor, thereby providing cheap thrills of horror for political or commercial entertainment, misrepresenting manual workers as a class without in any way helping the genuinely poor, and by melodrama retaining a welcome incommunicability.

The snobberies of the Southern Metaphor, the moral injunctions of the Victorian Metaphor, the workaday commands of the Northern Metaphor, and the boastings of the Imperial Metaphor floated as strange shapes above the manual-working families, sometimes producing disbelief or incredulous laughter, sometimes casting shadows in which families cooled their lives with uneasy imitations. The rhetoric of other classes created either Black

Sambos or Uncle Toms. The masters of England now increasingly prefer to see the working-class as Uncle Toms. Even the sympathizers of the manual workers despair of the 'Working-class Tories'. Yet, although large, these are only a minority group and of them, while some are genuinely deferential, seeing the Conservatives as their betters, others are seeking escape from class in their political preference, or simply believe that there is something in Conservative government for them. Two-thirds of the manual workers vote Labour and most of them live within the fraternal horizons of working-class life. The men may see as bullshit the exhortations of all the Metaphors, the kind of bullshit you are taught at school or the kind of bullshit the politicians talk at election time on the telly. Rhetoric can seem as remote as the other pleasures of the rich, or even a fraud, the lies of the successful in a world in which it is plain that all that matters is money. Their wives might enjoy some of the romance of celebrity life, but as a daydream. To the mass of the Average Britons the pomp and ceremony of Britain may be, at the best, a passing show and, at the worst, boss's bullshit.

Although an individual worker's son can move up to a higher occupational status group than his father, usually through education, the working-class *as a whole* is slow to change its status, slow to move into the condition that in the other English-speaking countries means that manual workers are accepted as an ordinary part of the community, sharing its aspirations, and not a class to go on about in some particular way. In Britain, to achieve a wider human recognition, a worker's son must leave the working-class altogether: outside its fraternity, he may find something inhuman in his new recognition. The old sense of strength, of a second nation armed with industrial weapons, has gone. Britain's 'Negroes' do not offer prospects of violence any longer. Nor is there any real myth of vitality about them. The middle-classes are not afraid that their daughters will be raped by the workers.

Average Britain

Average Britain is a fraternal and democratic country of little social snobbery. Running through it there is another society, an anti-egalitarian society, which makes a lot of noise and thinks itself better than everyone else, but not much attention is paid to it by the Average Britons in their ordinary lives. Members of this minority group can boss you around at work, and get the country into a mess from time to time, but they also have the great value of providing some excellent entertainment as you watch them on TV or read about them in the newspapers or magazines. The gossip and scandal you pick up about this other society is usually more interesting than what happens in your own street. If you meet a member of it in some situation that matters you can usually handle him by showing him deference, or by being rude to him.

In Average Britain you are a manual worker and you are more likely than not to be employed in the provinces. You're quite pleased to be yourself – what else could you be? – but you don't get very excited about being it. If the truth is to be told, the Average Briton's horizon of the possible is so low that to many the opportunities of the contemporary world are little known.

The Average Briton is a man whose job is a dreary necessity, its main pleasures those of escape – in companionship with workmates, or in feelings of superiority to bosses, or, at the end of the day, in knocking off work. But escape from work is often not very exhilarating. The senses can seem to be so dulled that the rest of the Average Briton's life can also be muted, producing that quiescence of mood of which some of Britain's propaganda men most humbly boast. From this dullness both the past and the future offer escape. The past offers the tough, rebellious, gregarious society, heroic and fraternal, of the old mateships. It is now usually confined to the crumbling terraces in the inner ring of the industrial cities. The future offers the HP escapes of the supermarket generation. Out in the housing estates they probably offer the future face of Average Britain, attempting a status which is often denied them by the members of the class to which they aspire.

3. THE UPPER ENGLISH

Upper England

When Kingsley Martin was in Australia, at the cocktail party I attended in his honour in the gardens of the house of a Pakistani in Sydney almost all of us saw him as one of the very springs of London radicalism. The cicadas were drumming in the trees, the human voices were crying out loud in drink, but above all the rest of the noise Kingsley Martin's voice rose, with that sense of command that to an Australian, however knowledgeable, still seems in itself a denial of the belief that men should be equal. He contrasted the poor publicity he was getting in the Sydney newspapers with the loud hails he had received in the Ghana press as a liberator, and then he lectured us on what our attitude should be to the Indonesians. There was an old Australian nearby who was perhaps the only person present who had never heard of Kingsley Martin and did not know he was supposed to be a radical. He recognized only the confident voice of the ruler. He came over and in the broadest of Australian accents said: 'You Englishmen want to watch yourselves in Australia now. The old days of the British Empire are over. You can't tell us what to do any more, you know.' Kingsley Martin crossed the garden and talked to another group.

I must admit a prejudice: the most extreme forms of upper-status English accents still get on my nerves so much that to me an Indian who talks with one is not really an Indian but an upper-status Englishman and I automatically react to him as such. In full flight, however decent otherwise they may be, Englishmen who talk like this do not realize how loud-mouthed they can seem. It is not just the volume of noise, but the absolute self-assurance of their clear, confident braying that cuts through all surrounding noises, as if all the lesser noises were being called to order. They have, as Nehru said, 'the calm assurance of always being in the right'.

However cosy their domestic qualities, and however professedly liberal, radical, or egalitarian the views of some of them, there was built into the influences that shaped the English of one of the educated classes (what I shall now describe as the Upper English) a sense of uniqueness and superiority. However much it may now have spread, in origin this sense of uniqueness was a matter of race and class. An Upper Englishman was reared in a way that made him a master twice over. As an Englishman he appeared to belong to the world's unique race. As an Englishman of one of the educated classes he felt, with various gradations of confidence, that he belonged to the unique group in that race. While it should not be forgotten that many Upper Englishmen still feel this way *explicitly*, the feeling of uniqueness has now been considerably democratized and modernized, even among conservatives, so that one may now speak of an Upper Englishman as one who still acts, whether consciously or not, from those habits of self-importance that were generated from his nation's history and sustained by sucking prestige from many of the peoples of the world and from most of his own people, even though the conditions that gave rise to them are gone and even though he may now deny their original basis.

That the craving for uniqueness cannot be fulfilled causes Britain's chronic crisis of identity. There is no generally accepted set of beliefs in Britain that can be effectively appealed to, to make sense of decision, *except a set of beliefs that cannot be fulfilled*. With the great subtleties with which Upper English self-assuredness protects itself, it can now hide its nature, or, with the English talent for whimsy, mock itself. But the old habits of self-importance can still be there or – and this is of equal importance – if they have crumbled there is nothing. No new thing happens.

The most widely acknowledged characteristic of Upper Englishness, the hierarchically gradated sense of domestic social difference, is sometimes misleadingly over-simplified as 'snobbery', as if it were like the kind of thing you find in other countries. An invention mainly of the Victorian era and coming from a new school system which tried to *teach* aristocratic manners and values, this hierarchic sense continues to be democratized (that is, spread more widely throughout the community) both in the continuing dissemination of education and in increasing social mobility, so that the inhabitants of Upper England become more and more numerous, and its standards become harder to challenge. Where the border falls between Upper England and Average Britain is a matter of infinite contest. For those born to it, Upper England is still a small place; their sense of where the border lies excludes most of those who claim membership. But among those who claim entry to it by education, if it is to include *them*, Upper England must seem a much bigger place. Even if they recognize in themselves only the second-rate or third-rate membership that comes from second-rate or third-rate schools they will see Average Britain as something they are not. The border of Upper England is where one stands oneself; on this side of the border are those who seem like oneself; on the other side are the outsiders. It is, of course, an uneasy existence being a border people.

One enters Upper England through birth and/or education and/or occupational group. Aspiring parenthood can be largely a matter of getting a child into the highest status school available in an order of status that descends from the most prestigious fee-financed boarding schools to the less prestigious, and then from fee-financed day schools to those government-financed schools that disseminate the manners of Upper Englishness. There are many other nations in which parents make sacrifices to push their children up in society by way of education (although none in which so many pay so much for it), but one of the great assets bought by education in England is to acquire a certain kind of accent, certain manners, certain styles in self-assurance, that are given value throughout society and that, irrespective of talent, ease entry into those occupation groups that are at the top of a generally recognized (if sometimes changing) hierarchy of prestige. A result of this system of social value is that to an Upper Englishman, sometimes despite himself, consideration of complex subtleties of manner, accent, attire, vocabulary, furniture, and a hundred other things, many of them subtly changing, becomes instinctive. Thus if he is in a new situation he sometimes even yet cannot stop himself from evaluating persons and circumstances according to intricate patterns of triviality. As a protection, his sense of good form is capable of so much wriggling that as soon as some aspect of Upper English triviality is widely imitated, it is abandoned.

Caught in a web of triviality, the Upper English cannot escape the tyranny of their irrelevant inheritance. It is not only that this system limits their own potential and the potential of those who do not belong to it. This can be true of any social system; it can certainly be true of societies in which there is a tendency to uniform enforcement of democratic manners. What is of decisive importance is that the system no longer works. Britain sometimes seems like a garden of miniature trees. If you stick your face right down amongst them you are in a forest where the trees seem in perfect relation to each other. But if you stand up you see that they are only toy trees, with clipped roots, but still tough and determined to survive as they are.

In Britain snobbery is over-simplified. Social mobility in Britain is no less than and sometimes better than that in other commercialist industrial societies – but these other countries have a *multiplicity* of snobberies. They are spared Britain's tendency towards a simple dualism of social value. In France and Germany, for example, there is a unified school system in which the sons of the less well-to-do and the sons of the rich can be educated together; this does not obliterate the multiple snobberies of these societies, nor does it eradicate privilege. But it does mean that there is not a simple two-nation division of social value as in Britain. In France it produces an intellectual élite and a managerial élite that have an arrogant sense of difference from the rest of French society, but these élites are only two social classes amongst many, two snobberies contesting not only against other snobberies but against themselves. Snobberies exist in all societies, but they are *contesting and self-confident snobberies, set one against the other*. The member of an intellectual élite sees a pattern of his society in which the greatest social value is given to his kind of person; an aristocrat sees his kind of person as the most valuable; a bourgeois prefers the bourgeoisie; a peasant the peasantry; and so forth. Attitudes towards social value are open and pluralist. Even in those few societies such as Australia into which the British system has partly penetrated it provides only one snobbery amongst others. It is only in Britain that there is a simple two-nation division of social values, the existence of which is recognized, one way or the other – accepted or despised – by almost everyone in the land. Britain alone has become polarized over a simple ideal of social division. And the ideal is irrelevant to the age.

Apart from its necessarily disappointed sense of uniqueness and superiority it is perhaps in its *style* that Upper Englishness is now most frustratingly important. The egalitarianism of Average Britain has pressed so hard on Upper England (even if the Average Briton's fraternalism is despised) that, in provision of educational opportunity and in the vocabulary of economic policy, Britain is more professedly egalitarian than most European countries. But this egalitarianism has meant, amongst other things, that more people have been able to acquire the style of Upper England, which they wanted not only because it opened the way to privilege but also because it was in itself an important social privilege. So the style of Upper England became most widely transferred through the community at the very time when its continued existence as an élite characteristic represents one of Britain's most intractable problems.

How that style, in its heyday, was envied or hated by other nations and classes! How absurd and irrelevant it can now seem! Once so formidable that it acquired imitators all over the world, it can now seem rather like one of those scarecrows you used to see in children's comics, done up in an old top hat with the crown out of it. All the understated elegance and aplomb that once caused so much discomfort in those who admired it can now cause laughter at the exaggerated manners of the stage Englishman.

In its ideal form, for certain kinds of Upper Englishmen, this style was everything. At its most subtle and comfortable, and among initiates, it was a relaxed cultivation of the apparently spontaneous, a ceremony of nonceremony, conducted in throw-away gestures and understated words, little hints of this and that, with nothing spelt out, a cult style that was quite inane to the noninitiate but which to its practitioners seemed the only true form of personal relationship. It was more a ceremony than a form of communication between human beings, part of its very essence lying in its incommunicability, and those who practised it entirely had to live in a superficially pleasant world deprived of all but cult meanings. Like so many other forms of privilege amongst Upper Englishmen, in its purest form it was assumed to be something that you were born with. You could not learn it or earn it. (In fact you could acquire it at the right kind of school.) You had it or you didn't have it. Between those who had it there was an ineffable sympathy, beyond words.

It was a style in which, in its pure form, it was possible

neither to conduct affairs nor to pursue intellectual interests. It did not allow for human awkwardness – in a sense its role was to avoid the awkward. But some of those supposed to be conducting affairs or pursuing intellectual interests would sooner preserve their style than the affairs or the interests. Others used it in its pure form only as an out-of-hours relaxation, but they preserved as much of it as they could when they were doing something that had some sense in it.

Seen from the interior it was a style of modesty: seen from the outside it was, in its self-assured cultishness, a style of arrogance. At its best it showed high standards of decency in human relations, but some of those who most honestly saw it in this way could not see decency in those who did not follow the fads of their style. In the company of men who did not share their style they felt at best inhibited, at worst contemptuous – as, in return, did the uninitiated whom they tried to put at ease. As a style concerned with fostering ease in human relations Upper Englishness caused a remarkable amount of unease in both those who practised it and those who didn't. Putting outsiders in their place was usually an accompaniment to the style; there was no subtlety about the methods used. The old school tie worn by the graduates of the most prestigious boarding schools was more a way of reminding most people that they had not been to 'a good school' than a sign of fellowship.

But among its Upper English devotees the style seemed all that was decent and human and now that its external brutishness has been so modified by the collapse of power there are many who see it as the important distinguishing characteristic of Britain, the characteristic that still gives England a unique superiority in the world. In believing this they are, of course, partly the victims of their own rhetoric: they are not as good as they think they are. But even on those occasions when the style is at its best – detached, contemplative, sceptical, amusing, fair – it is not the kind of style that can be enforced on a whole complex industrial society. In the conduct of affairs in particular, if it is a dominant style, it simply means that things don't get done. One can admire those cultivated and 'civilized' Upper Englishmen who despise effort because those who make efforts are incomplete in meeting the nuances of an incommunicable set of intuitive understandings. But one could admire some of them better if they would despise effort from the *outside*, instead of accepting preferment within the structures of decision, and then not making decisions.

One should examine with particular scepticism the Upper English 'love of order'. In one obvious sense – that of law-abidingness – this love of order is a myth: the British are just about as criminal as other societies of roughly comparable industrial development. Financial corruption in administration and government is probably less in Britain than in most comparable countries (although interlocking snobberies and old-boy circuits can provide a form of corruption of their own, without money passing hands), but what is meant by a love of order is different from that. It probably means above all that the Upper English detest disturbance in those areas that most affect them, in which they will often resort to face-saving compromises of complex deviousness rather than have one side clearly win and the other side clearly lose, and in which they will unite in resisting change.

It is notorious that they were able to use violence abroad against natives or foreigners without thinking about it; and earlier in their history they used violence at home against people outside what were then the magic classes, again without thinking about it, seeing their violence as police action taken in the cause of order and freedom. But beyond the speeches of war patriotism, there is now no significant philosophy in Britain of the role of the violent in human affairs. Nor, in the sense of physical violence, should there be, so far as domestic affairs are concerned, except in cases of severe repression or neglect, when the despised might well make violent protest against the violence that is being done to them. But there can also be a kind of peaceful violence, a decision to come down finally on one side or the other, that can enliven a nation, and it is this kind of shock that is avoided by the Upper English seeking of ease and order. It is true that this distaste for shock can also be an excellent thing and in the interests of a whole people. But what of the stability of stagnation, of the mere perpetuation of what has gone on before? Kindness, tolerance, and love of order become snobbery, woolliness, and love of the past. Effortless ease becomes the ease of not making any effort to do anything. Gentlemanly intuitive wisdom becomes the inability to make up one's mind. Doing the decent thing comes to mean that there should be no sharp clash of attitudes, no disagreeable new beliefs, that might disturb someone. The sense of fairness becomes the belief that competition is unfair: it might benefit some new person, but it might also harm some old person. Not being beastly means perpetuating existing beastliness so that those who practised it will not have the upset of changing their habits.

In the Southern Metaphor the ideal of Upper Englishmen's relations with each other was that they were kind, tolerant, orderly, decent, fair. The idea applied to outsiders only if the outsiders did not upset those relations, but in any case it was in practice a system of keeping things as they were, and a defence from the enterprise of the Northern Metaphor, which was therefore taken to be ruthless, bigoted, disruptive, ungentlemanly, and unfair. The Southern Metaphor seemed to work well because, although the reasons for Britain's achievements were different from the qualities in which Upper Englishmen delighted, Britain was for some time strong enough to survive having most of its affairs decided (or left undecided) according to wrong principles. But in a now enervated Britain the desire to keep things as they are is much stronger than impulses towards change (except changes in fashions such as clothing or Prime Ministers' slogans).

Once, in England, years ago, in the days of food rationing, I was living in a house in a country village with three old widowed Upper Englishwomen. Because of what had happened to their shares in Argentine railways and other crumbling investments, all three were rather down on their luck, but they kept up such appearances as they could. One of those old ladies was greedy. This meant that, since some food was short, she would steal small pieces of food from the kitchen. She usually put her broken victuals at the bottom of her wastepaper basket after she had emptied it, heaving herself back up the stairs and into her bedroom, where she would shut the door and eat in peace. Everyone else in the house knew what she was doing, but they would not discuss it with her because, if they did so, everyone would lose 'face'. She grew bolder. One night when we were eating supper I noticed the green tips of spring onions on her plate. I could hear a rustling of paper. A brown paper bag of spring onions lay on her lap and she was taking the onions out of it one by one and eating them. I asked her to put them on the table so that, if we wanted to, we could all have one. I was the only one to eat a spring onion. To save 'face', the others changed the subject, pretending that none of this had happened. It was not her selfishness but my outspokenness that had disturbed the propriety of their relations with each other.

It was only when they knew they would win (for example, by kicking a native in the backside) that the Upper English asserted 'face' by risking it in direct contest. Amongst themselves the main problem of 'face' was to save it. In the magic circles 'face' did not have to be asserted. Mutuality of 'face' was an essential belief of the cult and since avoiding awkwardness was one of its essential purposes there could be a general game of pretending when something bad happened, that it had not really happened. On the national scale, face-saving was one of the principal contrivances of complacency, perpetuating illusions that Britain was still of some special importance, that even though its Empire had gone and it was neither super-power nor world power, nevertheless there had been no great change. The Monarch still sat on a horse while the colour was trooped; British Prime Ministers and Foreign Ministers made sensational if meaningless flights to Washington or Moscow; and the Prime Ministers of the hastily fabricated 'Commonwealth' could still meet in London, to little purpose except that of London's self-esteem. It can be in the interests of change or growth that continuity should exist. But the appearance of British continuity became bogus, a national saving of 'face'. There was a falling-back on mere symbols that did not perpetuate any continuity except the continuity of themselves as symbols, thereby delaying intelligent concern with the realities of a changed situation. To some Upper English these symbols were all that mattered. The Southern Metaphor is playful, fanciful. It is at its best in Upper English self-denigrating humour. In itself this is a face-saving device: if you laugh at something you can make it appear not to exist, and when well done this kind of humour is still one of the delights of the world. If all Upper English face-saving consisted of funny things worth saying Britain's stagnation would at least be producing a lively by-product. But most of the face-saving is so trivial, because, beneath the crusts of much Upper Englishness there *is* little more than a dull triviality, not a vital kind of frivolity, but a delight in fiddling around with nothing much at all. In the cult, seriousness can be bad form, but perhaps one of the reasons why this is so is that many of the practitioners of the cult could not be serious if they tried. Some Upper Englishmen are simply *silly*.

Manufacturing the Upper English

You want to train an élite. You want it to be made up of more or less interchangeable pieces so that random selections can be joined in almost any situation anywhere in the world and they will fit snugly together with a common approach to the handling of affairs. Thus finally in some distant part of the world, you might put together a government official, a clergyman, and a service officer. They all three see each other as the same kind of person, following the same cults and practices. Two of them might even have been in bed with each other at some stage in their lives. Apart from protecting the interests of their own, which they will do with cool ruthlessness when necessary, their main concern will probably be with *fairness*. They will adjust claims and contests, but otherwise they will leave things to follow their own course, preferring to use power to no particular end beyond its own display.

To perpetuate this élite you choose the children of the rich. Some are children of the present rulers and are already being instructed in the manners of rulers. Others are the children of *arrivistes*, but the system will turn them into the right shape. You take them away from their parents at about the age of nine and put them into special boarding schools where they live until they are eighteen or so, visiting their parents' houses only in vacations. By arranging for them to enforce their own discipline you contort them into a cultish conformity so that they wear their manners like a caste mark, making them instantly recognizable. Certain idiosyncrasies are allowed, or may even be cultivated, but they must usually be connected with matters of laborious triviality. The general tone of the boarding schools must be hierarchic, concerned with birth, titles, honours, and place as important differences between human beings; but there is a brotherhood among the cult itself, trained to act as if from an innate superiority to all other humans, whether fellow countrymen, foreigners, or natives.

This illusion of innate superiority is the principal quality required in the new rulers since their most important function will be to wear power as if it belonged to them, but using it to no special purpose except those of self-perpetuation and of 'fairness'. Other than challenges to power or 'fairness', the events over which they are to preside are assumed to be static, with no need for intervention. The past seems sacred, the future a nuisance. One of the most important requirements will be to put on a stiff, confident public face, the face of a ruler, a somewhat different face from the one of relaxed charm enjoyed within their own circle. Since looking as if one has been born to wield power and being able to get on with one's fellow rulers are what mainly matter, the formation of 'character' is taken to be the principal task of education. To accentuate its importance the playing of games is given a special emotional prominence, thereby also reminding initiates that nothing is more important than the trivial. The scholastic part of education is taken to be the general education of a gentleman. It is assumed that no special training is necessary for ruling; to assume otherwise would be to erode the assumptions of what ruling consists of. The study of the classics is revived, because of its honorific uselessness, its very antiquity, and what is taken to be its value in mental training. Some of the new rulers are sifted out as being fit for one job or another by their facility to translate from Latin and Greek.

As this system of training is strengthened, more boarding schools and universities spring up to meet increasing demand. Those who are trained in the older schools or universities see the new ones as inferior, and in its more exclusive form their cult does not include those who have been trained in the mysteries of the cult at the wrong institutions. But the new institutions are imitations of the old. Then the state encourages the growth of free institutions for the sons of those who cannot afford the price of the boarding schools. These 'grammar schools' are mere day schools, but as much as they can they ape some of the customs of the more honoured institutions and spread their acceptance more and more widely throughout the community.

Roughly speaking, this was how the English public school system operated, and how its influence extended into the rest of the education system. Apart from the emphasis on games the particular form of these boarding schools was simply taken over from the few boarding schools that, in the eighteenth century, concerned themselves with housing the sons of the aristocracy and some of the gentry and giving them some schooling. But these forms were strengthened by new impulses and by the 1860s or thereabouts the use of them for the new purpose of creating a class of imperial rulers was boasted about and the whole mystique formulated. The new rich turned, whether knowing it or not, to a system that made their sons gentlemen. The public schools and their attendant universities not only shaped the face of power; they also swamped the Northern Metaphor with the Southernness of Upper England. By the 1890s some of the Northern Metaphor had also crept into public-schooldom: the rhetoric of fortitude, obedience, honesty, and industriousness was adopted (though not that of intelligence or enterprise), these being ideals that could be easily accommodated to those who saw seriousness of purpose as a desire to get into the school's First Cricket Eleven. The Upper English did not usually realize how unique was their system of training boys to be members of a cult. The public schools seemed so obviously necessary to them that they could not imagine that other countries did not have the same methods. Now there is plenty of criticism of them. But, while the evils of the social divisiveness of the public schools are often attacked, what now seems even more relevant is their anachronistic shabbiness, and the disastrous multiplication of their effect by the spread of their standards into lesser schools and into the government-sponsored secondary schools. They permeate so deeply into the social structure and promote so much silliness that if they could all be knocked down tomorrow the shock of change would make Britain a different and almost certainly a more decent, a more clever, and a more efficient nation. As it is, the influence and importance of these schools, and of their imitative multipliers, could be dissolved. Perhaps this is now happening, but it is a slow business. Upper Englishness is resilient, both subtle and tough in defence, sometimes even lulling its opponent by appearing to change its shape.

The hierarchic and the antique

While to most Average Britons, so far as they can judge it by their relations with each other, their country may have seemed democratic, to a large number of Upper Englishmen (and their imitators in Average Britain) Britain still seemed, even after the Second World War, to be a characteristically *aristocratic and antique society*. While in all other countries the aristocrats had been dug out of the constitution, sometimes left in neglected and isolated clumps, sometimes eradicated, in Britain the idea of the aristocracy, although taking on some protective colouring from its environment, continued to colour the environment in return, partly by its continued presence and, even more important, by the continued presence of its social values. Even now in Britain the most usual form of commemorating the success of a career is still to become a lord, or to enter one of the orders of chivalry. That one might now become only a 'life lord' rather than acquire an hereditary title is an expression not of the weakness of aristocratic values but of their strength: by this accommodation to the age the hierarchic idea extends its embrace to those who might otherwise reject it.

It is some time since Britain was directly controlled by the conspiracies of noble families, and the importance of the Labour Party and other forces continue to weaken their power. But it is not primarily because of whatever is left of its direct political or social power or influence that the aristocracy is important, just as it is not only because of the power of their old boys that the public schools are important: it is above all the *social esteem* given to the values of the aristocracy and the public schools that makes Britain a different country to live in from other countries, because this esteem has transmuted the social values of other classes.

Over most of the period of continuing crisis that has marked British history since the Second World War, many of the Upper English could still see their society as a classifiable hierarchy in which old things were best. Around the second top row of the pyramid sat the lords, next in social importance to the Monarch, and beneath them were the other hangers-on of importance. The House of Lords may continue to lose its political meaning and even its hereditary nature, but, improbably, it is *still there*, as much part of the constitution as the Monarch, an assertion of the value of antiquity, a proof that society should be organized hierarchically, a defiance of the democratic myth that the institutions of government are an embodiment of the people. To a large conservative part of the Upper English it has been these values of the hierarchic and antique that give life colour and meaning: they live in a society in which it is important that a man has become a knight and in which, no matter what kind of a dolt he may be, a lord belongs to a different order of humanity. Among Average Britons these values do not necessarily hold so strongly. But the nobs are now given contemporary meaning to Average Britons by also becoming 'celebrities'.

It would be different if aristocratic values were 'aristocratic'. Detachment from self-seeking, concern with the good or the true rather than the expedient, courage in a cause and so forth are sometimes taken by intellectuals to be the aristocratic values. But this is mere misplaced metaphor. In fact these very qualities were also to be found in the myths of the proletarian heroes, when there still were proletarian heroes. The aristocratic ideal in Britain is simply the hierarchic ideal *that this man should be better than that man because of his title or because of his use of the accent and manners of the aristocracy, or because he got there first.* It is a system of advantage to many racketeers who push their way up to success in the expense-account world that the ancient fol-de-rol of the aristocracy should still be there to add honour to their hypocrisy. It is a historically apt situation, since the honour of aristocracy was always a cloak for self-seeking.

I can imagine that some readers will think that I have confused beliefs with power; after all, just as the Empire has gone away and the Commonwealth has no power, so the House of Lords has been reformed and now has little power. The answer is that it is always hard to know where power lives, but what affects people more than their belief about the exact address of power is the set of beliefs they hold about what matters in life and where social values lie. If hierarchy, getting there first, and oldness for its own sake still seem to be among the most important values in life, this will have general effects of a kind to shape a society's actions much more strongly than the latest expression of policy, or the latest change in the façade of power. Such things provide the wisdoms of a society, stimulating if they are relevant, imprisoning if they are not. They provide the dividing lines between what can be thought and what cannot be thought, what can be done and what cannot be done. They provide a sense of what is important and what can be left over to some other time. They are a nation's identity, as liberating or as restrictive as a single person's style and sense of the possible.

The maintenance of the aristocracy and of the ideals of hierarchy and antiquity is still sometimes taken to be an example of the Upper English talent for compromise, of the ability to make social changes without tension. But another way of looking at this sense of compromise is that the tension that has been avoided has been tension for the hierarchy and their supporters. It would have been better if they had suffered their tension, and got out of the way. It is difficult to imagine Britain emerging out of its present state of arrested development without the abolition of the House of Lords and the abolition of the system of titles and honours, 'life' as well as hereditary. As with many other of the obvious ways in which Britain

could be restored to the sense of reality, it is equally difficult to imagine this being done.

The Monarch

Excluding odds and ends such as the King of Tonga and
the Grand Duke of Luxembourg, only eighteen hereditary
monarchies are left in the world. The list could become
smaller before this book is published. Of these eighteen
survivors only eight do any ruling, either directly or indirectly. And of the remaining monarchs in Europe all
but one have lost even their pomp and are better considered as hereditary presidents of *de facto* republics; only
the British sovereign is expected to act as if there were
some sacred or magic quality in a monarch which required
a loyalty to his very person.

There is much circumstantial evidence to support this
difference in the person of the Monarch from all other
persons. Apart from the £450,000 a year received from
the state along with a £2 million yacht and a whole flight
of aeroplanes, the Monarch is personally also very rich,
controlling a private fortune that may lie somewhere
between £50 million and £100 million. This fortune includes one private landed estate that is the richest in
Britain and several others of very considerable substance.
The Monarch personally owns five tons of gold plate, the
world's largest collection of jewellery and its most famous
collection of stamps, two thousand old masters and such a
stack of antiques that the catalogue of the furniture in
Windsor Castle alone takes up seventy-five volumes. The
households of the Monarch and of the Monarch's family
maintain somewhere between four and five hundred cour-
tiers and retainers; there are thirty-five ceremonial horses
in the Monarch's personal stable, apart from the famous
racing stable and the even more famous stable of the
Household Cavalry. The Monarch is expected to live in
various palaces, castles, and rural estates in a certain
sequence each year, as if the very ritual of moving from

one place to another was a magic ceremony that had to be performed annually in a certain way for the good of the kingdom. The Monarch's main associates are aristocrats. When the Monarch is crowned (in a ceremony which comes very close to meaninglessness) it is the aristocrats who perform the ceremony, as if it is by their grace that the Monarch becomes a sacred person, rather than by the grace of the people. In a moment of excitement the Archbishop who last performed this service seemed to see it as a popular sacrament, a kind of national communion service in which, presumably, viewers on their knees before their TV sets worshipped not their God but their Queen. Adding mystery to mystery, the Monarch is also seen as head of the Commonwealth. Extreme devotees of the monarchist cult see the Monarch not only as a transubstantiation of all human activity in Britain but also, owing to a titular relation to a titular Commonwealth, as the head of a world family. Some of the members of the Commonwealth acknowledge the Monarch as their own head of state although, as the old generation dies off, they now see the Monarch more as a celebrity than as a sacred person. The religious view of the Monarch as a person supernaturally embodying all loyalties extended for a while, as far as circumstances allowed, to the Monarchic Family, which was seen to share some of the sacredness of the Monarch. The privilege of the Monarch is convincingly instanced in the fact that the heirs of dead monarchs do not pay death duties and in the fact that one of the subtlest mysteries of this institution, one of its ineffable, elusive differences, is wrapped up in the question *Does the Queen pay income tax?* a question that is not asked about any other person in the kingdom.

The 'oriental' view that became attached to British monarchs dates only from the late nineteenth century. After the oligarchs of Britain clipped their autocrat's wings and until the end of Victoria's reign, when she was puffed up into an imperial symbol, monarchs were simply human beings who held office. When George IV died *The*

Times said, 'There never was an individual less regretted by his fellow creatures than this deceased King.' When William IV died the *Spectator* said he was 'a weak, ignorant, commonplace sort of person', whose 'very popularity was acquired at the price of something like public contempt'. To some upholders of the nineteenth century Northern Metaphor it seemed obvious that Britain would later become a republic, abandoning both Monarch and aristocrats. But the extravagances of Empire and the increasing idealization of the Monarch had it otherwise.

Disappointingly, the reign of Elizabeth II was initiated both with traditional pomp and aristocratic circumstance and with attempts at that fabrication of ideal 'personality' that modern media can provide. Hopes that the monarchic institution would be democratized on the Scandinavian pattern found no substance except in the Monarch's husband, nor do they yet except in the Monarch's children. In a Britain that needs to work out what relations its people should bear to each other and to the world, the most honorific symbol that the state provides of what life should be is still of an aristocratic multi-millionaire who is called upon to re-enact memories of a dead life, recalling the absolute value of privilege, hierarchy, and antique ways, and presented by the facilities available from the mass media as a permanent star attraction. In this way the Monarchy can be manipulated to excuse or glorify most of what is irrelevant or harmful in modern Britain. At times bad press relations and the simple impossibility of keeping to the unreal personal standards demanded of all members of the Monarchic Family have led to sporadic sniping, but to much of Upper England the Monarchy, along with public schools and aristocratic values, provide the most significant symbol of social worth. Even if belief in it lessens, nothing takes its place. This means that Average Britons live in a world in which what is most publicly valued is altogether out of their reach except when they are used as extras for the crowd scenes. The Monarchy is used not, as can be the case in the Scandinavian countries, as a symbol of the people, but as a symbol of the lack of value of the people.

The rational apologists for the Monarchy sometimes see it as a device for protecting freedom and order against the passions of the brutish populace. This modern defence of monarchism was first developed a hundred years ago by Walter Bagehot, who saw the Monarchy as a useful way of fooling someone he took for the sake of argument to be 'the labourer in Somerset'. According to Bagehot's theory, this simple fellow in Somerset could be so successfully tricked into believing that the Monarch was ruling everything that his faith in the Monarch's person would prevent him from creating disorder in the streets, or from venerating some great political leader who might use his power against the interests of existing order. In the generalizations on which it is based Bagehot's sceptical view of political passion was a realistic one, but to quote it now is to do too little justice to Bagehot, or to today's labourers in Somerset.

In its modern form, the Bagehot defence of the Monarchy usually follows some argument such as that adoration is better directed towards a meaningless symbol than towards a head of government. Considered in itself this seems civilized and reasonable. But on looking at more evidence than was available to Bagehot, one notices that if a nation's main political leader is also the head of state, this does not necessarily make him adored by the populace: thus the President of the United States, though both head of government and head of state, can be treated with more calumny than a British Prime Minister. Sometimes the argument runs to the effect that the ceremony of Trooping the Colour is less dangerous than a Nuremberg Rally or a Red Square ceremonial. But this shrewd and reasonable view seems to ignore the possibility that if British political life were such that it demanded a Nuremberg Rally, then it might get one and the Monarch might not be able to do anything about it; in fact the government would probably advise the Monarch to attend.

There is no quantum of demand for circuses in Britain so constant that if it were deprived of a peaceful ceremony of state it would then demand a brutal one. There are circuses on TV as well as in the ceremonies of state and they do just as well for entertainment. If this were not so, how could one account for the peace and order of those democracies that don't have ceremonies such as Trooping the Colour? They put on other kinds of festivals which have the advantage over the Monarchy that they bear no relation to political or social values or to anything of any importance. It is only the added *historical* value of Trooping the Colour that makes it objectionable; it is a parade of illusion, of fantasy strength, of fake value. Marching girls could provide exactly the same movement and colour and they would have the additional value of asserting vulgarity, or turning the past upside down and making fun of it, like a London swinger dressed up in an old Hussar's uniform.

So far as Canada, Australia, and New Zealand are concerned, when they become republics the symbolic break might shatter what remains of their provincialism and even lead to more rich (because more real) relations with Britain. So far as Britain itself is concerned, however, it is not so obvious that one should now start campaigning for the institution of Britain's Second Republic. The Scandinavian model seems to work reasonably well and it seems worth trying first. In an imperfect world, what is wrong with the Monarchy is not its existence but the role at present demanded of it. If Canada, Australia, and New Zealand renounced the British Monarch as their head of state and if the nations of the Commonwealth (assuming the Commonwealth survives) renounced the British Monarch as the head of their non-organization, this could be followed up in Britain by cutting out most of the dressing-up and ancient ceremonies or, if these were necessary for the tourist trade, devising new but meaningless pageants, mere shows. If the granting of new titles were abandoned and the holders of old titles were asked not to use them and if the House of Lords folded up altogether – if the state, in other words, ceased to give added social value to the hierarchic and the antique – the use of the Monarchy as a prop for the aristocratic ideal would be destroyed. The Monarch might turn Buckingham Palace into a museum to house the Monarchy's most valuable artefacts and the Monarch might be expected to live more simply in another of the available London residences, more in the style of a millionaire, say, than of a great prince.

Who runs Britain?

If one could find simple conspiracies of power in Britain it might be possible to be more directly and predictably optimistic about its future. What existed in such simple terms might be removed in simple terms. Not being able to find such a power network, some writers invent one. They purport to skim off the surface of British society to discover beneath it a kind of neatly describable clockwork contrivance of interrelated parts. They even draw diagrams of their invention. The members of this conspiracy go beyond the old-boys of the public schools (although the old-boy network is the motive force of the conspiracy); the power men are shown to be linked together with each other as power men. Unfortunately for simplicity, this view does not seem to be true. There is a diffuseness about the operations of power in Britain. Its power men do not seem to meet each other, except in certain recognizable groups.

It was from the recognition of difficulties such as these that the theory of 'the Establishment' emerged. The Establishment was seen as not so much a ruling class or a power bloc as an established body of prevailing opinion. However, instead of being described simply as a set of opinions the idea of the Establishment became, in mythology, embodied in actual persons. It, too, became a kind of conspiracy: it worked more by osmosis than by clockwork; and its network extended beyond power blocs; but one nevertheless personalized it by imagining the Primate ringing up the Warden who rang up the Editor and so forth. There is no doubt that people ring each other up, and that private pressures are applied and that conspiracies of influence operate – but these facts are too small to explain the nature of Upper England.

The familiar metaphor of a social climate may be more useful: a set of prevailing conditions in the social weather operating in such a way that those who are subjected to it tend to behave in a certain way, irrespective of their other differences or whether they know each other or not. In this one should distinguish between on the one hand opinions and policies and on the other hand style of approach. That there are differences of opinions and policies in Upper England is obvious enough. What is suggested is that even among those who differ there is a tendency to have *the same kinds of ways of going about things*.

To take some simple examples: even a 'radical' might really be a hierarch; he may have élitist views different from the more widespread values and still be élitist in his own way. Even a union official who sees himself on the side of equality and solidarity and against hierarchical deference may nevertheless have a deep respect for the antique, not only in society in general, but in his approach to the problems of his own union. And the conceit of Upper Englishry, although based historically in the self-importance of Empire and of an earlier nationalism, manifests itself in many other ways, even among those who hate the memory of Empire.

To those who believe that political or economic policies (in the narrow sense) are all that matter this general social climate might not seem important. It might seem a matter more of form than of content, of mere prestige or habit than of political or economic importance. This has been the usual view of the Labour Party, which has preferred not to make a frontal attack on the aristocratic values, or on the persons and institutions in which they are most entrenched, although attempting to reduce their power.

On the other hand it may be that what matters most are the dominant social values and world views of Britain and *the way the Upper English have of going about things.* All of the rest of it – the political and economic policies – may be of significance only to the extent that they are likely to alter these other habits. And these policies – both in formulation and execution – are often in the hands of those who are most deeply lost.

4. TWO INTERLUDES

Macmillan's Britain

At the end of the Macmillan era, when the Profumo case was causing great despair among the followers of the Victorian Metaphor, I went back to the village in which I used to live and which, for various reasons, I had not seen for some years. Everybody had the water laid on – no more carrying buckets over to the village taps. The picturesque hovels that were the village's most ancient cottages had been pulled down and replaced by an only moderately ugly council house estate. Almost everybody now had bathrooms, there were electric appliances in all the kitchens and – this would have been unimaginable a few years before – a few of the villagers had cars. There was regular bingo in the church hall, with enough profit to pay for its heating, so they didn't have to be polite to gentlemen with cheque books any more. When the Labour candidate had recently told the village that they must be saved from their feudal past, and that their squire must no longer order them around, some of the villagers had held up his car and would not let him leave until he had apologized. The idea that they would put up with a 'squire' was insulting.

This was bingo-debauched Macmillan's Britain. Weimar Britain, its morals eroded because it had the water laid on. Byzantine Britain, polluted by electrical appliances. A Britain where ordinary people were beginning to enjoy the things the top lot had long been used to enjoying. The fact that Average Britons seemed to be mildly pleased with life was taken as evidence of moral decay, even of the suicide of the nation. In retrospect it is alarming to consider how much violence was released by the statement that the Average Britons had never had it so good. It was true that the critics were right who warned that it would not last. But even some of the economic warnings seemed to have far too much of the Victorian Metaphor. There were overtones of the Victorian Metaphor's recessional sense of doom: in their new frivolity the people must perish.

Many of the warnings of moral collapse and national disaster were not based on economic problems; they were often based on a contempt for the economic in which the people were seen as corrupt because they could think of nothing better to do with their lives than share in some of the prosperity that the Upper English took for granted. For the first time since the civil war in the seventeenth century, the people were briefly called on to express a special initiative as if, for once, the nation *was* the people. Britain could not be 'great' (economically, politically, spiritually, culturally) if the people wanted electrical appliances and bingo games. Themselves desperate with their own meaninglessness, the élites blamed the people for their predicament.

Some British radicals were disenchanted with the Average Britons of the Macmillan era because their aspirations turned out to be different from what they were supposed to be. Instead of campaigning for the legalization of homosexuality between consenting adults and against nuclear stock-piling, capital punishment, and President Kennedy's Cuba confrontation, many Average Britons wanted to improve their houses and their domestic equipment and have a bit more fun in their spare time. It is one of the hazards of a radicalism that also professes to be populist that the people might let down the ideals of the radical: they might want something different from what he wants them to want. Most people anywhere want to gain an imaginable improvement in their material living conditions, and in an industrial society it usually becomes the ordinary aspiration of ordinary people to become 'suburban'. This desire to ease out one's life, to make it a bit more congenial, does not cause nations to perish: it is supposed to be essential to an economy's growth. But unless this seems a sensible and acceptable desire to a radical he must recognize himself as being radically against the people.

It can certainly be said of the mild material contentment Average Britons enjoyed in the twilight of the Macmillan era that it was not relevant to some of Britain's major problems. But since lack of material good things for some ordinary people is itself one of Britain's problems, this seems a curious complaint. Apart from increasing their material prosperity and asserting their own social values more confidently, the Average Britons cannot do much about the main problems of Britain – these are matters over which the élites have control. In the meantime Average Britons have received so little consideration in the past that one can only say good luck to them if, now and again, they can get something extra for themselves in the present. When, in the mode of the Victorian Metaphor, 'sacrifice' is called for, it should be recognized that the principal relevant sacrifice that can be made is in the life-styles and beliefs of Upper Englishness. Unfortunately one could hear the sighs of satisfied familiarity when, later, Harold Wilson took measures to stop the run on sterling which included an increase in unemployment, and when, in 1969, the Labour Government proposed tougher handling of the unions. In the sacrificial view of economic policy, this put the traditional sacrificial victim back on the chopping block even if nothing finally happened and, in the manner of Harold Wilson, the harsh events could be enacted only in fantasy.

Swinging Britain

Now one already looks back nostalgically even to Swinging Britain. The sub-generation that believed in it may go on believing in it, just as an earlier sub-generation may still believe that Britain is really a Welfare State, but some other novelty will take its place.

In writing about a contemporary society, since one cannot be sure of the strength of one trend against another, it is best to lay the trends out and imagine them conflicting. In this process what can be significant is whether one trend could *possibly* contend with another; that is to say that although two different trends may exist in the same society, they may not exist in the same field in that society, so that, although apparently in conflict, they do *not* conflict. Praise could be given to Swinging Britain, as it could to Welfare Britain, New Elizabethan Britain, Winds of Change Britain, and Never-Had-It-So-Good Britain. Young people should have a bit of fun; some of the old pomposities should be sent up; and it seemed particularly good that a new cultishness should have provided some novelty in a generation otherwise still divided by an old cult. Of all the guessing games about what Britain is, the swingers provided one that could have had some effect on at least one of Britain's problems: the problem of the kind of relations human beings should have with each other. But, even here, one can exaggerate the effect. That boys at Eton liked pop records, that Oxford undergraduates planned careers in the entertainment business, that peers' daughters went psychedelic, that the Beatles went to Buckingham Palace, that Princess Anne went to *Hair* and saw actors take off their clothes, and that at the investiture of the Prince of Wales Lord Snowdon designed himself a uniform that made him look like a stylish bellhop may be examples not of the breaking-down of prejudice but of that resilience of the aristocratic embrace which strengthens the grip of the hierarchic idea rather than weakens it, its very adaptability keeping it lively. If peers' daughters had *not* gone psychedelic there might have been some hope later of closing down the House of Lords altogether. It was the fundamental lack of conflict between the swingers' trend and any of the old trends other than the Puritan trend (which was done for, for other reasons) that made it weak.

It was wrong to describe it is an evasion. It might have been better to describe it as a new brand of oil, better than the old one, but one that was not going to make much difference – because the machine itself was faulty.

Even more significant than a lack of conflict between a country's trends can be that a particular trend is not there at all. The significant trend lacking in Britain is, of course, a strong and impetuous demand for relevant change. In this context the swingers provided a kind of comic relief. They parodied change, playing it for entertainment. They made believe that self-initiated change was really occurring. The metaphor became extended. Swinging Britain was not only fashion and entertainment: it was also strong-willed technologists from the North, determined to restore enterprise to an effete Southern England. Grammar school boys became leaders of the two principal political parties; provincial accents were 'in' on TV; Britain was the country that had invented the jet engine.

But the North is not what it was. It is the Northern Metaphor that matters: the real North has become one of the principal factors in Britain's economic obsolescence. Even the grammar school political leaders seemed to lack the zip and zing that, for a while, the newspaper headings proclaimed.

More than the Labour Party, the pop scene became the essential expression of the contemporary young working-class movement, even if the Upper English joined in. It was an expression of the joyousness of younger members of the forgotten two-thirds, joyful that most of them had a pay packet coming in each week and that they could enjoy a ration of self-indulgence; it was also an expression of some of that hidden contempt of the Average Briton for what seemed the hypocrisies around him. The pop Brits were making it new, saying to society with British good humour but saying it nevertheless: *Up your bum, mates.*

Part II

ABROAD

5. THE EUROPEANS

Where is the west?

Perhaps for want of something else, 'going into Europe' has seemed to more and more of the British to be a kind of universal remedy for all of the ailments they profess to find in their country. 'Going into Europe' seems like slipping into a cure-all mineral bath. Even if it doesn't work, it could be fun and one could easily slip out again. The intractabilities of reality are different from this. For instance, what *is* the Europe that Britain wants to go into? Before talking about Britain's relations with Europe one might quickly ask Europe to stand up and identify itself.

It was only with the Islamic seizure of the Middle East, North Africa, and later, Byzantium, that there grew the idea that the land mass conventionally titled 'Europe' had also a separate cultural identity. Before then the civilization of that part of the world was thought of as Mediterranean rather than European – the Arabs went on partly thinking of it that way – and in this concept most of the European land mass was barbaric. After the Islamic expansion, if there was a Europe it was Christendom.

Even after the Renaissance and the development of modern Europe, the word 'European' and the concept of a European culture had little meaning until the late afternoon of the period of European power – at the time when Europe was beginning to turn in on itself in a way that caused two wars which were to kill forty or fifty million people, and produced a gas-chamber civilization. The early periods of enterprise were Italian, Spanish, and Portuguese rather than European, and the later periods were seen as the enterprise of Frenchmen, Englishmen, Dutchmen and so forth rather than as European. Earth was seen not as a planet in which *Europeans* extended power but as an area in which some of the nations of Europe contested for power among themselves. As a political concept 'Europe' was not fully put together until Russia joined it in the eighteenth century; the word 'European' did not really have a political meaning until the nineteenth century. As a civilization the nations of Europe, when confronted with the peoples they conquered, saw themselves primarily in terms of their own nationalities, but if they saw themselves collectively it was not as 'Europeans' but as Christians contesting heathens or as the civilized contesting the savages.

It might be more useful to consider that the distinctive characteristic of Europe is that it was that part of the world (first in Mediterranean Europe) in which there developed the processes of modernity and of globalism. When scholasticism turned into humanism and creative speculation, when the spirit of discovery and the desire for wealth led to that continuing conquest of the seas and of the world that was to be Europe's role until all the seas were mapped and all the world was open to European trading posts, when Crusaders fighting old battles were replaced by conquistadors seizing new continents, there was the beginning of that combination of revolutionary optimism and concepts of world power that were the special and distinctive characteristics of modern European civilization and that made the fifteenth to the nineteenth centuries the 'European' centuries. Considered in this way Europe can be thought of as the distinctive home of western civilization.

But now that the word 'Europe' is used more than ever before, one finds, if one looks closely at the distinctive characteristics of western civilization, that they can no longer be given a special location in the European continent. For this reason, to say that Britain should 'go into Europe' may be to say that it should retreat from western civilization as a whole, confining itself to only one part of it.

As the centre of globalism, Europe is now irrelevant. In globalism's last contest the Japanese were as global as anyone else. After that contest, those powers that wanted to exert world power and prestige were the United States, Russia, China, India, Britain, France, and Indonesia. As even this list dwindled, the representation of Europe shrivelled almost to disappearance.

As the centre of modernity, of the belief that, by taking thought, things can be changed, the Europe of Copernicus and Magellan now reads in its newspapers of the contest in space between the Americans and the Russians. Europe is still a centre of modernity, but the United States, in every respect, exceeds Europe's importance and so, in some respects, does Japan. The curiously lop-sided development of Russia also includes prestige enterprise that is ahead of Europe's, although in other ways it remains more conservative. One of the words for modernity in Europe is now 'Americanization'. Much of the sense of change in European economic progress is now a sense of achievement that compares Europe's present with its past, rather than with the rest of the world, or that contrasts changes in continental Europe with the comparatively slow change in economic planning in Britain, once the very architect of change.

Even in democratic aspiration, Europe has always been in an equivocal position. It was a part of the world where, as the political expression of Christian humanism, the aspirations of freedom, equality, and fraternity received a significant and lasting expression. But its external colonialism was a system of tyranny and a denial of equality and brotherhood. In internal government Europe was as inclined to despotism as to freedom, finally producing in Hitler's Germany an industrialization of tyranny and, until very recently, its ideals of equality and fraternity remained, very largely, underground. It was in the United States, not in Europe, that eighteenth century European democratic radicalism first went into bloom and where its ideological aspirations were expressed most strongly, and then in Canada, Australia, and New Zealand. It is true that, except for Spain and Portugal, Western Europe is now, for the first time in its history, democratic in government, but it was too long about it for this to be a distinguishing characteristic: while India's democratic government is from Europe, Japan's is from the United States.

The true distinctiveness of continental Europe lies in its role as a museum. This is not to deny the diverse intellectual and cultural life of contemporary Europe, both as a producer and as a consumer, but western civilization is now not only European but transoceanic and, in particular, transatlantic. The knowledge with which educated Europeans grow up of the writing, art, and music of their predecessors is the most universally 'western' thing about them. But this knowledge is no longer distinctively European. It can be American or Canadian or Australian as much as European; in a minor way it can also be Indian or Indonesian or Algerian. Where Europe is distinctive is in being the place where all this started, the continent in which Dante, Shakespeare, and Goethe actually lived. Americans can stock their museums with old masters, but they have to create Disneylands to reconstruct Europe's past: they cannot buy Rome and reassemble it on the West Coast.

The most truly distinctive 'Europeans' (in the sense of 'westerners') are now the Americans. In globalism and the sense of modernity America leads Europe. It is as if Europe's distinctive characteristics had been skimmed off and turned into a substance different from the individual nationalities of Europe, more 'European' ('western') than Europe itself. Not only is American culture part of western culture: Americans are now taught the European part of western culture in a way not widely adopted in Europe, and in America the nationalities of Europe have been jumbled together. Europeans are still primarily Italians or Finns, Germans or Portuguese, French or British. Merely to take these six examples of

different kinds of Europeans dramatizes their contrasts.
Are a Swede and a Greek 'European' when an American
is not?

The present wide use of 'European', as if somehow the
people of Europe had already risen above nationality, is
a symptom of Europe's decline in power, and of its
jealousy of the rest of the world. To suggest that the distinctive characteristics of western civilization are peculiar only to the continent of its birth and that they are
common to its inhabitants was first (and still is) a weapon
against the British, but it is above all now a weapon
against the Americans, the true Europeans. And just as
materialist enterprise, one of the first distinctions of
European civilization, is now seen as Americanization, so,
if the sense of nationality goes in Europe and its inhabitants do become more alike, and a nation of 'Europeans'
really does begin to exist, then they will have become true
'Americans'.

Britain and Europe

I have gone through this diversion to suggest that it is
unlikely that suddenly everything becomes all right by
deciding that Britain is purely 'European'. If this were
taken to mean that Britain should see itself primarily or
exclusively as belonging to a community across the Channel it should be pointed out that this community does not
exist. That France, Germany, Italy, and the three Low
Countries, for the first time in their general history of
quarrelsomeness, agreed to co-operate in economic matters
marked an enormous improvement in their relations with
each other; it is also excellent that the nations of Western
Europe in general should now live at peace and know
more about each other. But these admirable trends are
not evidence that Britain's true essence is its continental
Europeanness (as distinguished from its global interests
or its Anglo-Saxonry) and that therefore Britain can re-
discover its true nature only by an affirmation of regional-

ism. At least it should be recognized that the mere fact of geographical contiguity does not settle the matter. How 'European' is Albania?

Among the perplexities of British relationships with continental Europe are these: There are feelings of difference between the nations of continental Europe, but are their feelings of difference of a kind different from the feelings of difference they have towards Britain? Do they see Britain as a special kind of different thing? Conversely, is the British sense of difference from them different from their sense of difference from each other? In particular, does Britain lump them all together, so that it is a feeling of difference from all Europe, not only from individual nations, as if continental Europe were the one different thing?

The last two questions are the easiest to answer. Yes, on the whole, more often than not, the British got into the habit of lumping all the nations of continental Europe together and damning the lot of them. While other great powers feared or dreamed of power and influence in Europe, Britain began giving priority to power and influence in the *world*, concerning itself with Europe mainly as something that might upset that power. It saw the world as an arena for its importance in a way that other European powers imitated, but could not so completely believe. In addition, in its relations with continental Europe, it suffered the enormous misfortune of having France as the main country across the Channel: this accentuated a feeling of difference that might have been impossible to sustain if Sweden had been its closest neighbour.

Individual intelligent and perceptive British people were not so ignorant or deluded. But, of necessity, if they drew sustenance from Europe it was not from all Europe but from some particular nation or culture in it. For the few who travelled in Europe and became familiar with it, and were not blinded by insularity, it would until a few years ago have seemed simply insane to speak of Europe as if it were the one thing. Even Hitler, the first of the modern 'Europeans', did not see Europe as the one thing but as an area in which to plunder, persecute, and massacre until it became the one thing – Germany.

Both the Anglophiles and the Anglophobes of Europe created out of Britain – more exactly, out of England – one main ideal, for which the Anglophiles praised it and for the lack of which the Anglophobes attacked it. This was, in essence, the ideal that the world's most powerful country was also the world's most truly aristocratic country. At the trivial level the Anglophiles admired and imitated what they took to be the dandy's elegance of the English in their clothes, their diversions, and their *hauteur*. The more fully developed Anglophile concept of English Puritanism was of *noblesse oblige*, of a courageous aristocratic honesty and decency, manifest most finely in the liberalism of some imaginary English Puritan duke. English Puritanism was seen as the equality that would now be described as simplicity of style. English disdain of even the most crass and brutal kind was an understandable expression of nonchalance towards a dishonest world. The Lion stood for power; the Unicorn for moral elegance. The Anglophobes attacked Britain for not meeting these ideals of aristocratic power. Hitler, the prime Anglophobe, sometimes seemed genuinely sorry that he had detected the smile of the pussycat on the face of the Lion. From Napoleon to Hitler, Anglophobes attacked English money-grubbing, the antithesis of aristocratic disdain, the nation of shopkeepers, the Jewish vampire bankers. Usually successfully intuitive in his propaganda, Hitler denied England those characteristics for which Germans would have most respected it.

It was nevertheless during Hitler's war that there shone brightest in its whole history the European image of a powerful England rising above the cynical parvenus and brutal go-getters of the Continent and, led by the aristocratic Churchill, determined to restore decency to Europe's affairs. It was the survival of the Lion that gave some sense of dignity to a conquered Europe. The haughty islanders, with their prestigious overseas power and their disdain for their neighbours, had accepted the responsibilities of neighbourhood. For a couple of years Britain was the standard-bearer of European civilization.

Britain's own image of itself during the war was different: the image was above all that of the embattled island, fighting for itself, betrayed again by the Europeans, hating Hitler but not loving overmuch the Europe he had knocked to bits. Despite Churchill and the dash of the Western Desert campaign, Britain had become somewhat matey and low key, most proud of itself as a nation that could take it rather than dish it out, over-extended, and later, anxious to be seen playing a role alongside the Americans.

In the difference between the European and the British images of Britain lies some of the unhappiness of Britain. When the war was over, the nation Europe had seen as a leader was debilitated and soon it took no significant European initiatives, except as expressions of its relations with the United States. The nations of Europe went on with their business in their own new ways, with most of the British not even understanding the opportunities that had been missed. When the British again took an interest in Europe it was not as aristocrats moved to an honourable action, but as shopkeepers who wanted to sell their goods. The Lion was begging for his dinner. That their society, although aristocratic in the sense that it is hierarchic, can lack the impulses of a moral aristocracy is, in their pussycat moods, sufficiently apparent to the British for them to be unable to understand the part their admirers in Europe have expected them to play.

In British attitudes towards going European there were to be found most of Britain's attitudes to the world. Of the opponents, some showed a simple historic distrust: Europe, all Catholics and Communists, was the place the wars came from. Others felt that Britain should improve its own Welfare State and to hell with Europe, or in other ways expressed their confidence in the superiority of British institutions to those abroad, even fearing a loss of 'British freedom'. Some, while not necessarily opposing closer relations with Europe, saw Great Britain as more a part of the *world* than a part of Europe. With the antique disdain for mere makers and sellers of things some saw the new Europe as a moneybags world of technocrats and big business, association with which would corrupt Little England.

First among the supporters of the Europeanization of Britain were those who felt that somehow it might fix up the British economy; there was something in it for them. Although, as the discussion continued, some of the ways in which it might happen were seen to be painful there was nevertheless an un-British acceptance of the need to shake Britain out of itself, to give it a shock, to see what would happen next. Some opportunity for continuing to play governess was also seen; it was Britain's task to reduce the dangers of a largely Catholic Europe; an expansion of Europe might lead to co-operation between other nations; with British moral leadership, Europe might attempt concertedly to raise world living standards. For a few there was the mysticism of a Europe that was all Britain had ever really belonged to – the Empire and the United States had not really existed. For some there was the anxiety of wanting to belong to something, of not wanting to be left out of everything. But what emerged more and more clearly was that entry into Europe seemed to provide a chance to again exert superiority. The desire to make a fraternal contribution to the growth of Europe received little mention even in rhetoric: what excited the imagination was that it might be Great Britain Again, this time in Our Europe. The British policy was simply de Gaulle's policy: to attempt to use Europe as an echo-chamber for the grandeur of one's own nation.

It is in a humbler way that Britain could most gain from enmeshment in Europe, Common Market or not:

the shock of finding commonsense in a Frenchman, or aristocratic and disdainful honesty in a Spaniard, or elegance in an Italian, or incorruptibility in a Swede. The muddled and conflicting ideals of British behaviour have become claustrophobic shadows, as if they did not really exist. To find them scattered among the nationalities of Europe might restore some substance to them. But why only Europe? There can be equally therapeutic shocks in finding pragmatism and good form in a Chinese or a sense of fair play and self-control in a Japanese or a sense of whimsy and self-criticism in an American.

Little Europe

Being human, Western Europe is tough. Its toughness, surviving the catastrophes of two horrible wars, lies not in its factories, its buildings, its highways, its electric transmission systems and so forth, but in men's relations with each other, in their habits, memories, knowledge, and aspirations which, as long as *they* still exist, can reconstitute a society even after the factories have been blown up and the communication systems sabotaged. Western Europe's despair after the first of the two great wars it caused came not so much from the debilitations of slaughter and material destruction as from an exhaustion of creative belief, a desiccation of meaning. Old habits were carried on, but in travesty. A Nazi rally was a send-up of old European things; the British Empire of the 1930s was a wooden dummy. In its beginnings even the second great war was a re-enactment, a parade of war, tanks pushing over cardboard frontiers, victims killed like rabbits.

However, in these tragic re-enactments Western Europe rid itself of the habits which had no meaning. Western Europe's revival after the war meant a greater acceptance of one of the two distinctive characteristics of western civilization. Its sense of globalism was weakened, but it now accepted more fully the spirit of change – and, as an extra, there was more general acceptance of democratic aspirations. Western Europe was now becoming more characteristically 'American', although its Americanism was still diluted and flavoured by the specific traditions of nationalities and regions.

It is with this Europe that the most 'European' British believe their nation can find a new sense of having a place in the world and belonging to something. Yet this 'Europe' is still one of those words like 'Commonwealth'; it is a post-war word, manufacturing identity where it does not exist. Unlike the paper castles of the Commonwealth, the actual economic mechanisms of the Common Market are a reality, but these are only a bit of Europe; the idea that Britain should go 'European' meant more than entry into the Common Market: it had some of the magical meaning of a word like 'Asian'. 'European' is not as meaningless as 'Asian' – there has been a European civilization, although manifest in diverse nationalities, whereas in Asia there have been only national, not continental, civilizations – but 'European' has the same rhetorical quality about it as 'Asian'.

Economically the nations of Europe are trying to catch up with America. Internationally they are concerned with consoling themselves for their collective loss of importance. At its most ambitious the dream of Europe is that it might become a collective Third Best, a Third Power, thereby doing America, Russia, and 'Afro-Asia' all in the eye in one go. Yet Japan alone might seem a more likely candidate for Third Powerdom than Europe.

It is not so much the insularity of Europe as its barrenness in relation to the future that is relevant to Britain's predicament, since barrenness in relation to the future is also characteristic of Britain. To understand this one must ask: What most seems to matter now and in the future? To these questions there seem two main sets of answers. (Like most answers, they interlock.) One is that human beings now stumble around looking for forms of equality and brotherhood – between classes within a nation, and between nations and races. The other is that those human beings who can raise their heads from the struggle of mere existence must now contemplate the processes of continuing *change*, exhilarating or frightful, but apparently inexorable. The economic question is a by-product of these forces: the belief that everyone should enjoy at least a certain level of material comfort is an expression of egalitarianism and brotherliness, given sense by the belief that change is possible.

These two central obsessions both come from the Pandora's box of western civilization, as does their global nature. When, however honestly or hypocritically, however intelligently or stupidly, the doctrines of equality are proclaimed in Russia or America or China or India or Indonesia, it was the impulse of Europe that put them there. And the western belief that change is possible was planted by the Europeans all over the world like bombs, often destroying like bombs, as it destroyed in Europe itself. Just as when a European follows the tradition of privileged liberty he is a *Greek,* or when he follows the tradition of rationality he is a *Greek* or an *Arab,* or when he follows the rule of law he is a *Roman,* so when a Japanese or an Indian or a Chinese wishes to uproot what exists and to plan a new situation to replace it he is a *European.* The distinctively modern turmoil of the world is European: that the world is moving from its traditional cyclic patterns to a sense of disruption and thrust means that the world is becoming European. But whether one means by Europe the nations of Europe or the 'Europe' of the speeches, it is obvious that Europe, the unlocker of the turmoil, is now no longer central to those world obsessions its unlocking caused.

6. THE EX-NATIVES

How moral was the Empire?

It was in imperial terms that the Upper English were most confident of their *moral* leadership and this is a subject that they cannot yet leave alone. It is in Britain's inability to find new ways to play governess to the world that a significant part of its crisis of external identity now lies. The habit is still to judge external relations in terms of their potential contributions to the rhetoric of moral leadership: the Commonwealth was to have been, among other things, an echo chamber for this leadership; some of the British saw such an opening in entry into Europe. At times one of the most flattering roles that could be found for the Americans was that they should play the Romans while Britain played the Greeks. It might take the pain out of this quest for purpose if the British recognized that much of their concern with moral leadership was manufactured as a kind of deodorant against the smells of imperialism, and that its function was more cosmetic than hygienic.

How moral was the Empire? In the settler colonies, settlers simply seized the land and pushed aside the natives or killed them. In North America, as in Australia, New Zealand, and South Africa, and then later in East Africa, the process was the same: acquire land by seizure or trickery and then ignore the native, or shoot him if he acted as if he still owned the place. What happened to the natives depended on their strength: the New Zealand Maoris got the best deal because they fought the British in a war and got some terms for themselves in the peace. The Tasmanian aborigines got the worst deal: they were exterminated in man hunts. When their countries had been stripped of natives, as one strips a countryside of trees, just leaving a clump here and there, Canada, Australia, and New Zealand then provided evidence for British moral leadership by becoming self-governing. Along with the appearance of self-government in South Africa (where the absence of native representation was not seen as a fault) and the establishment of India as a 'dominion', it could be made look as if the Empire was a kind of world federation of free states, with a suggestion of promise to the other colonies, where the natives had not been destroyed, and where settlers were small in numbers (because it was too hot) or where there were no settlers: this was the promise of eventual self-government; but it was a small promise, far off in the future.

In these colonies the imperialists, in the name of preventing anarchy, caused it. Taking advantage of the natives' powerlessness, they imposed their own civilization within the native civilization but as something apart – not destroying the native civilization, as the Spaniards destroyed the civilizations of the Incas and the Aztecs, not, except superficially, attempting to change it but mocking it and eroding it, walking through it as if it were not there, and pulling off any bits that got in the way. The natives were expected to conform to the conquering civilization only in those aspects of that civilization that suited the conquerors' comfort or that were judged fit for the natives. A native's wish to conform to the more privileged aspects of the conquering civilization could seem laughable (that babu!) or dangerous (that agitator!). The principal aspect of the conquering civilization to which the natives were expected to conform was the sense of orderliness. They were to become more orderly in their relations with each other, and in their relations with the conquering power. This eliminated acts of savagery among the conquered; but when civilizations turn their rough edges on each other they can merely seem rival barbarisms, there was also for the natives a violence in the order they were subjected to. The natives' sense of nationality was suppressed as fully as the sense of individuality of the subject peoples of that stereotype of oriental despotism, the Ottoman Turk. Even the Irish were treated as natives and even their sense of nationality was put down.

Such acts of barbarism were seen as acts of civilization because natives were taken to be essentially savage and disorderly. Since the Upper English saw a policeman as a symbol of their own liberty, Britain was seen as a world policeman, and it was in the interests of world order that British strength should be deployed wherever it was required. As a guardian of civilization, Britain was a missionary of order and good government, burdened with responsibilities for others, unthanked for the heavy tasks it assumed, but carrying on with a sense of service. There was a determination that this greatness must not pass. Some of this determination was sheer pride in the bigness of the Empire, but, along with the increasing readiness to boast of bigness, the rhetoric of service and duty also grew more outrageous and to protect and extend British power seemed a duty to the world. Calmly certain that they were right, the British began to boast that a quarter of the world now enjoyed British justice. The incorruptibility of officials, their just arbitration in disputes, and their suppression of disorder or native barbarism were the ideals of a civilizing power. Good government was better than self-government. And while in Britain it was an attack on British freedom to suggest that a restriction on the liberty of the élites might nevertheless be for the benefit of the people, in the colonies good government was taken to be in the true interests of the mass of the people. The discontent of the native élites at the small part allowed them in the government of their own countries was dismissed as mere 'agitation'.

In fact there was more pretence of government than government itself. The problems of India, for example, were not primarily those of fair administration, arbitrating in disputes, not taking bribes, and keeping the railway stations clean; as Gandhi said, India's real problems were social and religious, and the British were neither fitted to intervene in such problems, nor even aware of their importance. Although they brought much impetus in the European sense of change into India, throwing up new commercial and industrial forms, new concepts of education and communication, new views of life and, by their key decision to Indianize the Indian Civil Service, giving India something to go on with when it became independent, they preferred to adopt an old belief of government: that society was merely static and that the main role of government was to hold the ring. Although they generated change they would take no responsibility for what they had done, except to suppress manifestations of change that threatened disorder. They accumulated bits and pieces of knowledge about native societies, but they preferred to do as little as possible about what they had discovered. Beyond the maintenance of power itself, they were concerned more with the pretence of government, the display of their power, than with actual government. In many matters perhaps this had to be so; perhaps they were matters in which the foreigner could not finally intervene; but in the whole range of activities that go under the name of 'welfare', matters in which they *were* competent to act, they were rather mean. They were paternalists, but they were not generous.

Behind the display of pomp and the rhetoric of duty there was often a certain crumminess to be found in the style of British rule. After two generations of power in Cairo the nearest British officials could get to the Egyptians was to speak bad French. Their clubs in every conquered city were hated for their exclusion of the natives. Preferring the distinctions of race to those of class, they showed no sympathy for the hopes of western-educated natives. Their public attitude to native women was more prudish than that of other European colonialists and their wives seemed to be more stuck-up. There was a kind of parochial cosiness: wherever they went they tried to reconstruct the atmosphere of a second-rate English club. Of the civilization they took with them one of the most respected and jealously guarded elements was the tennis party. Their main concern was to maintain the reassuring trivialities of English life, and often they lived in greater ease than they could have managed at home. In fact one of the great attractions of life in a colony was that it could be softer, more pleasant, less demanding than life at home. When they went back to England to retire, their wives complained about the relative lack of servants. Talk to the old colonials in their most nostalgic moods about 'the East' and you usually discover that what most attracted their imagination in their old life was its privilege and laziness. In this narrow world in which he lived, entrenched in Upper Englishness, untouched by the exotic, the cautious man went about his conventional tasks in a conventional way, enjoying the softness of life, the spells in the hills, the long vacations at home, and the pension on retirement in a nice English county. For many of its employees, the Empire was a way of getting through life in a familiar way.

The Cardboard Commonwealth

For most people in Britain the Empire was one of those things, even more remote than the Monarch, that could give them a sense of importance. They did not need to know much about it. It was enough to see all the red on the map without even noticing exactly where it was, to hear the boasting songs without understanding even their qualifications, to learn the slanted history texts, and to absorb the most vulgar parts of the imperial speeches. As whites they knew they were better than niggers and as inhabitants of Great Britain they knew they were better than white colonials, even if the Australians could beat them at cricket. This indifference to the detail of Empire is now sometimes taken as an example of how easy it was to slough the Empire off, of how most people in Britain were not really interested in it. But it is not unusual for people to have a view of their place in the world that is based on matters in which they are not interested in detail and which they may not understand. It was enough to know that Britain was the most important country in the world. Those who did the public talking and writing, even if they had no interest in the Empire, were also affected by the assumption that Britain was the most important country in the world, an assumption of which the Empire was the cause and the proof, so that even when they talked of matters that had nothing to do with the Empire they talked in their own version of the imperial manner, backed usually by the easy assurance of the class manner. It is the absence of all this assurance that makes things seem odd in Britain now. When the Empire ceased to exist, it had to be re-invented. The function of the Commonwealth was to provide an ersatz assurance.

This suited the two kinds of influential persons who were most interested in the Empire: those who were for it, and those who were against it. The old imperialists could, for a while longer, add up all those natives and white colonials and still see Britain as a world force; it was not quite a super-power, but the weight of numbers made up for a super-power's nuclear stockpile, and of course there was British moral leadership to back it up. The old radical opponents of Empire could also see the Commonwealth as an example of moral leadership, setting new ideals of racial tolerance. In both cases the Commonwealth was a useful stick to beat Europe and the United States with. To the old imperialists it still gave Britain the look of a great power, almost as good as the United States, bigger than any nation in Europe; to the old radicals it gave Britain the appearance of a sense of mission, distinguishing it from the go-getters in Europe and the United States. For some time it remained one of the props of self-importance because nobody could find anything else to put in its place.

Yet the Commonwealth was almost entirely without political meaning except for its value as propaganda. It suited London's self-importance to have regular meetings of Commonwealth Prime Ministers, even if the meetings were to no purpose except for those Commonwealth Prime Ministers who used them to drum up support for their own policies. Schemes were produced to give it some other meaning, but the schemes themselves became mere propaganda. The central political question in the Commonwealth became that of its own survival. Its main use was that it should continue to exist and this meant mainly that the name should still be used and the photographs taken. The drama of its annual power manoeuvres was: *Will the Commonwealth survive another meeting?* When it was learned that once again it had not broken up, the Commonwealth had served its purpose. Britain was still important. The fact that the Commonwealth's main use was as a prop to self-esteem was illuminated when Britain made its Common Market applications: the Commonwealth didn't seem to matter so much then; Britain could now become important by entering Europe, or by appearing to do so.

The French lost Vietnam and Algeria in anguish, but they disembarrassed themselves of their tropical African Empire in the British way – by acclamation. They do not boast about this, however, as the British boast of their colonial disengagement. The loss of their Empire caused much more disturbance in France itself than did the loss of the British Empire in Britain, but (perhaps for this reason) they make no attempt to pretend that it is still there. What they have done is to put up some cash: they provide bigger aid programmes to ex-colonies than the British and exert more influence.

The British did not prove to have an interest as deep and practical as that of the French in what happened to the former colonial peoples. At a number of levels various institutions were, of course, still entangled with the natives – business firms, universities, families – and the use of English as the main European language of the natives maintained a mesh of general cultural and intellectual links. But no new initiatives came from British governments. The principal function of the Commonwealth was to be useful not to the natives but to the British, and its very cumbersomeness and contradictions meant that if it were to be used it would fall apart, since it was a cardboard cut-out, put up for show. The disparity between the industrialized member sections and the economically underdeveloped societies meant that it could not be seen as an economic unit; its geographical spread gave no sense of contiguity; its cultural diverseness, although one of its charms, did not lead to a natural unity; each unit was concerned with its own sense of mission in the world, and its relations to the others could not follow the British pattern. For example, Australia discovered its South-East Asian-ness to be more stimulating than the masquerades of Commonwealth. To Australia the formerly Dutch Indonesia was more immediately significant than India; of ex-British colonies, Singapore and Malaysia alone were more important than all the ex-British colonies in Africa; it was the future of the formerly French Laos, Cambodia, and Vietnam that might most affect Australian interests, not the future of Aden; and, in the destruction of Australian provincialism, while new relations with Japan were creative, to imagine that there was a special relationship between Australia and Tanzania or Cyprus was to fall back on the old provincialism.

It was because the British pretended the Commonwealth was more than it was that it came to nothing. If they had really wanted to make something of it, if they had really wanted to turn it into a free association of nations, racially and culturally diverse but holding some interests in common, it is just possible that they might have achieved something. But this would have meant removing the Queen as the Commonwealth's head and abolishing London as its meeting place. It would have meant chucking out some of the Commonwealth's present members and perhaps adding new member-states that had never been 'British'. It would almost certainly have developed along diverse, limited, and regional lines. All such measures would have dramatized change instead of providing reassurances of stability.

A useful test of British sincerity in using association with its former subjects to some purpose other than show lies in its relations with Singapore and Malaysia. Here British policy was admirable. The long task of putting down communist insurgency was concluded skilfully and intelligently and then, later, when Sukarno put on his show of 'confrontation' against the newly formed Malaysia, the British again acted both with determination and with cleverness: holding back their main power, they deployed no more than was necessary to hold Sukarno's bluff. By this means they gave Malaysia a chance to sort itself out and they created tensions in Indonesia without destroying the Indonesian Army's prestige, a necessary act of prudence since the Army seemed the main alternative power to the Indonesian Communist Party. When events blew up in Indonesia the Army still held credit and, in alliance with politicians more pragmatic than Sukarno, set up a new government, abandoning Sukarno's adventurism which had proved disastrous to his own people. All this, combined with sensible policies in dealing with Malaysia and Singapore, represented the most responsible and successful withdrawal from power in the whole pullout from Empire.

Yet its presentation to the British was ruined by those most interested in it. To the old imperialists, the actions in Malaysia were pumped up as parades of power – Britain was still Great in Kuala Lumpur; by the old radicals they were paraded as examples of imperialism, so that Sukarno, the imperialist, looked like a true Asian liberal and the enlightened British policy was presented as oldfashioned, reactionary meddling. Perhaps neither old imperialists nor old radicals are interested in Commonwealth countries except as excuses for maintaining their rhetoric so that they can continue to confront each other in London, playing the only roles they know. When Harold Wilson entered the London imperial theatre he played mainly to the other actors. Announcing an East-of-Suez policy he played to the old imperialists; announcing its cancellation and the withdrawal of British forces he played to the old radicals.

That Singapore and Malaysia did not want the British to give a time-table for their departure, that they wanted Britain to stay there a bit longer, *that the British were still welcome*, were facts that did not move the emotions of the old actors. To the old imperialists British power was better imposed than requested; to the old radicals British power was not asked for – its function was to be overthrown.

Black Britons

The British created 'the West Indians' as the Americans created their Negroes. They took them to the West Indies from Africa as slaves or from India as indentured labourers, destroyed their language, their laws, their sense of being, then created a new sense of being, that they were 'West Indian', a British people, dark perhaps and of different racial origin, but British all the same, acknowledging Britain as the Mother Country and, indeed, as the mother of the free. In all of the pulling out of Empire, this created people, the West Indians, seemed a special responsibility. Believing, despite their skins, that they were indeed 'British', a number of the West Indians went to Britain, where there are now 500,000 of them making up, with 200,000 Indians, 150,000 Pakistanis, and 150,000 Africans, a million in all of these non-Europeans who took the word of an Englishman as his bond. Some are direct immigrants, some are the children of immigrants, born in Britain, educated in British schools. This immigration has been almost stopped. When race bigotry against the blacks produced some open expressions of violence and many lesser tensions the government was impelled by that British sense of order that is greater than its sense of freedom. Fearing that even a little violence, even a little discord, might destroy existing freedom, but at the same time fearing that an openly expressed policy of racialist bias in immigration would bring the Commonwealth into disrepute, it set up elusively defined systems of control that displayed British fairness by appearing to discriminate against all Commonwealth countries but let in people of European origin more readily than it let in the blacks.

Some Black Britons live in ghettoes like those in Southall and Ladbroke Grove in London, Sparkbrook and Balsall Heath in Birmingham, or Moss Side in Manchester. These settlements display some of the characteristics of the American ghettoes – built-in poverty, high rates of baby deaths, malnutrition, delinquency, violence, drug-taking, and madness, disgusting and overcrowded housing for which racketeering rents are charged, a lack of public amenities, and a feeling of separateness from the rest of the city: 'integration' can be achieved most easily in prostitution, drug-peddling, hustling, and show business. There is even developing some aspiration towards 'Black Power'. Until recently too unsure of themselves to make trouble, the immigrants, as they begin to feel some strength, begin to return the hostility that was directed at them.

The most obvious manifestations of hostility are in attitudes to jobs and houses. A survey sponsored by the government in 1967 confirmed what was already obvious: that most employers rejected the blacks when they asked for jobs or, if they did employ them, did not promote them; that about two-thirds of the owners of rented houses would not accept blacks as tenants; and that if they bought a house, the blacks had to pay higher deposits and higher interest rates than whites. The result is that the blacks are housed mainly in decaying, sub-standard streets of old houses near the centre of the cities, where they are lumped in with white throwouts.

What seems worse is that even in the big conurbations

where most blacks live, only about one in twenty become tenants in council houses; when they do become tenants of the councils it is usually in inner city sub-standard housing, specially bought and patched-up for the purpose of keeping the blacks off the more respectable main council housing estates. In fact of all the types of housing available, the main council house estates are most likely to have no blacks at all. Deprived of council housing, they are more likely to use council mortgage schemes to buy houses of their own, but at least one council disbanded its mortgage scheme when it found that more blacks were using it than whites. To the councils the blacks represent a troublesome stimulus to voters' bigotries, so that it seems dangerous or undesirable to make any special efforts: it seems safer to act as if no problem existed. In detail prejudice is often exercised piecemeal: the official investigators of claims for council houses exercise their personal prejudices, either directly or indirectly, or without knowing it.

The special pain is for Black Britons who were born in Britain. They go to integrated schools where, with the innocence of children, they at first share their humanity, but with adolescence they become sharply aware of the prejudices of the society around them. Their white friends become un-friends, unable, as they acquire the ways of their elders, to include blacks among them. The whites pick up the distinctions of their parents ('We don't mean you, of course – you're different'); the blacks pick up the distinctions of *their* parents ('You can't trust Pinkie'). It becomes a challenge to the stability of society for a black boy to take out a white girl. Cut off from the special culture of their immigrant parents, educated in English ways, offered English history as if it were their history, they are nevertheless suddenly aliens in the place where they have grown up. This shock grows sharper when they discover that, although they have had the same education as their schoolfriends, they can't get the same jobs. They have a sense of minority. They have been done in by 'the

English'. British fair play is not to be theirs after all. As outsiders they become sceptical observers of the society around them, detecting its hypocrisies and seeing all aspiration as hypocrisy. It can seem a society with which you make communication by chucking a brick, or breaking electric light bulbs, or knocking dustbins over. Lacking identity with the hypocrisies and bigotries of the enveloping society, they seek identity in the colour of their skins. Some form peaceful duplications of white life: black child-minding centres, black credit clubs, black cricket clubs.

The blackness of Inner London is developing so fast that in the 1970s one in six of the children who leave school in that area will be Black Britons; yet there seems to be no strong local initiative intended to encourage them to belong to the city where they have been born and educated. The Wilson Government attempted to restrain discrimination in housing and employment, but electoral pressures blunted its attempt at liberalism. In a panic because Indians in Kenya had taken seriously an earlier statement that they were United Kingdom citizens and had attempted to come to Britain to redeem its pledge, the government passed legislation which limited their entry: only sixty-two members of the House of Commons voted against the Bill. It was an unreality for the Upper English that black men should become a domestic problem: the liberal rhetoric of the Commonwealth as a brotherhood of races was not meant to have been taken as seriously as that. Just as the particularities of Singapore and Malaysia were less interesting than the continuance of an old debate, so were the particularities of Southall and Wolverhampton. While liberal England spoke in protest in the newspapers and magazines, the broader liberal conscience, alive enough to condemn racialism in the United States, became weary when faced with the practicalities of a much smaller and more malleable manifestation of racial bigotry at home. What was most alarming was a lack of even practical interest in the material welfare of the million blacks already in Britain. It might have been expected that even those who opposed further immigration would be interested in extending British fair play to the blacks who were already British. But it did not prove to be so. Speeches were still available about moral leadership in the world, but the leadership was to be the old imperial one of the governess, lecturing but not acting. Those who sought great new roles for Britain did not seek them in Wolverhampton.

The ex-natives

If Britain is to move with the world it must attempt to understand the humanity of the ex-natives. This is not a question of moral leadership or playing a great role in the world, but simply the question of becoming a contemporary society, fit for the future. But while recognition of guilt might well suggest a continued sense of obligation, it does not suggest abasement, which can blind understanding as much as the old arrogance. Shocks of recognition are its essence, not the charity work of the guilty. One can contemplate, for an exercise, orientalism in Britain and materialism in Japan, or enterprise in Singapore and traditionalism in London. Or one could ask who, at the time of the Suez Crisis, was the bigger crackpot: Nasser or Eden? One might wonder what kind of a job Whitehall would have made of the mess Sukarno left behind him: would it have done as well as General Suharto? Or one might imagine Lee Kuan Yew as leader of the British Labour Party: with the resources he would then possess, might he not do a better job than Harold Wilson? How would the Lord Mayor of Birmingham make out if he were Prime Minister of Laos which, in numbers, has much the same population? Compare and contrast Westminster Abbey and Bangkok's Temple of the Emerald Buddha, or the role of King Phumiphon with that of Queen Elizabeth. From answering such questions one should acquire not a sense of abasement but a sense of modesty and equality. It is in the searching for similarities and differences between men that a sense of liveliness might be acquired in the future. Many Asian leaders, for example, although they sometimes confess despair about the intractabilities of the traditional societies that they are trying to push along, can nevertheless provide a fresh stimulus to understanding western societies: 'westerniza-tion' is what they are about in their own countries and they have sometimes thought about 'westernization' more sharply than most of the 'westerners', seeing more clearly its distinctive attributes, whereas 'westerners' sometimes see their 'westernism' in traditional terms that can also apply to Asian societies.

It would be an act of indecency for the British to lose all interest in all those places their predecessors looted and from whose possession they drew such self-importance. It is not abasement to recognize responsibility. Despite their own economic difficulties the British should attempt to increase economic assistance to the French level and to maintain various kinds of commitments to at least some of their ex-colonies – for several more generations, if necessary. This is an act that should be done for its own sake, but by maintaining such relations the British would also be enlivened by them. For Britain to remove itself altogether from the world of the ex-natives would be to withdraw Britain from the world itself. The demand that Britain should still play a leading role in the world is often too ambitious. Its eyes are bigger than its soul. But while the ex-natives will accept handouts if they do not offend pride, they don't want to receive lectures, especially from the British, whom all the world now lectures in return. This means a change in role. There is no longer a question of shoving a superior civilization into an in-ferior one, but of getting down to detail, of trying to help a society change itself. What the more pragmatically-minded ex-natives want is something that is likely to work. This is a field of speculation in which the British have been unexpectedly weak. In the first flushes of decolonization the approach to the new nations was that to become democratic they should set up political institutions copying those of Western Europe or North America, and that to become prosperous they had to go through a certain specified ritual that represented some ideal of what had happened in the prosperous countries but in fact did not happen. Since neither of these approaches worked, there has been a more open casting around for new ideas. How many British academics are making themselves reputations by analysing the problems of underdeveloped societies? How many institutes have been set up in Britain to study the problems of economic take-off or political freedom in traditional societies? There have been many roles the British could have chosen to play in the world after they lost their Empire; it was almost as if they did not want to play them, because they were all less than the old one big role.

Anglo-Saxondom

Are there *really* Anglo-Saxons? Do the people of the United States, Great Britain, Canada, Australia, and New Zealand have common characteristics that override differences and distinguish them from all other people? Or to put the question more realistically: Do these nations *seem* to be significantly similar? Do the *images* held of them significantly contrast with the images held of the rest of the world?

To continental Europeans the Anglo-Saxons are the maritime nations of European civilization – the European nations that are *overseas* and that, in some indefinable sense, are not fully 'European'. They make up an Oceanic Europe of powerful islands, with even the United States and Canada considered as a kind of island, floating exotically between the world's two greatest oceans. When Oceanic Europe expresses its heroism it does so globally, not within continental Europe. It throws its lot in with continental Europe only when it has to, to serve its own interests; it does not really *belong*. Great Britain looked across the seven seas, to Asia and Africa and to the Anglo-Saxon nations; in its own way, the United States pursued its ambitions in South America and across the Pacific. At first Great Britain professed to run the world; then came the turn of the United States. The two main Anglo-Saxon powers may differ, but they seem nevertheless locked in a trans-Atlantic embrace.

In another way, the Anglo-Saxons are seen as the true Puritans. As Roundheads, they are unintellectual pragmatists, lacking a sense of civic beauty, or of personal style, bigots who know nothing of values different from their own and who, when they break their hypocritical moralism to indulge in excess, do so not from any sense of joy but with a low vulgarity: Anglo-Saxons really do not know how to *live*; in their shapeless cities money is the only true measuring stick of worth. As Whigs, on the other hand, the Anglo-Saxons are the Reformation's finest flowering, the creators of modernity in both science and industry whose unique respect for constitutionalism and the rule of law makes them the only truly free societies.

In the Anglo-Saxon camp things do not seem so simple. In their period of power the British preferred to see Upper Englishness, not Anglo-Saxonness, as the centre of virtue, sharing esteem with the Americans only so far as they imitated England. In the crudity of 'White, Anglo-Saxon, and Protestant', or in less crude ways, the Americans drew to themselves some of the English virtue, seeing it as a transoceanic characteristic. In the period of deprecation of their own importance, the Americans were the true Anglo-Saxons, ideologizing Anglo-Saxon virtues in a way sometimes incomprehensible to the English. When the Americans entered their period of power they took some of the Anglo-Saxonry out of their virtue, converting it into a more general Americanism.

It is significant that, even when they speak of themselves nationally, the Anglo-Saxon nations tend to speak of the same things. They can all see themselves as pragmatic, empirical people given neither to pure logic nor to emotional excess. They can all boast of their practicalism, denying the influence of intellectuals even when it is most evident. Thus the Americans still have an ideology of pragmatism even when political debate in their society is highly conceptualized by intellectuals, and when intelligence and rationality are put to greater uses in America, with its tens of thousands of computers, than in any other nation on earth. And the British speak of their pragmatism, although less ideologically, when they mean their traditionalism. In the Anglo-Saxon societies political decisions – sometimes all decisions – are believed to be made on rational analyses of 'self-interest', whatever that may be. Things can be cut and dried in Anglo-Saxondom. It was in Britain ('the Manchester school') and then in America that the most austere ideologies of capitalist enterprise were manufactured. It was believed that if the iron laws of rapacity (the profit motive) and vindictiveness (competition) were scrapped, prosperity would fall to pieces. In a sense Manchester was the first modern American city.

With the exception of the Upper English and their imitators throughout Anglo-Saxondom, one of the crucial characteristics of Anglo-Saxonry is its apparent respect for an equality of manners amongst men. The muted aspirations of the British provinces and fringe lands broke loose throughout the rest of Anglo-Saxondom and now – if you forget for the sake of this argument the accompanying racial bigotries – Anglo-Saxondom can be seen as providing strong rhetorical support for those yearnings for equality between men that were first expressed in religious terms in the Reformation and then in secular terms in the eighteenth century. If Britain were all provinces and no Southern England, all Average Britons and no Upper English, all Northern Metaphor and no Southern Metaphor, the links between America, Britain, and the minor realms of Anglo-Saxondom might be indestructible.

But these differences provide the main ideological tensions of Anglo-Saxondom. The differences between Britain and America are less the differences between Birmingham and Pittsburgh than the differences between Upper Englishness, the minor but dominant cult of Britain, and Anglo-Saxonry, the global expression of British provincialism. The Upper English show disdain for Americans or Australians to the extent that Americans or Australians display British provincial characteristics: in the 'colonials' the democracy of the provinces becomes flagrantly manifest. To the Upper English the trans-Atlantic 'special relation' was not a relation between peoples: it existed most happily when one top dog could talk to the other with unique ease – a Churchill to a Roosevelt, a Macmillan to a Kennedy.

Another way of looking at Anglo-Saxons might be this: they suffer a feeling of foreignness when visiting any nation other than an Anglo-Saxon nation, but nevertheless what can absorb them most are their differences from each other. Perhaps it is in this sense that they constitute a family – members of a grown-up family who feel that something must still bind them together to distinguish them from the rest of the world, and who are absorbed in discovering if this something really exists. In this quest one English-speaker admires or detests another English-speaker by his own standards of what the English-speaking civilization is supposed to be. Since conducting arguments that nobody else understands can be a strong family bond, there may still remain some imponderable sense of family relation among English-speakers. Their differences still bind them, however loosely, since they cannot find such interesting differences in anyone else. One might define Anglo-Saxons as those English-speaking people who have a special interest in their differences from each other, such differences often being related to the differences between the Northern and the Southern Metaphor.

The man in the Hawaiian shirt

America was once the paradise on earth of Europe's radical humanist yearnings. In this paradise Americans took several forms. As the *free man* the American moved through the wilderness as the simple trapper (becoming a cowboy when he later reached the prairies); liberated from the cramping convention of effete civilizations, he was finding again the creative innocence known otherwise only to the noble savage: in this new naturalness he could stretch his soul as expansively as he could discover the vast freedom of his continent. As the *democratic man* the American was not only the new Athenian, recovering the forms of true self-government; he was also the first to seek a true equality between men, something unknown to Athenians. As the *revolutionary* he gave form to the aspirations of revolutionary Europe, throwing up great heroes who, unlike the Europeans, could produce revolutions that succeeded. As the *electrician* he was Stalin before his time, throwing up great powerhouses of industrialization.

Then began his terrible decline. The noble savage became the gangster, or the racialist Southerner, or the brutal general in the Pentagon. His son was a rebellious teenager, or even a drug-taker, seeking freedom in hallucinogens. The democrat became the party boss or the demagogic senator; if he was seeking equality he became the vulgar loud-mouth, the pedlar of barbarism, the man in the Hawaiian shirt. The revolutionary became the insane anti-communist or the man who didn't believe in income tax. The electrician became the plutocrat, the corporation executive or, if he couldn't qualify for executive status, he became the Coca Cola salesman mucking up picturesque views with advertising hoardings.

American civilization was empty and materialistic, a useless abundance; its symbols were roadside litter in Vietnam or old cars in California, piled together and smashed. Although gluttonous, the American did not know how to cook. In his inane organization hierarchies a stiff sense of status cramped and desiccated his life with its trivialities. His liberty was the right to make fake advertising claims and his pursuit of happiness was a liking for homogenized milk. When he was not devoted to the Almighty Dollar he was a shallow, depraved, sentimental, and stupid blunderer who did not understand how things went in the world. As Europe absorbed these new images of Americans, all first manufactured by Americans themselves, its loathing was equalled only by its envy, and then by its imitations.

It was America that first projected Europe's modern dreams and then realized them: since achieved aspiration is usually not according to plan it was America's role to disappoint European dreams by fulfilling them. Then as America took over Europe's power it took over a second role – of re-enacting Europe's old nightmares. Humiliated because America had saved them from a gas-chamber civilization, the Europeans could project their own past militarism on to the Americans: when the Americans accepted responsibility for the results of French dirtiness in Vietnam, the Europeans could see their own colonialism in the Americans. European diplomacy became a game in which a nation's policy was invented either to distinguish it from America or to distinguish it from a rival nation by supporting America. Attitudes to the communist countries became determined by attitudes to America. Even the friends of America-in-Europe sometimes saw the American as a blunderer not understanding what it was about as, like a travelling husband, he was faithless to Europe in Asia.

While Western Europe dreamed of doing without America, America was beginning to buy Western Europe up. The European capital and skill that first exported the industrial revolution to America generated such a monster that a hundred years later American capital and skill exported the new technological revolution to Europe. At first this was welcome. When Western European industry slowed down the Americans kept on inventing useful things, and in the wreckage after the war their capital helped to put Western Europe together again. But as Western European industry reconstructed itself, American industry generated such high steam that it had to expand. Profits beyond previous conception provided the new capital; the research and development fostered by government spending on the military and space programmes provided the new technology; and the Western Europe of free trade areas provided the new markets, not only because demand rose but also because the Americans, used to thinking big, and in terms of a continent, were able to set up rationalized continental sales structures more quickly than the Europeans. The 'brain drain' of Western

European scientists and engineers to America increased the technological gap. And the answer to the American challenge was more European 'Americanization'.

Special relations

One of the most obvious special relations existing between Britain and America is that the Americans invested more money in Britain than in any other European country. It is also from Britain that America takes the greatest number of European scientists and engineers; something between a fifth and a sixth of the total world brain drain consists of the haemorrhage from Britain, partly because in the new research-based industries Britain still provides Europe's main competition with America: the British alone maintain a research and development expenditure that is proportionately close to America's, so that, by training young scientists and engineers, and then frustrating them by the ancient crafts of British management, they fatten them up for American employment. Meanwhile the more lively parts of British management see American marketing approaches as their own. There begins to develop a transatlantic business and research community, young or youngish people to whom there is a cosmopolitanism of interest and opportunity (made easier by Anglo-Saxonry), to whom it is not particularly significant whether they live in one country or the other. Technocracy can be a more universal language than English, but speaking English makes it easier.

So far as formal political relations are concerned, the impetus that developed between Britain and America during the war continued to run down. Then Britain was the only European ally America had. After the war this fact and what appeared to be Britain's global interests, continued to give relations between the two governments a special importance, not least because British governments, although sometimes taking care to distinguish their policies from American policies, nevertheless supported

American lines more consistently than most other governments, even when the tone of British 'public opinion' worried the Americans. British Prime Ministers were anxious not to appear American stooges, but although they would fly to Washington, or Moscow, or both, during a super-power crisis, appearing to be moderates between two extremists and thereby crashing into the act, they were nevertheless moderates who were on the American side; in the United Nations they did not usually vote far away from America; in South-East Asia, after the French fiasco in 1954, they were the only European power still concerned with the part of the world where America was most controversially enmeshed; British Prime Ministers and Foreign Ministers seemed to clock up more hours per year in the White House than political leaders from any other country; there were special defence equipment entanglements; and the two countries shared a tightly binding interest – between them, their two currencies were used to finance the world's trade. Now that Britain seems less important in the world, particularly since its declared disentanglement from Malaysia and Singapore, what special relation is there between the two governments? In 1967 Harold Holt, the Australian Prime Minister, seemed to be photographed in the White House more often than the British Prime Minister, and President Johnson went to his funeral. In 1969 the Canadian and Australian Prime Ministers were the first heads of government to be invited to Washington by the new President.

America's sense of special political relationship had long become polycentric, beginning with its interest in the defeated nations of Japan and West Germany and then in its alliances against Russian and Chinese influence, but it is likely that British governments would have attempted to maintain a greater façade of special relationship with America if it had not been for the increasingly anti-American and sometimes chauvinistic tone of what appeared to be British public opinion. Britain's anti-Americanism developed both earlier and later than

Europe's. It was in the frustrations of being the junior partner in the wartime alliance that the modern forms of political anti-Americanism in Britain first developed. Here the criticisms of the Americans were mainly from the right: American generals and their soft-living troops did not really know how to fight and American statesmen were both too kind to the Russians and too hostile to the British Empire. During the 'Ami go home' period in Europe, although there was still criticism in Britain of the softness and naivety of the Americans, there was not much political anti-Americanism, and what there was existed mainly on the left: this was the period of the mythology of America's germ warfare in Korea, of the American introduction of the potato bug into East Germany and of Joe McCarthy's march towards fascism back home.

However, British governments were expected to 'play a role in the world'. Of the two main attempts at real independence one (the Suez incident) was absurd; the other (in Malaysia) was excellently performed, but there was no audience in Britain for it. In the logic of the situation, since they could not play the hero – at least not in areas that 'public opinion' was interested in – British governments began to play the hero's wife; an intelligent and emancipated woman who saw marriage as a partnership of equals and whose loyalty to her husband was manifested mainly in her attempts to save him from what she considered his own excesses. Attlee's flight to Washington during the Korean war was the first try-out in this performance; Eden's intervention at the end of the French war in Vietnam was the most significant. However, as a theatrical performance the role was developed more fully during the period of Khruschevian rodomontade; during the 'summit' crisis over Berlin, British leaders were so busy buzzing about that one cannot now remember the details of what they did. Hysteria of another kind developed at the time of the Cuba missile crisis, if to no point; and, although the government gave P.R. support to the American action in Vietnam, the self-importance of 'public opinion' expressed itself in its most positive anti-Americanism. One of the reasons for the decline in their special political relationship was that, apart from their joint concern about the use of their currencies in world trade, the British and the Americans did not have much to talk about any more. The intelligent wife started to get up to strange tricks to recapture her husband's flagging interest: the British flights to Washington at the time of the 1967 Middle East crisis were merely an absurd getting into the act without having anything to say. The symbol of their importance was that when, on one of these visits, the Union Jack was hoisted at the White House, it was hoisted upside down.

With that uncertainty about how she is supposed to behave that makes her policy so jumpy, Britain, in playing both the role of the special relation and the role of the honest broker, seemed to play both roles out. There was still suspicion in Europe that the special relationship had an inter-governmental meaning and that in some European crisis the Anglo-Saxons might be found wanting, but it was the British who were more distrusted than the Americans, not because of the special relationship but because of the game of honest brokery. There was equal distrust in America of the honest broker, although this distrust was tempered with cynicism at the highest levels of the American administration, where there has usually been an understanding that British Prime Ministers have to do some play-acting for their own people.

Some British hate the Americans. Some Americans hate the British. In the period of so-called American 'isolation' (which is to say the period when America's active interventions were confined to the two Americas, the Pacific Ocean and East Asia – that is, more than half the world) American anglophobia was at its most virulent. Perhaps if Britain continues to become more 'isolationist' (which is to say, interested only in Europe and Africa), British chauvinism against the Americans will become more virulent. There was a special edge to the attacks on American action in Vietnam that would probably not have applied to a similar situation in Africa. But forces of a different kind may be working as deeply among those significant sections of British society that do not get around to manufacturing 'public opinion'. The most firm supporters of a feeling of special relationship between the two countries used to be those Americans who saw in Britain something that they recognized in themselves and that they thought the British did better. It might be a knowledge of old silver; it might be a feeling for European culture; it might be an understanding of the springs of liberty. Now the most firm supporters of a feeling of similarity between the two nations may be those British who see in America something they recognize in themselves and that they think the Americans do better. It may be a marketing programme; it may be a research project; it may be an understanding of European culture. At these non-political levels Britain could detach itself from America only by committing an act of self-asphyxiation.

Dominia

'The Dominions ... are for me *tiefste Provinz*, places which have produced no art and are inhabited by the kind of person with whom I have least in common,' said W. H. Auden in *Encounter*. 'For the Low-Brows – I am thinking of the Low-Brows of my generation and older, for the development of cheap mass travel since the war must have changed the young – for them, the Dominions are inhabited by their relatives and people like themselves, speaking English, eating English food, wearing English clothes, and playing English games.'

About thirty-five million people live in Canada, Australia, and New Zealand, about as many people as in Poland or Spain. They can be differentiated in significant ways, but they share sufficient characteristics for it to be illuminating to treat them as if they were all the one nation. For this exercise one must temporarily exclude the French Canadians and also imagine New Zealand as a bigger place and with a different terrain from the one it has. (Since the peculiarly New Zealandish part of New Zealanders is mainly a cultural transfusion from Australia this is not as misleading as it sounds.) We shall call this imaginary land Dominia and its nationals the Dominials.

In origin Dominia is not 'English' but 'British'. It is made up of a mixture of all the nationalities of the British Isles, with the proportions of the ingredients less English than in the original mixture, and its original class mixture and emphasis on social types also different, so that it is predominantly provincial-egalitarian in aspiration, 'Anglo-Saxon' rather than 'English'. This mixture is further changed by historical and environmental differences. Like America, Dominia is big and was once a wilderness, and there is still a sense of a vast hinterland to the North that something must be done about. Despite their day-to-day suburbanness, in which they carry out the materialist hopes of Average Britons, the imaginations of Dominials can be moved by dreams of a perpetual motion of change, which is thought of nationally as 'development' and which internationally manifests itself (alternating with caution) in a global idealism. The hero of Dominial history texts is the *pioneer*. When Dominials examine themselves it is their lack of enterprise, the slowing down of the 'pioneering spirit', that they are likely to criticize. They make ritual confessions of guilt about their high urbanization, but they do not seek a return to a simple rural ethos: in their remaining emptiness they want to create more cities. Despite the economic importance of farming, the city is their characteristic social form. In their cities, again reflecting their history and their environment, they dream, like Americans, of a return to the *natural man*, of the rediscovery of the humanness of humans, the only road to true freedom. Superficially, their 'Americanization' is part of America's general cultural and commercial conquest of European civilization – they wear jeans and they buy Esso; but more deeply their similarities to Americans come from similarities of history; the Dominials are part of the English-speaking New World.

Within Dominia there is no overwhelming megalopolis. As in America, a sense of regional identity suffices: wherever one happens to live is important enough. The megalopolises of Dominia are external – Britain and America – and they can reduce Dominials to a sense of provincial insignificance, or excite them into a sense of provincial self-importance of the kind that defines itself only by its superiority to the megalopolis. Until the collapse of British power some Dominials saw themselves as agents of Upper Englishry, despising the Dominial characteristics of Dominia and acting as if Dominia's main role were to increase Great Britain's importance. Others defined Dominial national identity in terms of its superiority to Great Britain: Dominia's living standards were superior; Dominials were not so lah-di-dah in their ways; they had more enterprise than the Brits; they weren't so bogged down in petty traditions. Dominial nationalists even saw themselves as taller and better-looking than the British – and they washed themselves more frequently. Some of the prejudices of the British against Europeans and against the natives were transferred by the Dominials and directed against the British themselves. When the British Empire vanished the Dominials exercised their true British pragmatism and recognized the realities of American economic and strategic power, and although some of the older Dominials still drenched their relation with Britain in sentiment, the true role of Britain in the imaginations of most was to act as one side of a spectrum in which America was at the other side and Dominia was in the middle. For Dominials this spectrum represented the horizons of possible life-styles. One of the advantages for a Dominial of his equivocal position was that he could criticize the British for not being American and the Americans for not being British. However, the post-war immigration of continental Europeans into Dominia also made some of the population of Dominia more immediately 'European' than British.

We can now abandon Dominia and speak directly of Canada, Australia, and New Zealand. These three countries are not interested in each other. Even their 'Low-Brows' (of Auden's nightmare) are bored with the thought of each other *because* they are relatives. They share a common interest in taking attitudes towards Britain, but a sense of tedium overcomes them when they contemplate each other. In Australia, where this indifference is most strong, not only does Japan seem overwhelmingly more interesting than Canada but, of Australia's two neighbours, Indonesia and New Zealand, the interest lies in Indonesia, not New Zealand. Of 'Commonwealth countries' the only ones that can seem interesting to Australians are Singapore, Malaysia, India, and Pakistan, with even the last two fading.

Canada is one of the world's few fully industrialized countries and since it enjoys material living standards almost equal to America's, it belongs to a different world from the other industrialized countries. Its industry is highly derivative – America owns proportionately more of Canada than of any other industrialized country – and more scientists and engineers leave Canada each year for jobs in America than leave Britain, despite Britain's bigger population. Of all the countries in the world its strategic security is most intimately related to America's. In spite of these bonds, Canada seeks differences between itself and America, but such differences do not seem as great as those it finds within itself – between Canadians of British origin and Canadians of French origin. Its 'identity crisis' is twofold: What is there that is *Canadian* that overrides the difference between the two Canadas and that also distinguishes Canada from the United States? Its internal seeking for a sense of nationality clearly demands the breaking of its remaining constitutional link with Britain – its allegiance to the British Crown; however, its relationship with Britain (although increasingly vague) is one factor that distinguishes it from the United States. Canada can make its external distinctions from both Britain and America by looking for novelties in foreign policy. Although finally tied to America, it could become on the world scene a kind of super-Sweden or, indeed, a kind of super-Scandinavia, doing good works: an economic assistance scheme here, a contribution to a United Nations peace force there, externalizing by such means a confident sense of identity.

If there is such a thing as a homogeneous society, Australia is now becoming one of the most homogeneous societies on earth, and among its ordinary people there is a strongly felt sense of nationality – but the expression of this nationality becomes muted and confused among its élites. Australians *learn* an overseas culture, but they *live* in a variant of it that is not confidently expressed. They first recognized the strategic dominance of America in December 1941 when the Japanese were pushing over the European imperialist structures of Southern Asia. They now recognize the economic importance of Japan as it replaces Britain as Australia's main customer. R. G. Menzies remained their Prime Minister for so long (because the opposition party collapsed) that his woman's magazine view of the British Crown sometimes made Australia seem more British than Britain, but even Menzies saw the importance to Australia of America and Japan and he did not let his speech-making impede policy. Externally, to Australia – unlike Canada – even American power is not final. Australia is the only European country that, geo-politically, is part of Asia: progressive liberalization of its immigration policy combined with increasingly detailed involvement with its South-East Asian neighbours and its other principal Asian associates could liberate Australia from its provincialism and turn it into a laboratory for the future.

Canada can lose its provincialism through an enlightened internationalism and Australia through an enlightened regionalism. It is doubtful if New Zealand can lose its provincialism at all. When it distinguishes itself from Australia it falls back on its Englishness; when it distinguishes itself from Britain it falls back on its Australianness. Unlike Australia, which builds up steam by immigration and development programmes, New Zealand would prefer to stay as it is, concerned with preserving its Anglo-Saxonness. Anxious not to be ruined by Britain, it is distrustful of Australia, America, and Japan.

All three of these politically independent nations are successful *de facto* republics: the monarchic fiction does them harm not in any constitutional sense but because the absurdities of overstatement finally damage the genuineness of the relations that do exist between these English-speaking peoples, as does the fake rhetoric of the 'unity' of the whole Commonwealth, which disguises the reality of the similarities between Britain, Canada, Australia, and New Zealand. In this, Average Britain may be wiser than Upper England. Dominia can be as tedious to many of the Upper English as it is to Auden: it is an area where they cannot find self-importance. But the ordinary British people are more easily satisfied: at home they are Average Britons; abroad they are Anglo-Saxons.

8. A WORLD FIT FOR BRITAIN

Multi-focal vision

The guessing games about Britain's identity puzzled and depressed the British, but they aroused ancient suspicions among those other countries with which Britain seemed to flirt, only to jilt them, and then to flirt with them again. Britain, first of the Commonwealth countries. Britain, more European than Europe. Britain, America's Special Relation. Britain, the Greatest Little England in the World. Britain, the Third Force. Britain, Great Britain Again. Sometimes one role was played at a time. Sometimes they were all played in one contradictory season. The result was to confirm the suspicion of British perfidy which is in the minds of most other peoples and which, when expressed, so surprises the British themselves.

The traditional idea that Britain could pick and choose amongst options towards 'Abroad' gave its peculiar character to the long British debate about Britain's role in the world in the 1950s and 1960s. The old belief that decision could not be *forced* on Britain was maintained more strongly than might have been expected by those who did not understand the strength that was left in the old idea of 'glorious isolation', a past tradition of decision-making in foreign policy rare among nations. Whether or not this was an illusion, in the period of Britain's world power, especially in matters that affected Europe, there was a certain habit of detachment in the Foreign Office and in British governments, a greater feeling of choice between alternatives than usually occurs in the making of foreign policy. In particular, because of the specifically expressed policy of balance-of-power in Europe, Britain was a country, that, at least in theory, always looked as if it might change sides. In such a situation, with the permanent possibility that Britain might choose to break one friendship or alliance to make another, and with the habit of publicly pausing while its statesmen contemplated alternatives, it was not surprising that a characteristic of British diplomacy appeared to be its potential perfidy. It was a policy more of aloofness and of unpredictability of intervention than of isolationism: the isolationists (almost always a minority) were men to whom Britain's moral superiority in the world was so clear that they saw a danger of contamination in diplomacy; since their faith rested on sea power they were not really Little Englanders but anti-European big-heads, and their concern with sea power in itself pushed them in the direction of war, if not of diplomacy. The contradictoriness of both isolationists and interventionists heightened distrust. At the same time, because so much of the world was cut away for so long as a big separate bit that belonged to *them*, the British have had peculiar disabilities in seeing the world whole. The members of a British Government used to have many different eyes on the world, each, like a lizard's, seeing only one section of it. One eye, through the India Office, looked at India. One eye, through the Dominions Office, looked at Canada, Australia, South Africa, and New Zealand. One eye, through the Colonial Office, looked at pieces of South-East Asia, East and West Africa, the West Indies, and a rash of small states stretching across the world as far as the Fiji Islands. One eye, through the War Office, was itself split in two, most of it looking at the imperial garrisons, the rest of it looking at Europe. The Foreign Office looked only at what was left over. It was a weak instrument for helping to generate or propagate a new British world view since it could not have a general theory about what the world looked like until 1968 when the Commonwealth Relations Office, itself an amalgam of three older government departments, was put into the same harness as the Foreign Office.

There was also an enormous strain on both bureaucratic resources and public interest in the endless crises of disbanding the Empire. This was a much more important influence on Britain's international relations than could be observed at the time through all the muddle, taking up considerable energies and affecting other parts of foreign policy in complex ways. Even most of the British themselves did not understand how complicated and demanding the complex of their world involvements had been since the Second World War. Colonial names and faces, as they went in and out of newspapers and on and off television screens, must sometimes have had a fracturing effect on the minds of ordinary people, and on most of the élites as well – as they learned what a lot of Empire they had to give away. To take one example: in the first three months of 1959 there were simultaneous crises with Malta, Ghana, South Africa, Basutoland, Nyasaland, Cyprus, India, the Cameroons, Nigeria, Tanganyika, Somaliland, Kenya, Jamaica, and Singapore. These 'crises' must sometimes have seemed too diffuse to reveal meaningful patterns; perhaps finally they gave the impression that none of it mattered very much. As Britain's power declined, British Governments went through a greater period of general diplomatic activity, more demanding in its confusion than had ever been known before.

At least until the pull-out from East of Suez, the military services also helped cast some of the images in Britain's view of the world. Old habits still impelled them to nostalgic views of a world role: they were reluctant to think of new policies for a purely 'European' Britain. The Air Force was the first to lose a grip on the world. It became more an instrument of action than a prompting to it and it was continually perplexed by changing policies towards the expensive British aircraft industry, and changing relations with America. The Navy, traditionally the most global-minded of the services, seeing beyond the imperial garrisons and naval bases as its province, and a British peace as its objective, was the most shattered by change. Its preposterous dream was never really fulfilled, but the pomp and show of naval strength, spread out across the world, played an important part in sustaining the British sense of uniqueness. The First World War was really the end of the old Navy. The world could not be 'ruled' by a Navy; its bluff was called and, after the Second World War, as Naval technology changed, the Navy, like the Air Force, was caught up in the conundrums of equipment decision and obsolescence, so that there was a continuing doubt as to what it would consist of. Because of its desire to maintain some of the old naval stations, and to play at least a limited world role, it nevertheless provided a pressure for a continued, if limited, world presence. In the long withdrawal of power traditional naval strategy played some part in foreign policy, but eventually it was brushed aside and in two of the three main oceans plans were made that would pack almost all of the Navy away.

Even more than the Navy, the British Army was devoted to the idea of aristocratic lightness of style in action. Despite the incessant drumbeats of power in the late nineteenth century, it was not strength that inspired the imagination of officers in the Army, but the idea of doing a lot with a little, of looking for a way round, of seeking out the open flank. Service in the Empire consisted mainly of showing the flag with garrisons so small that they could have been overwhelmed by local populations, or in mounting modest expeditions against 'troublemakers'. Ubiquity, versatility, and economy of effort were essential to the bluff of British power. The slaughterhouse of two world wars turned it into a mass conscript army, but in the long series of counter-insurgency campaigns and police-holding actions after the Second World War the British Army scored more regular successes than it had done since Wellington, using what it liked to consider its characteristic methods. The world continued to be interesting for the Army, more interesting than Europe, and it tried to keep Britain in the world. Having failed to do so, after several centuries of a contrary tradition, it must now learn to merge itself in the mass armies of continental Europe.

Looking both ways

If Britain is to continue to play a full role in the Anglo-Saxon world it may be able to do so only by becoming less Upper English and more Anglo-Saxon, seeing itself, among the other Anglo-Saxon countries, as merely one of the inheritors of that civilization, not as its creator. Anglo-Saxonry is a matter of common social and intellectual ancestry, to which the present inhabitants of Britain can make no more particular claim than can a New Zealander. The ideals of the seventeenth century Puritan revolution were expressed more adequately in America than in Britain; the nineteenth century Chartist ideals were expressed more adequately in Australia than in Britain. Although all of us who belong to the western civilization make our ritual obeisance in the direction of Athenian democracy and Roman law, we do not consider the present Greeks and the present Italians to have more connexion than we do with the Greece and Rome we are speaking of. If the British are prepared to accept themselves as cousins of the other Anglo-Saxon nations, no more important, no less important, except in terms of contemporary performance, they have a chance of making their mark in this particular world not from their present geographical location, but by the excellence of what they do. If there is any field in which they want to lead, they will have to earn their leadership. Meanwhile the special significance given to them by the other Anglo-Saxons continues to fade. Anglo-Saxonry could go on without Britain.

Could Britain go on without Anglo-Saxonry? This is what some of the extreme supporters of 'going into Europe' seem to suggest, yet the question seems as senseless as *Could Britain go on without Britishry*? Auden is right when he says that British low-brows see Dominials as 'relatives'. He said nothing about how they see his fellow countrymen, the Americans, but he may as well have lumped them in too. It was the violence of the extreme Upper English supporters of the 'going into Europe' campaign, their wholehearted exclusiveness, that suggested that going into Europe meant going out of the rest of the world. For Britain this is close to being impossible. Special economic or political links with Europe are probably advantageous to Britain: the shocks that would come from them might knock some of the rubbish out of Britain – it would be part of the Upper English tradition of going into Europe for a health treatment – but this is not a whole-hog matter of *nothing but Europe*; if it were, it could be disastrous. The whole-hog idea of 'Europe' lies not in political and economic relations but in a national entity that does not exist and, for some time ahead, *cannot* exist: to swap the 'Commonwealth' for 'Europe' would be to swap one illusion for another; there would be no final comfort in it. The 'European' extremists in Britain are top people whose ability to conceptualize is very high. This year they say one thing; next year they say some other thing. This has little more meaning for the ordinary people than a change of advertising image: it is disturbing when an image changes, but life goes on. An attempt to take the 'Anglo-Saxonry' out of Britain would be absurd. Even after South Africa was rightly excluded from the Commonwealth, rightly vilified (although as a distant and safe target, not like apartheid towards West Indians in London), the British low-brows continued to emigrate there, because of the partial Anglo-Saxonry of South Africa. If 'going into Europe' meant merely the *rhetoric* of 'nothing but Europe', this might be supportable to the ordinary people, who can suffer nonsense in rhetoric with great patience, although it would not be as familiar as the rhetoric of the Commonwealth; but if it meant what it said (and it seems unimaginable that this could be so) it would cause the kind of social disruption in Britain that Upper English policy has for so long avoided. For instance, imagine that 'Europe' really became a political entity (although still an entity made up of diverse nationalities), and on some great global issue of supreme significance confronted the rest of Anglo-Saxonry (America, with attendant Dominia). Would the British people stand by a British government that was part of such an entity? Would the British, for that matter, be prepared to fight the Americans, the Canadians, or the Australians? The French could imagine themselves doing so. The British could not even imagine themselves fighting the Anglo-Saxons in Rhodesia.

Anglo-Saxondom and continental Europe together make up most of European civilization. (The case of Latin America is ambiguous.) Britain belongs both to Anglo-Saxondom and to continental Europe, with, for most of the British, a greater sense of belonging to Anglo-Saxondom than to continental Europe. For the sense of identity of most of the ordinary people it would suffice if their image-setters said simply that they belonged to Anglo-Saxondom. This would simply confirm what they know to be true. There is, however, no political or economic form of Anglo-Saxondom which the British can join. Anglo-Saxonry is a language and a set of aspirations and habits, even a set of employment opportunities, but it is not a political or economic system. In a sense, if decisions on national politics worked by some calculus of majority motives within a community (that is to say, if they were assessed in a truly democratic way) it would be *natural* for Britain to suggest that Anglo-Saxondom be bound together by economic and political forms. But the idea is absurd. It is impossible for the élite of Britain to find a fully satisfying sense of importance in the Anglo-Saxon world – because the Americans dominate it. But they will also fail to find this in 'Europe'. 'Europe' is a relationship between equals, some more equal than others, deploying bluffs and pressures in the democratic way, but finally balanced against hegemony. It is true that British governments might play a more actively interesting role in 'Europe' than in America: there is more room for manoeuvre, for crises, editorials, debates; it would be more interesting for the public opinion-setters; they could lead fuller and more satisfying lives. But the Anglo-Saxon nature of Britain finally inhibits it in its relations with Europe: there are some lengths to which it cannot go. It is in the nature of Britain to be caught between what are geographically the two camps of European civilization. Perhaps Britain should follow its nature.

This is not to say that there are not good and important roles for Britain to play in Europe. But there is no world role. A world role is impossible without meaningful relations with some of the ex-'natives', with whose future the besetting problems of the world lie. It will be argued in the last chapter that the British – or the British élites – are over-ambitious for world roles. The point to be made here is that they won't find one in Europe alone. The point to be made later is that they won't find what they want anywhere. The 'identity crisis' of Britain is not a crisis of the people as it is, say, of Canada, for roughly speaking, the people know who they are. It is a crisis of Britain's élites caused by their over-ambition. It can end only in a change in ambition. In the meantime the chopping and changing in concepts can have an unnerving effect on the ordinary people: if they are carried out too adventurously into policy the effect could be of the most serious kind, finally perhaps fracturing the immense social and political stability of Britain.

Part III
At Home

Mother of whose Parliament?

British schoolchildren used to be given a very simple view of the growth of freedom: freedom was a British invention that spread to the rest of the world. Freedom began when in an age of innocence the Anglo-Saxons gathered under oak trees to settle their differences in moots. There was a set-back from the Continent when the Normans conquered Britain, but out of their kings' Great Councils there developed in the fourteenth century the beginning of the present forms of the Houses of Parliament. Parliament steadily increased its power and as other parts of the world became more enlightened they learned how to conduct their affairs by imitating the British, so that the British Parliament became the mother of all other legislative bodies. In an accompanying process, beginning with Magna Carta, there was a steady growth of the liberty of the subject, which was manifest above all in the Common Law. The freedom of other countries was gauged by the extent to which their legislative bodies and their law courts approximated British institutions; in this process a particular safeguard of freedom was believed to be that constitutions should not be written down and that the law should not be codified. This cartoon view of history became fixed in the minds of even those who did not believe it. It was one of the proofs of British moral leadership.

Before kings developed more absolute powers it was a practice of other European kings as well as the kings of England to call together gatherings of leading taxpayers with whom the king would bargain to raise money, sometimes being forced into concessions. The English Parliament was no more prominent in this process than some of the similar bodies in other kingdoms. Although dominated by nobles, the Swedish *Riksdag*, for example, was more representative than the English Parliament, including, as it did, peasants as well as nobles, prelates, and burghers, and it was probably more influential than the English Parliament. The Danish *Rigsraad* actually elected the king and the king had to sign a charter guaranteeing the constitution (even if this charter was not enforceable once he got his power). French kings were forced to summon Great Councils; the French Estates-General took shape about the same time as the English Parliament, and it showed the same interest in getting concessions from the king in return for raising taxes. In none of these kingdoms were such assemblies related to democracy, nor did they have any necessary relation to freedom. It is better to think of the period as one in which the king, the feudal magnates, the towns and the peasants had different interests; these assemblies played some part in this difference of interest, usually representing the interests of the most powerful and richest landholders. To peasants, the power of the king sometimes represented the only protection they had against the demands of the landholders. That names such as *Rigsraad* or 'Parliament' were later used to describe legislative bodies in the democratic era may be no more useful in understanding their present role than the fact that English monarchs are still called 'queen' or 'king'.

The role of these feudal organizations was weakened or even abolished in the clash of interests between monarchs and magnates, which the magnates lost. As the kings destroyed feudalism they also tried to destroy the assemblies that had provided the main collective form of feudal pressure. This royal absolutism began earlier in England than it did in some other kingdoms. The Tudors dominated their Parliaments with the self-righteousness of newcomers. By the beginning of the seventeenth century the kings of England and France seemed determined to govern without parliaments. The English king dismissed Parliament in 1611; the French king dismissed the

Estates-General in 1614. When Charles I became King of England he adopted the style of a protector of the common people against the special interests represented in Parliament and, although he called a Parliament in 1628 to get some money, he dismissed it again in 1629, and for eleven years ruled without it.

It was when Charles called a Parliament again (because he needed some more money) that there began the treating of monarchs as disposable objects that marked the first true achievement in the history of English Parliaments. Parliament beheaded one king and later exiled another; it imported a foreigner to take the place of the latter and then imported another foreigner when the first imported line ran out. As part of its propaganda against Charles I Parliament had legitimized its actions by claiming ancient rights (which it did not possess) thereby giving rise to the boasts of its unique antiqueness – but Parliament's important characteristic was not its unique oldness but its revolutionary past.

In broad terms Parliament represented a way in which England's Top People successfully contested the power of the king, so that England became an oligarchy rather than a monarchy; when 'Great Britain' was formed the oligarchs of the fringe lands were allowed to join in if they wanted to. The special relation of this type of power to freedom was that its oligarchic nature meant that there was among the privileged a greater outspokenness, general liberty of action, and greater freedom from arbitrary government than in the absolutist kingdoms, although any challenge to the power of the oligarchs themselves and to the state they had created was met with no less harshness than could happen elsewhere in the defence of kings.

The Revolution of 1688 itself soon became a prestige antique: romantically-minded conservatives saw some kind of perfection in the constitution it threw up. Not only was there no longer any necessity for further change: in this view change itself seemed to become the principal enemy of British freedom. At the same time there also developed an idealization of parliamentary government and of the liberal state, founded ultimately, although somewhat mystically (since most of them didn't have a vote), on the consent of 'the people'. This view of things, which imagined that change was not necessarily the enemy of freedom but often its servant, became the basis of British liberalism: it over-idealized the role of Parliament and it found more liberalism than yet existed in British society, but it formalized aspirations that may have had more influence outside Britain than the deliberate imitation of British parliamentary forms. Although the British claim too much for the antiquity of their Parliament, they may still with honesty praise their history for the development of a liberal spirit that was to grow strong enough to contest with older views of the world. This liberalism was founded in a belief in reform, in a belief that what had been did not necessarily determine what should be; it was optimistic; and it believed that there was a natural state of reasonableness in which men could be equal and independent, no one harming another in his life, health, liberty, or possessions. In the form in which this liberalism was developed by John Locke, most famous of its early spokesmen, it was democratic as well as liberal: but democracy was only an optional extra in early liberalism so that in the eighteenth century it was, in effect, very largely a liberalism for men with property. However, the belief in the natural reasonableness of human society hung over into the democratic age and became one of its contradictions, sometimes beneficially, sometimes disastrously. It is still the basis of British liberalism.

Contemplation of eighteenth century Britain's oligarchic freedoms helped create new doctrines in France and the rest of Europe. To Voltaire intellectual life seemed more lively in England than in absolutist France; in England thinkers were not only given greater freedom but also greater respect; the name of Newton was venerated in a way that would be unimaginable in France. But it was the oligarchic liberty more than the parliamentary forms of England that impressed Voltaire: he was as impressed by the Royal Society as by the Parliament in Westminster. And to Montesquieu it was the aristocratic nature of England that, along with the apparent independence of its judiciary, was the reason for its liberties; the power of the aristocrats checked and balanced the power of king and people. It was through ideas such as these, rather than through imitation of a supposed antiquity in its parliamentary forms, that English oligarchic liberty of the eighteenth century was transfused into those general ideas that became associated with political changes in Europe in the late eighteenth and in the nineteenth century.

As a direct influence on later forms of representative government the American Revolution was of greater consequence than the eighteenth century British Parliament, and the American Constitution was as much French and American in its inspiration as it was British, although part of the American approach to law was to remain English. The British colonies in America were thrown up partly by the same impulses as threw up the Puritan revolution in England, and although these colonial societies were also oligarchic their initial impulses were carried further than in England. Both landed gentry and self-made manufacturers could express a theory of the nature of men and a belief in 'the people' of a kind that can still come awkwardly in Britain. Since their revolution was a revolt against the attempted absolutism of a distant government, it was not the contemporary British constitutional system that they directly imitated: they took spirit instead from the French theorists whose theories had been inspired partly by a misunderstanding of the British system. They wanted, above all, a system of checks and balances, of powers balancing powers. They controlled their own local assemblies: what they now wanted was a means of limiting the powers of the central government they were about to create. Working empirically from an existing American situation, but also work-

ing 'rationally' from French theories, they developed
that system of federalism that has been a model for the
world, that has been as important in countries like
Canada, Australia, and India as the imitation of British
parliamentary forms, and that, if the fringe lands of
Britain ever achieve home rule, may finally prove to be a
model for Britain itself. In addition, in a most un-British
way, they wrote their constitution down, in what was to
become the European manner.

When, in the nineteenth century, the nations of Europe
established new forms of representative government, or
strengthened existing ones, none of them drew any strong
special and direct inspiration from Britain, except perhaps, in several cases, in the reduction of their old
chamber of three or four estates to two chambers. The particular influence of British forms had been on eighteenth
century French theorists who admired their oligarchic
quality; the impulse in the nineteenth century was towards democratic government and in this the British were
not notably ahead of the others in practice, although their
theorists were busy. The nations of Europe and of Europe
Overseas lumbered towards democratic forms, writing
down constitutions in defiance of the British example,
with their eyes on the American constitution and the
French theorists rather than on the British. In Sweden the
Riksdag, in Denmark the *Rigsraad*, in Norway the *Stort-
ing*, in Holland the *States-General* all acquired a stronger
democratic flavour more quickly than the Parliament in
Britain, mainly because they fell into the control of
peasant parties. Manhood suffrage was established somewhat sooner in some other countries than in Britain;
almost all other countries provided for some form of
direct election of their second chamber, the British House
of Lords remaining as a freakish survival.

The rule of whose law?

Although the English preferred the word 'English' to
'British' to describe most of those things about which

they were vain, for some curious reason in moments of self-congratulation one did not hear of 'English justice' but of 'British justice' – even though 'British justice' is one of the prime pieces of evidence produced to justify English conceit. Yet 'British justice' is a purely English achievement: the Scottish system of justice is separate from the English and more directly based on Roman Law, and even in the other countries that took over English Common Law traditions their written constitutions introduce some very un-English elements. In its purest form, 'British justice' is the system of justice carried out in England and Wales.

There has been claimed for this system of justice characteristics that would make it not only unique among all other forms of justice, but also the only true form of justice. The phrase 'the rule of law' came to be used as if only England and countries influenced by 'British justice' really operated under a rule of law. It was made to look as if the English, not the Romans, were the principal law-givers of European civilization. Attempts to maintain the 'rule of law' as the unique trademark of English justice have been justified in a dozen different ways; as each crumbles another takes its place. The facts are that there are differences between the legal systems of England and most other democratic countries, but that these differences are exaggerated and that in any case they seem to be by the way – eccentric rather than significant. The quality of justice (as distinguished from its procedures) is much of a muchness in all liberal countries and it seems likely that the efficacy of legal institutions depends more on the general habits of the society in which they exist than on particular legal forms. English lawyers purport to see the law courts as the prime cause of the growth of liberty in England, yet this claim is impossible to sustain. At some periods in English history the judges seemed to extend liberty; at other times they were the principal enemies of it. In any case the growth or retreat of liberties is a matter that depends on circumstances working through whole classes of a society, or throughout a whole society. A fake history was fabricated to sustain the fiction of the law courts as the principal guardians of liberty, just as a fake history was fabricated to sustain the fiction of the historic rights of Parliament. Insofar as this fiction is still believed, along with the myth of the significant uniqueness of English justice, lawyers swell with conceit, and the many inadequacies of the practice of English justice, as distinguished from its theory, are claimed as its virtues.

One of the principal pieces of evidence to sustain the uniqueness of English justice has been the English belief in Common Law. In extreme cases English Common Law is claimed to be the foundation not only of civil liberty but of the whole English way of life. The claim is significant because the defences of it provide almost definitive symptoms of Upper Englishry. When examined they reveal the backward-looking reverence for the antique, the anti-intellectual pretence of practicality, the whimsical concern for the merely trivial and the plain conceit of claiming unique goodness where it does not exist.

In its classic form, this boasting about the Common Law compares English justice with the justice of France. The English are seen as highly practical, untheoretical chaps who patch together in an empirical way a legal system that really works; the French are seen as highly logical and therefore unpractical people who try to define too much and write too much down. They lack the indefinable excellences of the English: they don't really know how to behave, so they have to make up a lot of written rules. According to this nightmare the French made a grave error in writing down their laws as a code: this leaves them in an inflexible situation in which they are always having to look up their written code, and when the code is found wanting add another bit to it. The English have a much better system than that. They write down their laws as a mixture of statutes and precedents: this leaves them in a flexible situation in which they are always having to look up their written statutes and precedents, and when the statutes and precedents are found wanting add another precedent to them. In short, the certainty of the code and the certainty of recorded precedents produce much the same effect: lawyers have to look up books to find out the rules. The English Common Law provides the rules; English scholars sort this all out and systematize it for reference. French judges make precedents and French scholars sort them out into case law.

The English also have a nightmare about French judges. In France a lawyer decides at the beginning of his career whether he will be an advocate or a judge. If he decides to be a judge he is trained in his profession and devotes his whole working life to it. In England the cult of the amateur is preferred; judges are appointed in their middle age from the ranks of advocates, with no special training for their new job. Their gentlemanly status is strengthened by the salaries they receive, by the hallowed seclusion in which they live, and by the extraordinary flattery and adulation with which they are cosseted for the rest of their lives. The French judge, on the other hand, is less well paid, maintains more open contacts with the rest of society, and, if he is treated with esteem, it is not as a sacred person but as an expert professional. While the English judge, when he is working in court, is seen as an umpire, ensuring that there is fair play, the French judge is seen as an inquisitor, butting in and asking questions; his aim not fair play but the truth. English justice is ordered so that judges can live in London; French justice is ordered so that judges live wherever they have to do their judging. The result, in quality of justice, is probably much the same in either nation: the importance of the comparison is in national style.

Into these fantasies of national character purporting to be comparisons between legal systems the role of the jury is sometimes produced as the trump card of English justice. It is, in fact, very largely an illusion that juries are either dominant in English courts (where most of the civil cases are personal injury cases in which juries are very rare) or missing in continental courts (where the use of juries is widespread, especially in criminal cases). The role of the jury in English imagination does not seem primarily to be democratic but to be made up of two other strands. One is that a jury fuzzes over the violence of a decision, thereby saving the impeccability of the judge, who can get on with the fair play. The other is that the jury system is antique.

The antiquity of the treatment of juries is strenuously preserved. Since juries were originally incapable of reading or taking notes or giving any kind of sustained attention to complicated matters, they are still huddled together in a box, under conditions that judges would find impossible for their work, and treated like idiots. The rules usually prevent the two opposing counsel from rationally presenting what they are trying to prove, so that it is hard for the jury to know what some evidence is supposed to be about. In long and difficult cases, in which the sense of fair play allows counsel deliberately to introduce all kinds of confusion and deceptions, it is impossible for the jury to go about its work rationally. It is probably true that the jury is as likely as the judge to decide correctly whether a witness is lying. Since judges live in the manner of well-to-do hierarchic persons, it is probably true that the jury, which lives in the manner of ordinary persons, is better equipped than the judge to decide matters that rest on 'the common opinion of sensible men'; but the mumbo-jumbo of formal legal presentation and the deceptions of advocacy combine with the stupefying antiquity of the jury's accommodation and treatment to make it unlikely in some cases that the jury can know in what way it matters whether a witness is credible or not and in what way they are supposed to exercise their common opinions as sensible persons.

Meanwhile, there are two thousand or so tribunals of various kinds that lie outside the honorific part of the legal system, some of them existing publicly and independently, some absorbed within departments of government, so that a great number of matters in dispute in Britain are settled outside the courts. The English have shown a traditional dislike of this 'administrative justice', thoroughly misunderstanding it and for some time acting as if it did not really exist. It was the kind of naughty thing one found abroad. The result was that while the French went about it systematically, making their administrative tribunals work well in correcting abuse, the English went about it furtively, with less guarantee of effectiveness. As it happens, some of England's despised and distrusted public tribunals work very well (although there is justifiable concern about the departmental tribunals). They have their own concern for precedents and usually they engage in that applying of rules that is the basis of law; they can be cheaper and quicker than the law courts; they adopt easier and more efficient procedures; and they go about the marshalling and assessment of facts in a sensible and logical way. They represent one of those continuing quiet victories of the Northern Metaphor without which the future of Britain would not be possible to contemplate.

Parliament as a work of art

Among the relatively small number of people who give the workings of the British Parliament much detailed thought, some have in their minds an Ideal Parliament of some other time, stocked with independent-minded men who said what they pleased, beyond party discipline. So great was the power of this Other Parliament that sometimes when a great orator spoke in the debating chamber a whole government fell. Apart from these dramatic moments of righteousness, individual ministers were responsible day by day directly to this Other Parliament: once a minister lost this Parliament's confidence, he resigned. When this Other Parliament was not breaking or making ministers or whole ministries it gave a steady flow of high-principled advice to the government about how to run the country. Knowing this, the Prime Minister and his Cabinet sat in the House of Commons afternoon and night, diligently taking notes on all the good ideas that Members of Parliament were passing on to them as they spoke in parliamentary debates. In the nation at large this Other Parliament was respected as the nation's most important institution and the true organ of its government.

To these idealists Parliament now seems to have sunk into a decrepit institution which is in every respect the opposite of what it used to be in the days of the Other Parliament. But this Other Parliament never existed. The task of governing the country by Parliament was attempted only once – during the seventeenth century revolution – and, like other revolutionary attempts at government by assembly, its failure led to an authoritarian régime. Nor has Parliament usually made governments or unmade them. There was a period in the middle of the nineteenth century when, during a collapse of old parliamentary alliances and a grouping of new ones, something like the Other situation existed; but at the time it was seen as an unusually disorderly period in Parliament's existence. Both before then and after, most members have been voting fodder. The impeccability of the relation between Members of Parliament and government, without representation of special interests, has never existed. In fact in the general corruption that marked British politics before the democratic era, in which a large part of politics was mainly about patronage, special interests not only controlled the votes of members, but had such direct forms of pressure on ministers as would now seem scandalous. As now, the usual role of debates has not been to instruct the ministry in ideal forms of government, but for the opposition party to try to make fools of the ministry and for the government party to make fools of the opposition. Outside their party discussions, Members of Parliament are *worse* fitted than many other individuals to provide the kind of public debate that can help a government determine its priorities and policies, because their main public role is forensic: it is the job of some to appear for the plaintiff and some for the defendant. So far as the reputation of Parliament is concerned, it is customary for it not to be as high as the self-esteem of its members' demands; although inaccurately and unfairly, it is usual for Parliament to be blamed for what seems wrong with the country; whenever the country's fortunes seem low, Parliament gets some of the blame; when they seem high, Parliament gets little of the credit.

Not only are the inventors of the Other Parliament deluded in their sense of decline; they may also be deluded in imagining that their Ideal Parliament would work in the way they imagine. A Parliament of government-by-assembly, with ministers waiting for its instructions and then getting the sack if they did not carry them out, with a debating chamber in which the affairs of state were decided by free individuals forming and re-forming in different groupings on different issues, would not be so much government as a revolutionary situation.

The complaints about the inadequacies of present Parliaments, and the suggestion that they are in decline, come from a small group of people who would find life more interesting if, somehow, Parliament could be made central in national life. What they are really trying to imagine is that, together, they would form a band of brilliant men who really ran the country, some of them by debating in the House and others by writing critical estimates of the debates. This view of Parliament as a kind of artistic performance, as something that should in itself be *perfected*, expresses an arrogant misunderstanding of the necessarily crude nature of its main function which is that it is a rough and ready way of giving governments legitimacy. It does this by relating governments to the 'wishes of the people', but its members are not 'the people', nor are they 'representative' of the people; they are men, who for some reason or other, got selected by their parties as political candidates and who were elected for the most part because the voters in their constituencies preferred one party to the other, often without knowing the names of the candidates. What they personally 'represent' is the political balance within their own constituency parties; what they collectively 'represent' is the voting balance of the last election.

As parliamentarians most of them have no important personal political role; a few learn how to exert pressure within their party; a few become good at asking questions or raising grievances or criticisms that are then taken up by the media; for most their principal function is to act as welfare officers for aggrieved members of their constituencies. In fact many of those back-bench Members of Parliament who enjoy Westminster do so because they *like* being welfare officers. But the main consolations of parliamentary life may be that it allows its participants to enjoy the combination of prep school, club, and debating society. As a prep school, Parliament is an institution in which newcomers are expected to be patient and obedient in the processes of initiation. As a club it provides the delights of knowing gossip that hardly anyone else knows, watching the play of familiar personalities, and watching at close hand powerful men, who, in theory, are nothing more than fellow club members. As a debating society, for the lucky ones who can get a chance to speak, Parliament can be an arena of showmanship in the normal and necessary childishness of political fashion. This is in no way peculiar to the British Parliament.

The elected monarch

If there is a true monarch of Great Britain it is the Prime Minister. He is the real 'Crown' to whom the people are subject. He is, however, an elected monarch who can be dismissed from office by the people at an election and he is bound by the habits of convention so that if he wants to act against the laws of the land he must first change them. This gives the people freedom from arbitrariness and, since he must face elections, when the Prime Minister changes laws or makes new ones he keeps in mind the possible reactions of the people. It is not, however, as a law-maker that he is principally judged, but as a chief executive: law-making is merely subsidiary to this principal role and, on most important issues, irrelevant to it, although the Prime Minister wastes a lot of time sitting around in Parliament pretending otherwise. As with the President of the United States, the main job of the Prime Minister is to get on with the government of the country. Although he lacks the powers of appointment of the President, in one respect he is – at least potentially – enormously more powerful: while Congress can independently check the President's actions (for example, by not giving him money), the Prime Minister can control Parliament more effectively than any President can control Congress. Gaining his strength directly from the people when they vote his party into office, the Prime Minister can sometimes manipulate Parliament as successfully as did a Tudor king. It is not Parliament but his own party that matters to him and he controls Parliament to the extent that he controls his party.

Apart from his general concern with public opinion and with interest groups, the main limits on his power are held not by Parliament but by those with whom he shares the government. These limits may sometimes take most of his power from him; at other times they mean that he can get away with a great deal. Most of the ninety ministers are of little importance. Fifty of them are mere junior ministers. Forty of them are full ministers, but of these only twenty sit in the Cabinet and of those twenty few have real influence on anything except their own departments, where they must also reckon on the power of the Prime Minister, or of the most influential of the other ministers. But some of his ministers are powerful in their own right and he has to keep an eye on them, and sometimes give in to them, just as a feudal king was confined by his consideration for the activities of the powerful magnates. Here the Prime Minister is in a weaker position than the President of the United States, whose ministers cannot use party political support against him as do British ministers. His power, like that of any other ruler, is also limited by the fact that its instruments are the government bureaucracies, complex institutions with impulses of their own that largely determine how detailed administration is carried out. Even in the development of new policy, in determining the possible from the impossible, the role of the bureaucracies is often decisive.

For the Prime Minister the most important of all roles for Parliament is to act as the formal electoral college that puts him in. Parliament is the mechanism by which the voters change the government. After an election is held and it is known which party won the most seats, the leader of that party becomes the Prime Minister, appoints his ministers, and is 'the Crown'. He then has at his disposal the bureaucracies that are the significant instruments of state. After this act of power, Parliament as a thing in itself is of much smaller importance than rivals within the Prime Minister's own party. It cannot investigate what the administration is doing as thoroughly as the American Congress can: its members can make inquiries of the government about what is going on, but this can sometimes be a game in which ministers engage in any kind of subterfuge except a direct lie. Parliament has a use as an assembly in which grievances can be expressed and in which formal criticisms of the government can be made; but it is doubtful if, in this part of its role, Parliament is as effective as the mass media, and the main effectiveness it has depends on the publicity the media choose to give it.

As a legislative body Parliament's most important courtly function is to enact an honoured ritual, hallowing the passage of the Prime Minister's Bills or the Bills of his chief associates through Parliament into law. The Bills are 'debated' in Parliament in the sense that members get up and down and say things, but, except in very extraordinary cases, what members say has no effect on the Bill. What the Bill is to be is a matter that has already been decided by the balance of power between the Prime Minister and his main associates. The 'debates' are the means by which the prior decisions of these great men, often put into order by government officials, are given the honorific value of laws: they are a kind of religious chant to hallow an occasion. Apart from their fundamental role as digits in the tally that elects a man Prime Minister, the true parliamentary role of most Members of Parliament is the ceremonial one of adding honour to the passage of the Prime Minister's Bills by saying something when required and by walking through a door to be counted when there is a vote, thereby affirming what is already known, that the Bill will be passed.

Parliament plays court to the Prime Minister, who is its elected monarch. This does not mean that his power

is absolute, any more than the power of hereditary monarchs was necessarily absolute. Their degree of power was
up to them and to habit and circumstance. Parliament's
true power is that of a feudal court in that it contains
other powerful men, with whom the Prime Minister must
reckon and to whom sometimes he may have to yield.
There are the pretenders to his office in the opposition
party, and there are those in the Prime Minister's government who may, in their dealings with him, defeat the
Prime Minister's plans and force their own plans upon
him. The Prime Minister, however, has a very strong
reserve power: opponents within his party know that
the overthrow of a Prime Minister by his own party is
usually catastrophic to the party.

In its role as court to the Prime Minister Parliament
provides a theatrical setting for the great dramas he un-
folds. Oratory magnifies his presence, so that there is a
constant recitative of the good or evil of his great actions.
Whatever he does is gossiped about, partly in the form of
speeches, and then written down. Appeals are made to
him; he is counselled; he is warned. He is the embodiment of the great happenings of the world; he flies off to
other countries and speaks to Parliament on his return.
He is the source of office, enthralling Parliament by the
dispositions of power. (Sometimes re-arrangement of his
ministers seems a necessary part of the show, as if power
was a series of impressive *tableaux vivants*.) And it is in
praise of his power that Parliament chants the rituals
that hallow his wisdom as a legislator.

The parties

In a big unit such as Britain, perhaps in any unit larger
than a small tennis club, a 'true' form of representative
government does not seem possible: the 'representative'
nature of Parliament, and of the government, is limited
by the limits of the 'representative' nature of the two
main political parties. These two parties have their own

histories, only related to the rest of society in a general way, and sometimes in part running in a direction opposite to general social movements. The choice that voters have is to vote for one party or the other; but they cannot choose to change the nature of the parties or invent new ones, so their choice is very limited.

Perhaps most limiting of all is the fact that most Members of Parliament are Upper English – by birth, by training, or by imitation. In the sense that Upper England is above all a product of education, this is not unexpected. Politicians are usually educated above the general mass of the voters. But given the special function of education in Britain this fact in itself probably accounts more than any other single factor for the inadequacies of British politics.

Conservative Party members are almost entirely Upper English; three-quarters went to public schools and two-thirds to universities. There is a public school atmosphere about the party, and a tendency to accept hierarchic values, that usually makes it more cohesive than the Labour Party. At its top its Upper Englishry becomes even more important: for most of recent times almost all its leaders went to public schools and three-quarters went to Oxford or Cambridge; about a third of them went to the same school – Eton.

Upper Englishry suffers greater challenge in the Labour Party. About a third of the Labour Party members begin life as manual workers. Although they have usually worked as union officials before entering Parliament, they make up the main group in Parliament of those who grew up as Average Britons, untouched by even a grammar school education. However, there are more grammar school old boys than anything else in the Labour Party, but even in the Labour Party about a fifth of the members went to public schools; there are more old boys from Eton alone in the Labour Party than there are ex-manual workers in the Conservative Party. At the top reaches of the Labour Party Upper Englishry in origin or education becomes more prominent: up to a third of the top men come from public schools and most have been to universities. But there is not a dominant social tone in the Labour Party as there is in the Conservative Party, since the Labour Party is made up (in broad, somewhat caricatured terms) of unionists (who tend to be bread-and-butter men), of fairly conventional public school or grammar school old boys who have acquired Upper Englishry (who tend to be 'moderate'), and of a mixture of grammar school old boys and renegade public school old boys who make up a kind of intelligentsia (that tends to be 'radical', if often in an Upper English way). The 'moderates' and the bread-and-butter men are dominant; the 'radicals' are less important in the parliamentary party than they are in the party generally. A Labour Prime Minister assumes office with the knowledge that there are endemic divisions within his party. To a Conservative Prime Minister his party does not matter so much; his greatest opponents are likely to be the reactionaries within his party, but this is also the section with whom schoolboy appeals to loyalty can usually be most effective. At least this seemed true until the outbreaks of Enoch Powell.

Having some relation to these Members of Parliament are the two big extra-parliamentary political machines, arranged in a hierarchy of local branches, constituency organizations, and regional and national leaderships. Both party machines are among the biggest in the world, but their influence on the parliamentary parties is not as great as their mass membership might suggest. The main jobs of local branches within a constituency organization, apart from providing a feeling of 'belonging', are to raise money and to help get in the party vote at election time. Most members don't do anything except join. The main influence the constituency parties have on affairs is that they choose the local party candidates (except in those Labour constituency parties where this role is handed over to a union that will pay the bill), although the central party organization also tries to affect the result.

In the case of the Conservatives, the mass organization doesn't really matter much. Apart from picking candidates it has no direct constitutional relationship to the parliamentary party or to the official party machine. Democratically based, although with a disproportionately high number of Upper English leaders, its national conference is no more than a body that can express moods. Until recently it was a kind of mass rally, acclaiming the leader; now its debates reach a higher level of intelligence, but they provide nothing more than one of the factors that the parliamentary leader might care to take into account. It is the parliamentary leader who picks the leader and the main officials in the Conservative Party's Central Office and it is the Central Office, not the democratically organized National Union of Conservative and Unionist Associations, that is the controller of the party's national affairs. It is the job of the constituency associations to provide some feeling of sustenance and belongingness and, on polling days, to get in the vote.

The National Executive of the Labour Party has a closer direct connexion with the constituency parties, but even this is limited. The trade unions contribute almost seven times as much to central party funds as the constituency parties (who put up most of their money for the local parties) and this gives them a majority of seats on the National Executive, both directly and indirectly. Half a dozen or so big unions put up most of the money and these particular unions tend to 'own' most of the trade union representation on the Executive (although they can be divided among themselves). This gives the Executive a somewhat different tone from that of many of the constituency branches, which tend to be more 'political' and 'radical'. The undercurrents of difference within the parliamentary Labour Party merely reflect undercurrents within the party as a whole, making it much more a self-consciously defined coalition of interests than the Conservative Party.

In the first eighty or so years of mass democracy in

Britain, the Conservatives usually ruled the roost. In the period of manhood suffrage (from 1884) the Conservatives ruled Britain until the big Liberal Party breakthrough of 1906. In the period of universal suffrage – after women got the vote in 1918 – they also ruled Britain for most of the time, the significant exceptions being the Attlee governments of the late 1940s and early 1950s and the Wilson governments of the late 1960s. This Conservative dominance of British politics is obviously due partly to the fissionable nature of its opponents. The main opposition parties – first the Liberal Party and then the Labour Party – both split, while the Conservatives, after a decline under the Liberal government, regained cohesion and adaptability (or 'opportunism' as their opponents would call it), despite disasters such as Chamberlain's appeasement policy and Eden's Suez intervention.

One must, however, recognize what an unsatisfactory technique voting is. Of the 75 to 80 per cent of the British electors who vote at general elections almost the same number will vote for one party as for the other; the widest variation in recent years was 49 per cent Conservative, 43 per cent Labour; the narrowest was in the 1964 election when Labour defeated the Conservatives because it got 44 per cent of the vote and the Conservatives got 43 per cent – which, in terms of electors rather than voters, meant that Labour won the government with a 31 per cent vote against the Conservatives' 30 per cent. It can even happen that a party can win an election with fewer votes than its main opponent. In the 1951 election Labour scored 231,000 votes more than the Conservatives, but the Conservatives won by getting their votes in the right places, gaining 321 seats in the Commons against Labour's 295. With neither proportional nor preferential voting, under the British system votes for minority parties are usually nothing more than a protest or an expression of aspiration. The minority Liberal Party can win up to 11 per cent of votes cast, as it did in the 1964 election, but gain only 1 per cent of seats in the House of Commons.

Putting on pressure

It is arguable that the interest groups of Britain are more significant in governing the country than Parliament, and that Parliament itself is sometimes most significant when interest groups make it work; but the operations of the interest groups have not been widely accepted as a necessary part of the processes of British democracy, except amongst the specialists, to whom this question assumes critical importance. Yet in some ways interest groups can provide a democratic element in government more effectively than Parliament, or even provide a balance against the undemocratic aspect of Parliament; and in other ways they are so necessary to effective government that they provide some of those elements of order without which government might become both more inefficient and more arbitrary. Their apparent lack of antiquity means that to some their operations seem unnatural, 'not right'; yet the main result of not accepting them as part of the process of government is not to limit their power but, by this privacy, to increase it, and to make it less likely that abuses might be reformed.

Only one kind of interest group is given recognition by all (except the confessedly undemocratic) and that is the kind that functions openly, not in special self-interest (such as trade unions or professional or business associations) but in some altruistic cause (e.g. the Royal Society for the Prevention of Cruelty to Animals or the Committee for Nuclear Disarmament). These kinds of groups are less significant than they were in their heyday in the nineteenth century. Yet the traditions of the high days of reform are now accepted. It is understood that it is essential to political liberty that new causes should have the opportunities to triumph over old habits and that those who push these causes, using the pressure techniques of public occasions and general publicity, may affect government as much from their open activities as from their influence on Parliament by specific lobby pressure or the infiltration of parties.

Not much of this still happens. At least not in its classic form. No one really has to join anything any more. Controversy is something carried out on TV and, at various levels, in the newspapers and magazines: perhaps this is the reason why there are so many *passing* controversies. The most intense disturbances carried out by altruistic groups have been the street movements that came first from the Committee for Nuclear Disarmament and then from the various groups protesting against American action in Vietnam. This seemed the whimsy of the Southern Metaphor carried to a high degree: the most sensational disturbances had to do with matters in which the British government was insignificant. Even in these, one of the real interests among the wider public was not in the causes themselves but in the theatricality of the marches and demos and the style of the police.

The most successful campaigns in Britain have not been carried out by altruistic interest groups, but by groups of self-interest, helped by P.R. and even advertising to stir up instant controversy. An old example is the 'Mr Cube' campaign, run by the sugar interests against the Attlee Government's proposals to nationalize sugar: the lovable little 'Mr Cube', along with Locke and Mill, became one of the spokesmen for British freedom. Another was the campaign for commercial TV. Both have been attacked as examples of the manoeuvrings of rich men, yet in both cases the opponents of special interest were themselves very powerful. In the first case it was the government of the United Kingdom, no less; in the second it was an 'establishment' of B.B.C. supporters who seemed to hold most of the honours that accrue to men in Britain. And in both cases it may have been the spokesmen for special interest who were more 'representative' of the people than the government or the holders of high office.

These openly operated interest groups, using Parliament along with other platforms, are not the most regularly influential groups Indeed, sometimes the use of Parliament and other open methods is a desperate measure taken when a group has nothing more to lose. It is in dealing with the government bureaucracies that interest groups can most influence events, not usually in the grand manner, but in significant detail. It is they, not Members of Parliament, who regularly meet with important bureaucrats and become, in some instances, part of the apparatus of government. For example, the annual bargaining of the National Farmers' Union with the Agriculture Departments about subsidies to farmers and price guarantees has become one of the most predictable and significant ceremonies of state. When it comes to deciding what support goes to what section of the industry, and in which regions, the N.F.U. virtually makes the decisions. And so closely related is the N.F.U. to the departments with which it deals that they in their turn tend to be lobbyists for farmers' interests in their dealings with other departments. In fact it is not unusual for departments throughout the government to use interest groups in their struggles with other departments, particularly with the Treasury.

Set up within the government bureaucracies there are more than five hundred advisory committees made up of representatives of interest groups; some departments have thirty or forty committees. In addition there would be thousands of instances each year of 'informal advice' coming from interest groups. Just as a department can lobby for interest groups, the spokesmen for interest groups can lobby among their members for support of policies agreed with a department. It is in this way that many decisions become effective, just as private arrangements can provide departments with information necessary for policy-making, of a kind that they would otherwise find it expensive and difficult to collect.

What British elections are about

The great majority of voters vote for the same party from one election to the next. Many of them vote for only one party throughout their lives, and for those who once or twice switch their votes this can be an affirmation of a shift in their view of the world, of their feeling that things have changed. So far as these basic, unchanging, or almost unchanging voters are concerned, what their views of the world are is not hard to determine. There is the world of the Upper English and the world of the Average Britons: to basic voters of this kind a vote for the Conservatives is a vote for Upper England or in some cases for a 'classless Britain'; a vote for the Labour Party is a vote for Average Britain or in some cases for a 'classless Britain'. It is not usually specific political issues that affect basic voters: in some cases they vote for their party although they cannot name the specific issues raised in an election; in other cases they vote for their party even if they disapprove of some of its policies; in other cases, if they disagree with their party they prefer to change their opinions on specific issues rather than vote against their party.

About four-fifths of Labour voters are manual workers. About four-fifths of the non-manual workers vote Conservative, which makes up about half the Conservative vote. The other half is made up of manual workers who may fall into two main classes – the Alf Garnetts who feel that things should be run by their betters; or the supermarket generation that wants to deny a class division in Britain. These basic undercurrents of difference mean that for most voters at an election it is not a question of choosing between programmes or of voting, as in referendums, on particular issues. What determines basic voters is their conception of British society. They see it in terms of a fundamental social division and they support one side or the other, irrespective of most of their particular policies; or, choosing one party or the other, but more usually the Conservatives, they vote for a 'classless' middle-class Britain. One of the greatest emotional significances of an election is its use as an affirmation of basic voters' views about what British society is and what it should be, although it should be recognized that this division is not necessarily evident in politicians' speeches: the Conservatives now sometimes present themselves as simple bare-footed Average Britons; the Labour Party is sometimes cautious in attacking the social forms of Upper Englishry.

Perhaps the other main factor determining party images, and therefore elections, is the question of whether a political party is 'legitimate': *Does this party really look as if it could govern the country?* To the committed basic voter the two questions are one: the party that represents his image of British society is obviously the only party fit to govern and he sometimes hates the leaders of the other party as symbols of evil. To others, perhaps those who do not hold such settled views of the nature of things, the question is more diffuse. British elections attempt to determine which party is a 'legitimate' government, and thus bring about a change in voting habits. For most of the 1930s the Labour Party was seen as the party that *did not know what to do*. Then in the election of 1945 there was an insultingly big majority for Labour of more than two million votes over the Conservatives so that it went close to winning half the votes cast while the Conservatives did not quite gain 40 per cent. It looked as if there was a desire for Average Britain to triumph over Upper England and for the ordinary people to appear the nation's most important concern. In this situation the Conservatives looked the party that *did not know what to do*: given that the aspirations for their society which the British seemed to be expressing were so strong that even Churchill, the hero of Europe, fell. Conservatives seemed freaks from the past, muddlers of the Depression years, appeasers of Hitler, men who did not know how to run the country. But by following a path that was different from the aspirations of the people and becoming over-concerned with its particular economic theories, which did not interest even most of its suporters, the Labour Party then drained itself of its new legitimacy.

Tests of the 'legitimacy' of the Labour Party are sometimes seen as tests of its ability to imitate the Conservatives, but in a situation such as that of 1945 in which the voters were expressing changed social aspirations, exactly the opposite might have been the case: the Labour Party might have been a more 'legitimate' government than the Conservatives only to the extent that it did things that the Conservatives could not do, so long as those things were commensurate with the aspirations of a majority of the voters. There were some matters on which it was expedient (as well as, in itself, good) for the Attlee government to have maintained a traditional form of legitimacy, most notably in its opposition to Russian influence in Europe and its readiness to co-operate with America. But, while its extension of welfare benefits fitted in with the expectations of a change in priorities among those who voted for it, in the narrowly doctrinaire economic base of its radicalism it proved a failure in legitimizing new social aspiration.

The Labour Party acquired a new illegitimacy as men obsessed with doctrinaire trivialities about the ownership of industry ('nationalization') and to that extent they became men who *did not know what to do*. Except for their welfare programme, they went for the wrong targets. And when their welfare programme was implemented (no sooner was this done than it was threatened by the chronic economic crisis), there was nothing much else they could think of to do, apart from causing arguments about purely economic theories, which bored some people and irritated others. They became a party that argued in public about what it should do. They had a philosophy of approach they could not use.

If people had voted for them because they wanted society changed (beyond narrow economic fields), Labour had not acted like the government that people wanted. To have dressed up in the same clothes as Conservatives, to have turned up at the Palace in the same way, to have come from the same schools, to have played games in the House of Lords and so forth, softened some of the sense of change. But perhaps the new legitimate role was not softening a sense of change but strengthening it. An intuitively strong government can sometimes sense that doing new things once considered illegitimate may legitimize it by fulfilling new aspirations. There may have been a stronger desire for social change in Britain in 1945 than the Attlee government fulfilled (or was interested in fulfilling), obsessed as it was with the economic in a narrow and tendentious way. If it had satisfied the desire for social change more strongly, including views of what Britain was supposed to be about, it might have legitimized itself more strongly than it did by conforming. By creating new habits it would have made irreversible changes that the Conservatives would have also adopted, since it would be only by adopting them that the Conservatives could be rescued from their illegitimacy. Otherwise the Conservatives might have remained the party that *did not know what to do*.

As it was the Labour Party fell into years of exile as an 'illegitimate', tendentious party. The impulses that could have made social change real began to weaken. The Conservatives took over the welfare policies of Labour, dismantled some of the more doctrinaire controls and began to act with the pretence that British society was classless after all. There was some satisfaction of the desire among the ordinary people of Britain for the ordinary things of life which the more doctrinaire men in the Labour Party dismissed as 'materialist'. Beneath this façade of easygoingness, with its inferences of that suburbanism that Average Britons aspire to, basic problems still remained. Senses of snobbery and hierarchy recovered their confidence, taking strange new shapes. With the silliness that can come over political parties, the Conservatives then put in the aristocratic Home to replace Macmillan, then, swinging the other way, they replaced Home with Ted Heath, a grammar school old boy of such apparent ordinariness that one could easily forget who he was.

When Labour returned under Wilson, it no longer

appeared that the potential for social change could be successfully dramatized by shock action. Some ministers began to unpick bits of the social structure, but there was no excitement about it. Wilson spoke the language of expertness and technology with more enthusiasm than he spoke the language of social change. He was concerned with being 'with it', falsely mistaking passing fashions for deeper impulses, but he seemed to want to legitimize himself in the traditional way, without having Attlee's pragmatic ruthlessness. India got in Attlee's way, so he got rid of it. A new turn in the sterling crisis got in Wilson's way, but it took him three years of standing by sterling, as if it were a flag rather than a currency, before he was prepared to get rid of its over-valuation.

Among the élites especially interested in politics the questions of 'Britain's place in the world' were discussed at a length quite out of proportion to the interest ordinary people had in the subject. What also interested people – their relations with each other, the kind of society Britain was supposed to be – remained unsettled questions. Some of the shrewder politicians in the Conservative Party recognized these impulses, but it was apparently impossible for their party to fulfil them, since fulfilment would involve the destruction of much of the party's nature. It would seem the role of the Labour Party to enact those dramas of social change that could lead to a permanent shift in emphasis in British society; but this is a drama the Labour Party finds it hard to play since some of its central obsessions are irrelevant to what people want.

Voters decide between governments according to broad aspirations as to what government should be and diffuse images of what society is. In a sense politics may be about 'ideas'. In this situation it may not be, above all, a government's individual decisions that matter, but the overall kind of approach to life that they represent: much more important than legislation, often more important than the brutal strategic and economic decisions it reaches, may be the government's role as an actor – as a dramatizer of the significance of events and of a view of life. If new senses of virtue are to be established in Britain they are likely to arise first within the community (as they have) , certainly not in Parliament which is usually less mobile in its attitudes; but perhaps they must finally be dramatized by the government itself so that Britain will seem a different country and British society will seem to have a different potential. It is in this sense that, in the democratic manner, the people are capable of creating better than they know. It is in this sense that British government has been weak.

11. EDUCATING BRITONS

Training for what?

After attacking the obsessive devotion to the classics, the Royal Commission on Public Schools concluded in its report that, on the whole, public school education had been a failure. Later, the Royal Commission on Technical Instruction, reporting on 'the widespread concern about the capacity of English industry to stand up to European competition', recommended that 'no portion of the national expenditure on education is of greater importance than that employed in the scientific culture of the leaders of industry'. The Royal Commission on Public Schools gave its report in 1861, the Royal Commission on Technical Instruction in 1876. The debate continues.

As a remarkable example of a system deliberately concerned with training élites, the English education system has obviously made a very bad job of it. Some of the reasons for this have already been recorded – the whimsical silliness, the concern with 'face' and manners, the reverence for things that are old or that stand still, the vain concern with British superiority and uniqueness. But there is even more wrong with English education than that.

The most publicized of the other disadvantages has been that neglect of specialist training that comes from the belief that general style is more important than particular knowledge or even brains. But what seems more remarkable, there was a slowness in and a distaste for providing good specialist technical training for *anybody*. In this, Britain was different from the industrial nations of Europe. When these nations industrialized they changed their education systems, but in Britain even when people got their jobs they were not supposed to learn anything in a systematic way that might be useful to them; there was not even any eagerness to train the 'technicians', the understrappers of the uselessly educated gentlemen. England has perhaps been the last of the industrial countries, in each field, to take vocational training seriously.

There is still a lot to be said for receiving a general education before specializing; and it can be argued that at its higher levels American management accepts a certain 'amateurism' (not of administrative style, but of technical knowledge) so that a McNamara can move from business into the Defense Department, put in twenty or thirty other new men, and go about changing it. There is also obviously something to be said for 'character' in making practical decisions – what is wrong with the 'character' produced by the English education system is that it tends to make the wrong decisions. The present vogue in England for talking about 'professionalism' could go too far (although one doubts whether it is likely to go anywhere much at all). What was remarkable was the refusal for so long to seriously consider the quality of *any* vocational training. The social values of Upper Englishry being what they are, this has meant that, in what is really a highly materialistic society, even the processes of increasing material wealth have not been taken seriously. For the Upper English, since prosperity grew on trees (preferably in a great family's park), it was demeaning to have to do anything about it. Whatever had to be learned was best picked up by physical propinquity, 'on the job'. Both apprentice and managing director muddled through in their pragmatic manner, the one at his bench, the other at his desk. The contempt of the humanities men for the useful in education may be one of the reasons why Britain is an incompetent society. If there are tests of intrinsic value in education there are also tests of intrinsic value in competence: a society that values incompetence should not be surprised at the result. Those Englishmen who wish to live in a state of contemplation and of oriental indifference to the material world should not complain if goods in the shops become more expensive and the trains stop running on time.

The indifference of the humanities men to vocational training remained, but their uneasiness towards science, 'applied science', and technology (a scale of un-prestige descending in that order) took the strange direction of leading to a boom in scientists, and the preference for 'pure' science led to a boom in applied research. When it was obvious that something was needed to stimulate British industry, to the humanities-educated men who made most of the decisions it seemed obvious there was nothing *they* could do about it so they urged that more scientists should be produced. Let *them* do something about it. Soon Britain was producing more scientists and engineers than its industries had the brains to use, so a lot of them went to America. In the same way, honouring the uselessness of 'pure' science, it seemed to the humanities-educated decision-makers that what industry needed was more 'applied research'. The connexion between the two was so un-obvious that one ministry handled 'pure' science and a different ministry handled 'applied research'. Cutting down on research projects in 'pure' science, which was honoured as being useless, and fostering 'applied research', which was dishonourable enough to be of some use, Upper England did its bit for Britain. The results were as disappointing as the over-production of scientists and engineers.

It is at this point that the faults of Britain also became the faults of Europe. Worried about the 'technology gap', the Organization for Economic Co-operation and Development in 1968 prepared some working papers comparing Western European nations and the United States. As a result of finding a new way of counting them, they found that most Western European countries produced proportionately more researchers than the United States, and that, of the Western countries, Britain produced more than any of them. As well as this suggestion that production of scientists was not in itself sufficient, it was also indicated that it was in the United States that the science-based industries that grew fastest were those most closely tied to 'pure' research. It appeared that the critical difference between the United States and Western European countries (and in this difference Britain may be the furthest from America) was not in the production of scientists and technologists but in their use, and in the education of those non-scientists and non-technologists who also make decisions. This is what the Americans mean when they say that it is not a technological gap but a management gap that distinguishes them from Western Europe. Their system of education, both because there is more of it and because it is different, gives them managers and workers who can accept new ideas more quickly and see their possibilities, so that new technology becomes effective more quickly. To some extent this comes from a difference in the use of technologists (who get more executive jobs in America), to some extent from a difference in the education of non-scientists and non-technologists, and to some extent from a difference in the number of people who receive some kind of education.

The feeling in England that science is a 'specialist' subject whereas the humanities subjects are 'general education' has led to an early specialization in the humanities. What this means is that English education, so often praised because of its general nature, in fact becomes specialist too early. Even from a non-vocational point of view, one wonders how a 'general education' cannot emphasize those sciences that have provided most of the principal intellectual developments of the century. From a vocational point of view, it is likely that a management, although not scientifically trained, needs some ingrained sense of the technological before innovations can be put more effectively into practice. In any case there is no disgrace in America in receiving an education that is related to future employment, so that one at least learns to think about what is one of the most important things in one's life – one's work. Even if they are not scientists, Americans can take an expert and intelligent interest in their jobs.

However, what may be even more at fault in Britain (and the rest of Western Europe) is that fewer people receive a full education of some kind or other) than in the United States. The United States produces proportionately far more university graduates than any other country, and Britain less than most European countries. Seventy-six per thousand working population in the United States; twenty-eight in Britain. And even as far as the ordinary working force is concerned, Americans stay longer at school. (In this Britain has a worse record than most of Western Europe, which is itself well behind America.)

Premature élitism in secondary education, with accompanying specialization, may be the factor that provides the real gap between Britain (and Western Europe) and America.

The system of early specialization is, of course, an extremely economical form of élite-training. It means that there are fewer of the higher-educated in Britain than in America, but at least the lucky ones have been educated in a short time and with remarkably little wastage. Handpicked and brought into prime condition by the Sixth Form, in the universities they are able to take a high-most other countries. The real standards of education, how-standard first degree of shorter duration than is possible in ever, are not the standards of Sixth Form work or of university first degree courses, but the standards of those who have finally finished their education. If they take longer over this, with more wastage and more post-graduate work, but end up better, they are of higher standard. All that has happened is that the process has cost more public money. The main economic role of the Sixth Form is to enable students to pass university entrance examinations at a standard that enables a short first degree course. If university places were easier to get and degree courses were longer there would seem to be no point in repeating a year in the Sixth Form.

There is antipathy towards the American idea that higher education is the right of everyone who completes a secondary education and there is even concern about the sudden raising of the school leaving age to sixteen for those who do not finish their secondary education. In both cases the main reason given for this, apart from money, is a concern with 'standards'. Yet the huge expansion in both school and university places that has already occurred since the Second World War seems to have been associated with a general increase in the quality of individual students. From the point of view of education (considered both in itself and as a form of training for employment) there seems every reason to believe that the education system that works best now is one that tries to achieve an average standard of attainment for everyone, with the more talented students sorting themselves out after the rush and then concluding their higher education as specialists in less crowded surroundings.

When he was Education Minister, Mr C. A. R. Crosland crashed ahead with comprehensive schools, which bring together into the one school the kind of children who were previously sorted out at the age of eleven into grammar schools or secondary modern schools. The number of comprehensive schools soon reached slightly more than 10 per cent of the total secondary schools (although a quarter were still grammar schools and the majority remained secondary modern schools). The comprehensive schools represent an attempt to break away from early educational élitism. However, élitism is not yet postponed to where it most belongs – in the post-graduate courses at the universities.

Oxford

In their intake of students the British universities are less related to class than they used to be: in fact a slightly higher proportion of university undergraduates in Britain come from manual workers' families than happens in any other country in Europe, and university staffs have very largely shed the crudities of the class system (although many of them have transferred its values to other purposes).

A new England? In some ways, yes. But what kind of a new England? Here are most of the future élites of the country, carefully sifted out from their fellows. Many good candidates, it is true, are still thrown away before the sifting begins, because of economic under-privilege, but at least the survivors are graded by exhaustive tests. To what effect? How much is the grading concerned with the talents that will be called into play when they move into the élite business? How much is it concerned with the kind of problems they will then have to face? The answer is: very little. Perhaps this would not matter – perhaps it might even be an advantage – if more students went on, after an undergraduate education, to advanced studies. There are, of course, many virtues in British university education for those who are not proceeding through it for a training in practical affairs, and even for those who are, a good general undergraduate course might provide a firm basis for more specifically vocational training. But here Britain is behind almost all the industrial nations. In the United States something like 40 per cent of the twenty to twenty-four age group pass on to advanced schools; in France it is 15 per cent; in Germany it is 8 per cent; in Britain it is 5 per cent. In the United States the selective processes of competition do not seriously begin until the age of twenty-one; in Britain the major part of the competitive process is settled in early adolescence, at secondary school, and much of it in the undergraduate schools. And even within the undergraduate schools there is another premature selection – between those who are chosen for Oxford and Cambridge, and those who are not.

Although most students attend the provincial redbrick universities, and a few attend some of the 'plate-glass universities' of the You've-Never-Had-It-So-Good period, the élite of the élites still moves towards Oxford and Cambridge. A third of all would-be university entrants in Britain apply for entrance to Oxford or Cambridge. They have good reason to do so. An Oxford or Cambridge education is the best way of having a pick at the best jobs. In this way, by specializing for years at school in circumstances of intense competition, students are sorted out even before they become undergraduates: this early sorting out determines which of them will have the best start in life. Even if the privileges gained for those children whose parents can pay for their secondary education disappeared and if all schooling in Britain were exactly equal, it would still seem that there might be a better result if selection were delayed until at least the second degree stage. But here Oxford and Cambridge have a strong defence: while providing second degree courses for provincials, colonials, and foreigners they prefer to elevate the status of their own first degrees so that it seems unnecessary for those who hold them to take another degree. In all the fields in which university graduates are important Oxford and Cambridge graduates are either dominant, or disproportionately represented. Does this mean that the sorting out at matriculation level really has chosen the best brains? Or does it mean that Oxford and Cambridge have England bluffed?

Although the elements of English élitism have many earlier causes, it seems likely that if one were now to look for the biggest single élitist factor in English and therefore in British society, it would be found in Oxford and Cambridge. If the range were made even narrower, it would be found in Oxford. Given this, it seems reasonable to examine the University of Oxford as one of the most important sources of infection for the maladies of Upper England.

Before doing so it should be pointed out that to criticize the special role of Oxford as an élite-trainer is not to criticize the idea of *excellence*, unless one took the lunatic view that all that is excellent in Britain comes from Oxford. One must distinguish between the role of a university as a trainer of élites (a role of which Oxford is unconscionably aware) and the role of a university as a promoter of excellence in the pursuit of the studies it fosters.

These are not matters that have to be determined here. It is as an élite-trainer that one judges Oxford. What does it have to offer? One obvious comment is that, although Oxford is so anxious to absorb the best examination passers in England that it is now worried that *only* a third of university entrants apply for Oxford, and although it produces the best job-getting degrees in the United Kingdom, it resists any demand for a sense of responsibility in its role as an élite-trainer. It is an institution that delights in its power to produce men of consequence: but in its conceit it believes that it produces graduates so eminent in talent and style that this is all that matters.

But *is* the Oxford style one that is so good that it is all that matters in any practical situation? This very indifference to the results of its existence is an example of two of Oxford's characteristics – its frivolity and its superciliousness. The frivolity is sometimes delightful, sometimes laboriously cliquish and allusive; more usually it is a simple avoidance of appearing to be interested in what one is doing, a horror of seriousness, a preference for chit-chat that can make Oxford one of the most difficult universities in the world in which to have a serious conversation, let alone an interesting one. While this is a style that can sometimes go very well with an academic approach – carrying learning lightly, bringing out complex issues simply, and encouraging generalization in a world given increasingly to detail – nevertheless, when transferred to practical affairs, it can produce a mildness of manner inadequate for the matter in hand, sometimes making those whose style this is appear merely silly. That this frivolity usually accompanies superciliousness may suggest that it is really a retreat from combat, a refusal to compete. It is a frivolity that is sometimes in itself a way of avoiding what should, by any standards, be faced, even of avoiding the accusation of superciliousness: *one wasn't really serious*. The supercilious is often applied to the trivial: while class origin might go, voguishness and cliquish manners flourish and there is an habituation to constant subtle denigration of others and therefore to self-congratulation. But it can also be applied to the important; if some important matter is to be disposed of it is made a joke of. That gets rid of it.

The buildings of Oxford are themselves famous antiques, great tourist attractions, and members of its staff can amuse themselves throughout their lives by defending little old things. One sometimes wonders, however, what the real substance of Oxford – its scholarly life – would look like if it were housed in a couple of big, 'functional' buildings, and if the concentration were entirely on academic matters.

The Educated Moderns

One must remember, of course, that Britain still provides some of the world's most clever people. What goes wrong with so many of them is that their creative energy seems to leak away: for some because of the nature of their education, for others because of their general environment. So many carefully educated people: so many people who feel their lives wasting away. Such a good potential: such a poor performance.

But there are others who are fully extended, particularly in science and technology. The Britain of Newton, Faraday, and Darwin is still one of the most important nations for scientific research. Of the Nobel Prize winners this century the British run second only to the United States in physics and medicine, and second only to Germany in chemistry. Financial support for scientific research in Britain is still proportionately one of the highest in the world, and the nation that invented the piston engine and the spinning jenny, Bessemer steel and the tank, continues to invent things – even if, as in the case, for example, of terylene or the swept-wing aircraft, its inventions are then developed in nations that are more advanced technologically.

The spirit of scientific speculation and of technological inventiveness, though strong, exists in a society that does not grant it full prestige. Business managements are sometimes incapable of turning inventiveness into products. In the 1960s emigration of scientists and engineers from Britain doubled in six years. It was one of the few statistics that did double in that time.

But new élite generations are now pushing themselves up through English society and growing stronger as they do so. Neither Upper-English nor Average British, they are what might be described as Educated Moderns, people educated in the 1950s and the 1960s who have somehow avoided most of the grotesqueries of the inheritance of Upper England. They can be part of social networks of like people in which they can get on with their own lives in a new and more modest way, giving sustenance and meaning to themselves in their own inter-relationships. Not only in scientific and technological achievement but within the general field of the humanities as well, there is plenty of evidence of talent that is finding expression for itself. But this does not really seem a generation that will take over, although colonies of new people may be building a base for some later change. The forms of power and prestige and influence still creak and strain with old stresses and distortions, even if they sometimes seem to be pointing in a different direction: old values are still maintained, even if in new words.

12. MEN AT WORK

Amateurs in Whitehall?

In the first century B.C., when the British were still barbarians, the Chinese Emperor Wu Ti, concerned with the arts of government, encouraged the growth of schools in the provinces and also set up in his capital a higher school for the training of future officials. It was from this time that competitive examinations to choose those worthy of office began in China. In the seventh century A.D., when the English had almost completed the conquest of Britain, the Emperor T'ai Tsung strengthened and extended this examination system to help break the power of the old aristocratic families, so that careers could be more open to the talents. As the centuries went on, the examinations became more extensive and more severe. There were examinations in history, law, mathematics, poetry, and calligraphy, and there were some questions of a practical kind, but the greatest honour was paid to those who had achieved success in the study of the classics. The examinations were concerned more with testing a traditional sense of style than with testing originality of thought: those who did best were those who could compose essays and poems on the topics selected, in the style that was most preferred. This system cultivated considerable intellectual arrogance and considerable conformity, although it did also prove to be a way of choosing men of greater than usual ability, with a capacity for concentrated application. It was in the 1850s, when the Chinese Empire was beginning its dissolution, partly because of this system, that the British Empire adopted a similar competitive examination system to choose those most worthy of office.

The system was introduced in the spirit of novelty and reform. The scandals of the Crimean war had revealed what a lumbering and rotting thing the apparatus of state had become. An Administrative Reform Association was formed and it campaigned with the lustiness of a nineteenth century reform group that believed its policies could be put into action. Thousands attended its mass meetings. By 1855 the campaign was won. The principle was accepted that important posts in the civil service would be filled not through corrupt patronage but through competitive examinations. Instead of the blunderings of the placemen there would be the competence of trained administrators.

Although the universities, which were to provide these administrators, were themselves in such a mess in the 1850s that in the first civil service examinations no university candidates passed, they soon put themselves together sufficiently well to set the new approach. They went about it in much the same way as the Chinese: the best way of training officials was to make them distinguished scholars of the classics. Oxford maintained that its sole business was to train the powers of the mind and that the study of the classics was the best means of doing this. In reply to its critics Oxford stated that it had reformed itself two centuries before and that the reforms then carried out were all that was needed in the way of change, since at that time 'the nature and faculties of the human mind were exactly what they are still'.

When Britain was enjoying its greatest appearance of world power, most of its important government officials were men of letters, mainly classicists, who believed that the art of good government was to do as little as possible. To outsiders they could seem more like Oxford dons than administrators; in fact they did not usually see themselves as administrators but as theorists of policy: the administrating, if it had to be done, was to be performed by those who were now being produced out of the new universities or the grammar schools.

The élite of the British civil service consisted of about 3,000 individuals out of the 400,000 or so who made up the civil service as a whole (excluding post office and industrial employees). These were the members of the Administrative Class, a thoroughly misleading title, since their role was more that of top policy-makers. They were assisted by the Technical Classes – scientists, lawyers, doctors, engineers, and so forth; and the actual administration was carried out by the misnamed Executive Class, a much larger number of persons who entered the service straight from school and who in turn presided over other lesser classes.

It was the nature of the élite Administrative Class that established the nature and tone of the home civil service. Who were they?

Something like 60 per cent of them, at the rate of about one hundred a year, entered the top Administrative Class straight from university after being selected by a highly competitive examination. Of these, for most of the century, something like four-fifths were graduates of Oxford or Cambridge. It was heralded as a sign of change in 1968 that only 65 per cent of the entrants to the Administrative Class came from Oxford and Cambridge. For most of the century a third were classicists and about the same proportion studied history. Almost three-quarters came from public schools; if private schools are added, more than 80 per cent came from schools in which parents bought their children's education.

The remaining 40 per cent of the Administrative Class came up through the non-commissioned ranks of the lower-graded Executive Class. Even after allowing for those who entered it through this back door, almost 50 per cent of the Administrative Class were graduates from Oxford and Cambridge alone, and almost two-thirds came from public or private schools.

It is inaccurate to see the senior civil service as having been manned by the sons of upper-middle-class gentlemen; for some time to become a senior civil servant has represented a reasonable ambition for some of the lower ranges of the middle-class and the lower-middle-class, who got into it by way of education. It is true that only 3 per cent of the senior civil service were the children of semi-skilled or un-skilled manual workers, but about a quarter were the children of routine white-collar workers or skilled manual workers, and while the majority (about 70 per cent) came from the upper-middle and middle classes, most of them came from the lower ranges of these classes. It is possible, however, to imagine that the higher civil service would have remained much the same even if it had been largely made up of the sons of unskilled workers educated, through grants, at Oxford and Cambridge.

For most of the century there was no specialist training for members of either the 'Administrative' or the 'Executive' class once they had entered the service. Entrants to the Treasury, for instance, almost all of whom were not economists, were simply given a reading list of books on economics (and not a comprehensive one at that); among the instructions issued for their use was the warning that the books should not be regarded as urgent compulsory reading: 'That way lies indigestion. The lists constitute a menu to be tasted with discretion and to return to if necessary over the years.' Now that a second reform movement is beginning, a fourteen-weeks course in administrative studies has been provided, with a further seven weeks for those who have been assigned to the economic departments; but this seems a small thing compared with the three years provided in the École Nationale d'Administration in France (to make that comparison with France that both fascinates and irritates the English). And while a junior bureaucrat in London may never have any special contact with either provincial life, or with the problems and styles of business life, a student in the École Nationale d'Administration spends his first year as an assistant to a provincial Prefect, and part of his third year in an industrial, commercial, or agricultural undertaking.

One of the simpler remedies proposed in the 1960s for reform of the British senior civil service was that more 'specialists' should be put in charge. By 'specialist' was meant those who in their training specialized in subjects such as engineering or economics or medicine rather than classics or history. This easy answer could have had its own dangers. In Britain some of the professions make up highly conservative bodies: one of the reasons why the Board of Inland Revenue, for instance, has a conservative effect on economic policy is because accountants are so strong in it. What seemed obvious, however, was that 'specialists' should not continue to suffer from their present disabilities: there seemed no sense in preventing a 'specialist' in economics, for instance, from rising to the top in an economics department, while encouraging a 'specialist' in classics to do so. What came to be recognized as necessary was a break-up of the traditional approach to the higher civil service, perhaps with entry to it only after a period of service within the bureaucracy and by consideration of merit relevant to departmental work. This would end the whimsicality of creating an early élite on the wrong grounds. The alternative would be to follow the French and some other countries and create an early élite on the right grounds.

The policy of switching members of the Administrative Class from one post to the next, within departments or between them, meant that they could not make up by 'work on the job' what they lacked in other training. It may be true that, at the very top, the problems of administration are sometimes best gripped by nonspecialists; but good administrators more usually spend their incubation period thoroughly grasping details about *something*. They learn what detail really feels like and learn how to care whether one policy or another is right. And usually they work within the one field for much of their lives. By comparison, members of the Administrative Class were constantly on the move, almost as if to test their improvising power. Often the result of this theory was that the senior civil servant became like the kind of barrister who overloads himself with briefs: he learned how to manipulate cases quickly out of anything, but he did not really know what he was talking about.

This superficiality came from the essentially political role that senior civil servants usually played and usually preferred to play. Usually they did not spend most of their time running their departments. The fun was to be found around the minister. The top men in a department saw themselves primarily as policy advisers to the minister, and the lesser members of the Administrative Class saw themselves as the assistants of these senior and privileged officials. Attempts at serious analysis would often come only from the young and inexperienced: everyone else was too busy helping the minister, or helping the minister's helpers, and perhaps too busy to spend much time even reading the analysis. Since the minister was usually and necessarily concerned with questions of expediency, the 'policy advising' was likely to be on little, urgent matters. 'Looking after the minister' could mean that, from one year to the next, wide questions of policy were not given any comprehensive and responsible examination.

It also meant a reinforcement of caution. Protecting the minister was mainly a matter of avoiding criticism. This consideration, combined with the timidity that comes from not knowing a subject thoroughly and the scepticism that comes from mastering briefs without really caring about them, could produce a worldly, charming cynicism about being able to achieve anything at all. The true official style was not always one of achievement; sometimes it was one of a mannered pleasantness in human relations, of conforming to traditional departmental lines, of patience and pedantry: its reward was a knighthood. Even the thoroughness of civil servants could be overstated. They had extremely methodical methods of documentation and of demanding standards of precision about small things, but there was sometimes an astonishing shallowness in what was produced by these precise and methodical methods. It could be the precision not of a rigorous intellectuality but of pedantry.

More secrecy still surrounds the affairs of Whitehall than surrounds the bureaucracy of almost any other democratic society. In the manner of Upper England, its affairs proceed as mysteries, things that only the initiated can understand. Most of the highly intelligent 'national debates' conducted in Britain are concerned with matters that in Whitehall seem 'unfeasible'. But Whitehall does not give its reasons. This secrecy has not only taken from Whitehall the stimulation of interchange: it has sheltered the sloppy and the second-rate, while protecting a sense of superiority that has not always been deserved and a scepticism that has sometimes been an expression of failure.

Business – going through the mill

The overall inhibition placed on the British businessman is that he is part of a society in which some of the strongest traditions and values go back before the industrial revolution. If he is himself relatively free of those values, he might be attacked as a barbarian; if he is absorbed by them, he might be attacked for his incompetence. He represents what is now a muffled tradition of rebellion against those values – a failed rebellion, attacked from without and weakened from within, the failure of North against South.

Business itself was not born in the industrial revolution. In its modern forms it was born several centuries before, in the Catholic countries of the Mediterranean; it was already flourishing in Britain before the industrial revolution. This was the business of merchants and bankers, its headquarters in London, its power spreading across the world, and its members respected by the aristocracy and the gentry. The special honour still given in the hierarchy of business esteem to bankers and other members of the City goes back to this pre-industrial time. Much of the prevailing social climate in Britain is still one that can accept finance and commerce, but has even yet not fully adjusted itself to the nature of modern industrial production and marketing.

In the early beginnings of modern manufacturing, in the eighteenth century, there was a sympathetic and even active interest in inventive skill among some of the aristocracy and middle classes, but somewhere in the nineteenth century manufacturing became dirty (unless it was very big – as in shipbuilding and steel-making). The more it succeeded, the dirtier it became. The business virtues of optimism, self-confidence, and a general sense of push, although they were also to some extent general virtues in the eighteenth century, gradually became particular vices in the nineteenth century: to believe that new things were constantly possible (the central creative drive of business) became un-English, and Britain moved into its first post-industrial economic crisis while other nations were still industrializing, often on British money or borrowed British skills. That Britain's pioneering acts of industrialization were going on at the same time as the expansion of the Imperial Metaphor also seems significant: honour went to the servants of Empire rather than to the industrial innovators and, with that praise of stagnation that makes things easier for imperialists, innovation itself became an enemy. Whereas in America some of its heroes became its businessmen, most of the heroes of Britain became its imperial servants.

Manufacturers became respectable to the extent that they were drained of the business virtues: the families of manufacturers became respectable to the extent that they moved out of manufacturing or became so rich that they could buy themselves aristocratic virtue. This kind of change was easiest to see at the top: whereas in other European countries the aristocracies despised the *nouveaux riches*, in England, if their affairs were great enough and their fortunes big enough, the *nouveaux riches* were accepted by the aristocracy, provided they changed their ways. By the end of the nineteenth century it was regular for the great manufacturing families to buy themselves landed estates and titles. At the lower levels, among the smaller-scale manufacturers, families would move into the suburbs of the industrial cities, adopting the polite ways of middle-class provincial life and then perhaps later move into the rural areas beyond the suburbs where they could take on the ways of the small gentry; as they became richer they would send their sons to public schools or universities, from which they might escape business altogether or, alternatively, enter their family businesses, but with an enervatingly irrelevant attitude.

In Britain, to achieve honour, businessmen had to cease being businessmen, or at least to act in some ways as if they were not businessmen. In America (whether they were honoured or hated or despised or tolerated) if businessmen were successful their success was respected. In this particular regard the difference between Britain and America was not that American society was nothing but a businessmen's culture, which is a crazy idea, but that success *in any field* in America was likely to promote open esteem, whereas in England it was not. This was one of the reasons why some of the Upper English treated their jobs in an off-hand way, almost apologetically, as if work could not possibly be a serious part of their lives.

In Western Europe, at the time of British industrial expansion, Britain was itself sometimes seen as the British grew to see America – as a vulgar, pushing society of businessmen. The subtleties of Britain's habit of easy ennoblement evaded most of the European aristocracies, who preferred to exclude the *nouveaux riches*, and by this deprivation successfully increased their own enfeeblement. In Britain the combination of a hierarchic society with social mobility allowed the hierarchic idea not only to survive but to flourish with a new sophistication. In the European nations businessmen could not find such easy honour as they could in Britain by denying their nature, but as the enfeebled aristocracies crumbled and as nationally accepted senses of hierarchy collapsed, businessmen found themselves in societies with more open values and with more varied judgements of success.

As new manufacturers established themselves in Britain they showed a belief in the uselessness of education except as a means of achieving social advancement. They bought education for their own sons, but only to give them a lift in status. Since uselessness was part of the prestige of education they despised it in its relation to business, so that sometimes in a business the only fully educated men might be the members of the controlling family, who had in any case been educated in the wrong things. A lack of interest in the value to business of an Oxford degree in classics or history was understandable enough: but this was accompanied by a contempt for thorough vocational training even for technologists and technicians. While the Americans, the Germans, and other quickly rising industrial powers were setting up whole complicated systems of training for technicians and technologists, the best the British usually did was to set up spare-time night schools. In America, even by 1910, about two senior business executives out of five had received tertiary education; ten years later in Britain even the professional engineers had been to nothing more than night school. For four or more generations technical training in England has been behind that of America, Germany, and other industrial nations, and so far as special business training is concerned it did not really begin until recently. Even the educated sons of businessmen who themselves went into business were expected to get their business training simply by going through the mill. Less than 1 per cent of Britain's 400,000 managers have received any form of systematic management training. Only one in ten of them are graduates, compared with five in ten, six in ten, or even more in other advanced industrial nations – and of those British managers who are graduates nearly all have degrees irrelevant to business.

It was the massiveness of big business in Britain that began to give business a greater respectability. At first it was the massiveness of the early starters – the shipbuilders, the shipowners, the steel-makers, the manufacturers of chemicals – and then the kind of companies that began to coagulate late last century or early this century. It is in the hundred biggest businesses that alone control more than half the assets of British public companies that graduates now most eagerly seek careers. With the Empire gone, young graduates are going for a new strength, but too often with the education and outlook of the masters of Empire rather than the masters of business. Happily, only about a sixth of the graduates occupying top positions in business hold Oxford and Cambridge degrees, although even this proportion seems ominously large. Altogether, somewhere between a quarter and a third of the top managers in British business are now university graduates. That is to say that in this respect Britain in the 1960s has not yet reached the American total of 1910, and at the lower levels of management the situation is even worse. Britain is now behind, perhaps critically behind, America, Japan, and Germany, where almost all of the top managers now hold degrees.

Watt invented the steam engine fifty years before the theories of thermodynamics were sorted out. The great industries of the industrial revolution in Britain – iron and steel, shipbuilding, chemicals, textiles, railways – were equally intuitive or pragmatic. They were splendid examples of inventiveness and enterprise, but they were different from the modern industrial world in which science stimulates technology so that whole new industries (electronics, computers, plastics, for example) come *straight* from scientific and technological research and increasingly the business of the businessman is to turn the results of this research into action. In this new age, on the one side Britain spends more on research than other European nations, and is ahead of them in most of the advanced technologies, but on the other side many of the managers of its business are, in a sense, the opponents of technological values and are even in a kind of implicit revolt against the age. There is enough knowledge available in Britain now to transform the British economy so that everyone could stop talking about it. But the tone and structure of British business management is such that knowledge is not turned into action. There is a wealth of research, but insufficient development; a disregard for expertness and skill; a dithering in making decisions about investment; an uncertainty in economic forecasting and market analysis; alternations of diffidence and arrogance towards the problems of overseas trade. In short, although the right men seem to be in the laboratories, the wrong lot seem to be in the executive suites and, perhaps even more, in the lower levels of management. It is notorious that, compared with the decision-makers in Japanese and German industry, decision-makers in British industry lack both technical and general business training and that the lower one goes in the management scale the greater this discrepancy becomes. What is not sufficiently recognized is that the gap is so great that it may become final.

The British businessman is just as fascinated by money as the businessmen of other countries, but he doesn't take business itself as seriously as they do. For a time this manifested itself boldly in the conspicuous waste of long weekends devoted to the pursuit of aristocratic sports. Until the post-devaluation panic at the end of 1967, businessmen who wanted to be honoured by the Monarch usually had to engage in politics or good works to earn their baubles. In the New Year's List of 1968 there was a sudden handout of forty or so honours to businessmen who had been good at exports – the first wide recognition of success in business as something that was of value in itself – but this apparent change in attitude was really a confirmation of old attitudes; what still really mattered was to be ennobled or to enter an order of chivalry. It is true that the number of public school old boys going into business has doubled and soon will treble, but this partly reflects a desire by firms to engage in a new style of interior decoration: it is not a sign of an increase in prestige for business but of its lack of prestige that it promotes the old boys of public schools so quickly.

There is still a strong element of frivolity in British business. Not just the obvious frivolities of telling jokes over gin-and-tonics in the board room about all those dull, provincial fellows outside who are running the firm, but also the less obvious frivolities – a whimsical preference for traditional techniques, even for the revered antiquity of certain kinds of machinery; a refusal to take serious problems seriously because to do so would require a vigorous and sustained application of expertness that would be ungentlemanly; a facetious superciliousness about the possibility of change; a nonchalance that sees business as a side-line, or a means to an end, and reveals its true interest by leaving copies of the *Queen* on the tables of anterooms rather than copies of *Fortune*. Just as high British government bureaucrats tend to lack the optimism of American or Japanese bureaucrats, high British business bureaucrats can tend to be equally cautious and sceptical when they look at the future. The notorious slowness of British management to exploit the inventiveness of its designers and technologists comes partly from a lack of faith that problems can be solved. An American or a Japanese can delight in the analysis of a problem and move on to the decision as to what should be done about it: a British business manager sometimes seems to see his work as finished once he outlines the problem – there's a problem, so what can he do?

It used to be believed that what made businessmen tick was the profit motive. There is no doubt that business attracts men who like money, but in the big business bureaucracies that set the pace in Britain there is no longer any special relation between a firm's progress and the financial progress of those who manage it. When a nineteenth century manufacturer put up a cotton mill there was an obvious direct connexion between how the mill went and how much brass the master could put in the bank. But when a young man now enters one of the

great bureaucracies of big business the money he makes
will not necessarily depend on his contribution to the
affairs of the business but on the success with which he
can capture a high position in the business bureaucracy. It
is his success in getting himself promoted within a business that has already been built up, and that it would
probably take more than his efforts to ruin, that will determine the size of his expense account. It is hard, under
these circumstances, to agree with those British businessmen who attribute most of the economic ills of Britain to
its income tax, which at its upper reaches takes all but
9d. in the £. According to this theory the managers of
British big business, who usually have little more than a
token shareholding in the companies they run, would
nevertheless run them more efficiently if they had more
take-home money. The usual circumstances in a big firm
are that the rewards of the top men are something they can
wangle for themselves. Lower income tax would mean
that they could keep more of their salary. It would not
necessarily mean that they would 'work harder' (or more
to the point, work better): it would be just as likely to
mean that they would have a greater incentive to get
higher salaries, without working harder or better.

Where government taxation policy may have crippled
incentive has been in not discriminating more harshly and
permanently between companies that earn foreign exchange and other companies, or in other ways discriminating between companies that assist government economic
policy and those that do not. (This could be accomplished
by allowing the executives of favoured companies
more extensive personal tax fiddles so that they would
have a personal incentive of a selective kind that they
would have to *earn*.) The idea of 'fairness' – by which can
be meant the idea of protecting the old against the new –
has had a very conservative effect in economic policies.
It was usually considered 'inequitable' to provide
special privileges for exporters, who were supposed to be
spurred on mainly by exhortation. In Japan, where busi-

nessmen can be stimulated by patriotism as well as by expense accounts, exhortation or indications of direction do seem in themselves to have an effect on businessmen and make them turn to exporting in the national interest. But patriotism does not seem to be an incentive for the British businessman, perhaps because for so long he thought the world really owed him the living it continued to give him.

There is now an explicit uneasiness in Upper England that if the way out of continuing economic crisis is by greater business efficiency, then this could challenge the standards of Upper England. When Arnold Weinstock of General Electric enjoyed a vogue as the paradigm businessman it was said: 'What Britain needs is to use the Weinstocks to build a world in which they will be out of place.' The Wilson era brought in a great deal of P.R. for the idea of efficiency in business and there were some attempts to make heroes of those business leaders who seemed to have succeeded most. Upper England began seriously to contemplate the type of action needed for greater prosperity, but it did not like the look of what it had to do, and was not at all sure that it really wanted to do it. It seemed easier somehow if the workers could just go on pulling in their belts. While the sharpness of success was appealing to many of the young of Average Britain, separated from their grandfathers' Great Depression by a gulf of history and wanting more take-home pay, to Upper England it could seem frightening. Perhaps because the sense of social conformity of the two-nation system suggested that diversity was not possible, there was a fear that if men engaged in practical affairs became more businesslike they would necessarily take over the whole nation. Belief that it might be possible to use economic essentials without applying them to everything was slight.

The use of intelligence in modern technological activity is not often properly understood in Upper England, which can still see decision-making in business in its older forms. As the first industrial society, it cannot even yet see fully beyond the old industrial society to the future technocratic society in which the use of technical knowledge will be no longer more or less confined to the particular end of manufacturing things but will broaden out, so that the technological and technocratic methods will extend to many parts of life (and possibly be used for a great deal more good than bad). In a period in which knowledge will finally indeed be power, and in which intelligence and talent will be the principal factors that entrepreneurs of new activities will assemble, it could be stupefying for Britain if Upper England were not prepared to use its brains.

The world's oldest union movement

In a nation which is prepared to grant itself more unique claims in the struggle for liberties than can be supported by history, it is instructive that the British do not make much of the fact that trade unions achieved legal recognition in Britain before they did in any other country, and that the British union movement in the nineteenth century attained a strength unequalled in any of the other great industrializing nations. The refusal of history texts to give unionism the significance that they give to every other outbreak of violence which resulted in reform is one of the symptoms of that continuing Upper English distaste for trade unions which now represents one of the union movement's problems. Unfortunately the antiquity of the British union movement also seems to be connected with a reverence for the past that makes it probably the most conservative labour movement in any industrial country.

The explosion of unions in the nineteenth century – at first among the spinners and weavers of the textile boom, and then among the coalminers, ironworkers, shipbuilders, and heavy industry engineers of the other main growth industries – was itself part of the general radical explosion that is one of the most impressive characteristics of nineteenth century Britain. In a restless dynamic society, exerting change, old things were ripped up and new habits created. In the history books it is usually the violence that is sensationalized – the burning of mills, the protest meetings and marches, some of them with thousands or tens of thousands of participants, the revolutionary Jacobinism of the Chartists, terrorization. From such lurid scenes Karl Marx constructed his images of a great, final revolution that would cleanse mankind of its pain and error and light the way ahead. Yet perhaps what was more sensational was the quick victory of the workmen's associations and their rapid institutionalization. The acts forbidding 'combinations' of workmen were repealed only in 1824, yet by the mid-1860s the Trades Union Council had been formed, with union representatives being welcomed to their annual congresses by mayors in robes of office, and holding religious services before they got down to business. By the end of the century, with their membership of almost two million and their networks of co-operative and mutual benefit societies, the British unions were a wonder of the western world. The older unions had become hierarchic guilds of craftsmen, attempting to limit entry into their industries by apprenticeship schemes and wrecking labour-saving machinery with more skill than the Luddites – by prohibiting its use. By the 1890s newspaper editorials were already warning that Britain's exports were suffering competition because of union restrictions. Carnegie and Krupp didn't have to deal with trade unions: in Britain one skilled man would tend one old-fashioned machine; in Germany three new machines would be tended by one unskilled man.

But there was no settling down. In the established industries the unions grudgingly lowered some of their standards to accept fellow workers of lesser skill, but out of fresh explosions in the 1880s and 1890s new unions were forming to band together the unskilled – dockers, seamen, railway workers – and within the older unions 'agitators' were restirring the pot, this time with French revolutionary syndicalism. There was talk of a General

Strike in 1911 and after the war rebellion again stirred – this time in some of the older industries; shipbuilding, mining, and some kinds of heavy engineering were now so long-established that the prosperity was draining out of them. There were two million unemployed as early as 1921, most of them collected in areas that were to remain slumped for nearly twenty years. The pit towns, oppressed by what now seems the primordial stupidity of the pit owners, broke into revolt with a strike of a million men in 1926; one accident led to the next and, with no great conviction, the union movement fell into the General Strike about which the unions had woven dreams for two or three generations and the collapse of which, after nine days, was to exhaust the belief of labour movements throughout the world in one of their sustaining myths.

For several generations the middle-classes had seen various successive threats of anarchy in the union movement. Its strength seemed exhausted now and Britain was soon seized by a depression that to the unemployed and those who feared that they would be unemployed seemed to be the final act of violence of their bosses. In the memories of the middle-classes there were two sustaining victories: they had beaten the Germans in 1914-18, and they had beaten the unions in 1926.

Union leaders now become knights, or even lords (although lords do not become union leaders). The unions have more than eight million members, with a £20 million annual revenue and reserves of £80 million. Their leaders are regularly consulted by governments. They sponsor a significant proportion of members of the parliamentary Labour Party and dominate the National Executive. Yet their position is not as strong as this might suggest. Two-thirds of the working population are not members of the unions and the whole union movement is built on a base of subsiding importance: they have failed to attract the membership of white-collar workers and some of their greatest strengths are in old industries that are now crumbling. Individual unions are often weak in resources, with underpaid executives who have to devote much of their time to the endless tugs-of-war of leadership struggles and with inadequate staffs who can do little more than keep up with each day's work. Since the Second World War members' dues have increased by less than one-eighth of the general increase in wages. The Trades Union Council can exhort or advise or offer conciliation: it has no final authority to speak on behalf of the unions, or to them. And while two-thirds of its membership come from less than two dozen big unions, these unions are usually divided among themselves and are surrounded by a host of little unions whose policies on the job are often divisive.

In an atmosphere of mutual suspicion two sets of strong criticisms of the unions are made by almost everybody – one of these (on wages policy) is questionable; the other (on hostility to productivity) is undoubtedly valid, and related to central economic weaknesses in Britain.

The attitude on wage policy sees unionists as capricious, greedy fools, constantly demanding more money which does them no good anyway because costs spiral up into prices, causing inflation, and robbing the unionists of their gains. This kind of criticism is against experience in other industrial nations and in Britain it has partly been by their 'irresponsible' wage demands that the unions have corrected some of the social injustices of their country. They have got their members, particularly the unskilled and the semi-skilled, a bigger slice of the cake. This may have had an inflationary effect, but *they* have not been robbed of real gains – because there are other parts of the community that do not gain from the rounds of wage increases, or other unionists that do not gain so much. Other countries gallop along after wage rises successfully while Britain does not, and these other countries are less likely to expect the prosperity of their economies to depend on 'wage pauses'. Wages rose more quickly in Germany than in Britain over the period in which Germany improved its position in relation to Britain; in the

United States there are still big strikes, tough bargaining, and subsequent wage rises of a kind that in Britain would make editorial writers look up new synonyms for 'anarchy'; in Sweden the unions push hard for higher wages, as if they were the real stimulus to greater efficiency (as in some cases they can be) and then help work out how to increase productivity.

The difference between Britain and these other countries is that in the other countries – Sweden for instance – although the unions brutally challenge industry with their collective power and force up wages, they are confident that industry can respond, flexibly and constructively, to challenges of innovation. In Britain there is probably more resistance to change, not only by union executives but by the 'lads on the job', than in any other industrial nation. This is not just a matter of job security. For a generation or so British unions and workmen have been criticized for their 'depression mentality', for their fear of unemployment and for their desire to stay with the one industry. This timidity and immobility is, however, also a characteristic of Japanese workmen – and it has not prevented Japan from continuing to perform its industrial miracles. In Japan business managers respect the desire of their workmen to remain with the same firm all their lives; they accept it as a stimulus to innovation: to achieve this end is one of the tests of their success. In Britain it is innovation itself that workmen reject. Not only do they want to continue to live in the same districts and work in the same firms – they want to go on working in the same kind of way. This opposition to changes in working methods drags down productivity. Suspicious of their bosses, afraid for their future, exerting their maleness in struggle, their prompting to stubborn inaction is: *what we have we'll hold.*

In this 'Maginot complex' any kind of change is a source of danger. Machines must remain overmanned, methods of training must remain antique, work restrictions of all kinds must be maintained; the more hands

there are the better. Britain is the only European nation
in which there are constant disputes about whether one
worker can do another worker's job. It is also the nation
in which 500,000 craftsman's mates stand around, each
paying court to the skilled craftsman to whom he is
attached, and waiting for the craftsman to give him something to do. Overmanning is not just a privilege of
manual workers. The office staff in some industries is five
times what it would be in an equivalent American concern.

Sometimes Britain's economic problems are attributed,
in the Puritan manner, to the leisure enjoyed by British
workmen. There seems no evidence for this. Working
hours are shorter in the United States and other big
industrial nations than in Britain: in fact British workmen, although they have increased their relative reward,
have gained little in reduced working hours, still clocking
up with overtime about as many working hours as they
did in the 1930s. Sometimes it is strikes that are seen as
the besetting problem. There seems no evidence for this
either. Strikes are worse in some countries (most notably
the United States, where they are three times worse) which
nevertheless have a more impressive industrial performance than Britain. Even the continuing agitation about
plant is no longer always relevant. Re-equipment in much
of British industry is good, in some industries better than
the United States. But the *use* of this equipment is bad:
it does not increase productivity because it is overmanned
and its use is restricted in other ways.

It is not generally true that countries get the governments they deserve. It might be more useful to imagine
that governments get the countries they deserve – if the
countries are modern, industrialized, adaptable societies,
capable of movement. In the same way, in this kind of
society, one might say that bosses get the workers they
deserve. The élites in a country generally, and the managers of its industry and trade in particular, are at the
controls: if they push buttons and nothing moves, that
is principally *their* problem, or the problem of those who

would like to take over from them. (It is even more their problem if they don't bother to push the buttons.) It is a sign of nervousness in élites generally, and in the managers of business in particular, if their complaints about their condition are levelled at the ordinary people in a way that suggests that nothing much is going to happen without a self-generating initiative from the workers. In fact this is a revolutionary belief. To believe that the sluggishness of British industry can be saved only by the workers' initiatives is to believe in the proletarian revolution.

The belief in low wages persisted for too long in Britain. When Britain's industrialization began labour was still abundant, and, compared with America, where it was more scarce, there was not such emphasis on labour-saving innovations. Because British businessmen came to regard cheap labour as a natural condition, their inclination was to try to get more work out of 'the men' for the same money, so that even when labour-saving equipment was introduced they were not ready to pay their workmen the higher wages its introduction warranted. The historical background of union opposition to greater productivity is the haughty greed of a business class that wanted one man to do the work of three at the same money he was getting before. Its effect was that labour-saving machinery was introduced without saving labour. It requires patience and determination to bargain with a union to increase productivity; it requires reassurances about security, a readiness to provide extra benefits (perhaps fringe benefits) out of extra profits, and a plan for softening the effects of redundancy; it requires co-operation between firms and a real sense of touch in industrial negotiation; and it requires a sense of confidence among workmen that the bosses really know what they are doing, so that the new arrangements really will produce the effects the bosses are talking about. To change other practices – such as the ancient institution of craftsmen's mates – is even more difficult. But if businessmen cannot create a more reasonable relationship with their workmen, no one else will.

That the present reverence for inertia among British workmen is one of the distinguishing characteristics of the British economy is not surprising: it means that Average Britain looks at Upper England with suspicion. Is this not the necessary corollary of a society in which almost all the values most publicly upheld by that society are not available to the ordinary people? Even the desire to get on in the world, to accumulate possessions – promptings of the kind that in other nations *force* acceptance of change and get labour forces moving – are derided by those who have already got on, or accumulated their possessions. On television on the one hand there are commercials enjoining people to buy things; on the other hand, perhaps in the very programme in which the commercials are embedded, there is laughter about the vulgarity of the hollowness of those who do. There is at least some justice in the fact that of the values that Upper England upholds there are at least some that are also available to Average Britain – fear of or a lack of interest in the future, hostility to change, a preference for things as they are, a reverence for antiquity. In preferring to maintain the antiquities of his ancient craft the Average Briton is able – in one respect – to behave like an Upper Englishman.

13. A HUNDRED YEARS OF ECONOMIC CRISIS

The long run down

The extraordinarily creative forces that were released in England in the seventeenth century and throughout the United Kingdom in the eighteenth century produced one of the most impressive examples of vigorous national enterprise history has recorded. The speculations of science, the novelties of technology, the developing sophistications in financial and commercial enterprise, the geographical discoveries, the impulses towards world conquest and world trade, the revolutions in agricultural techniques, the revolutions in communication, the revolutions in manufacturing, meant that for a time Britain was the world's laboratory of modernism. To take just one example of that British restlessness now known as 'Americanization', no sooner had the British furrowed through their countryside to produce a national network of canals than they made it obsolescent by replacing it with the world's first national railway network. British enterprise then emigrated across Europe and the Americas, building more railways.

After Waterloo London began to take over from Amsterdam as the world's principal financial centre: its merchant banks soon became central to the world's credit system in a way that is not likely to be repeated by any other nation. In less than fifteen years British exports doubled; by the end of the 1860s they were ten times more than they had been after Waterloo. But that was the end of Britain's remarkable export growth. Things have never again been as good as they seemed in 1851, the year of the Great Exhibition. At that exhibition Britain won eighty of the ninety gold medals. At the Paris Exhibition in 1867 it won only a dozen. It was at about this time that the national debate began on why Britain was not keeping up with its new rivals in new industrial products and why British goods were so comparatively poor in design. Not only – as was expected – did British exports now have to face competition from exports from countries that were industrializing, following the British example, but the new rivals were developing new industries, which British businessmen ignored. British industry became frozen in postures that were irrelevant. The coal, iron, steel, and textile industries continued to absorb a quarter of the labour force, to produce nearly half Britain's industrial output and to account for almost three-quarters of its exports. It was left to other countries – particularly America and Germany – to apply technological development to new industries. Electrical equipment, machine tools, domestic appliances, scientific instruments, telephones, petroleum – industries such as these developed without strong or immediate British competition. And it was in other countries, particularly America and Germany, that those organizational changes began which reduced the manning of machines and increased productivity. For a large part of the end of the nineteenth century and a large part of the beginning of the twentieth, Britain was providing the first instance of that modern phenomenon, the stagnant industrial economy.

But on the face of it Britain still seemed to be doing all right out of the earlier shove its economy had received. Its industrial exports still made up a third of all the world's trade, even if they were mainly the products of declining industries, and largely directed to uncompetitive captive markets. Earnings from the great network of financial interests in London, from the insurance brokers and commodity traders, from the shipping lines, and from investment abroad, made up invisible exports that in themselves produced enough to cover a third of Britain's import bill. In this period of massive self-congratulation and pride, Britain was becoming a rentier and an exploiter of tame markets and old industries. Each apparent economic crisis seemed merely temporary, something to be propitiated by sacrificing employment.

But after the Second World War progress was again remarkable. Dependence on coal and textiles withered away and the iron and steel industries developed new growth because of their relations to the newly developing industries. Instead of a quarter of manpower depending on the old staples for employment, the engineering and electrical goods industries now provided a quarter employment. The motor industry became another new staple industry, alone employing 10 per cent of the manufacturing work force in good years, and there was a remarkable diversification into the new industries that grew around developments such as petro-chemicals, synthetics, and plastics. Britain seemed really on the move again. The volume of exports continued to grow, at a rate remarkable considering the disruption of war and the loss of overseas investment. In volume the pre-war level of exports was doubled, and Britain then appeared to move towards trebling it, at the same time engaging in healthy diversification so that it did not depend for its exports merely on a few old lines.

The only trouble with both the increase in economic growth and the increase in exports was that, although they seemed all right in themselves, they were no good compared with the advances being made by other industrial nations. It was in the never-so-good period of Conservative government that industrial nations whose economies had been shattered by the war recovered their pre-war levels of activity, then accelerated in both economic growth and exports – of all the European industrial nations and Japan, Britain scored almost the worst.

In domestic economic growth there were investment drives, but investment often moved in the wrong direction – too much into the nationalized industries, too little into the export industries. In terms of investment in industries from which the greatest growth could be expected, Britain was behind America, Japan, Germany, France, Italy, Sweden, Belgium, and Denmark, and even where investment was correctly placed its effects were inhibited by overmanning, bad management, and inferior marketing. In ten years the British share of world trade in manufactured goods fell from 19 per cent to 13 per cent. From being second, Britain became third. Not enough investment went into *human beings*, into the kind of revolution in education and training that might have broken through the caution both of management and labour. In the 1960s there were some timid attempts to introduce economic planning, but they were laughable compared with Japanese planning and inadequate compared with French planning. There was a diffidence about really interfering with anybody, of really upsetting things as they stood, and such changes as were introduced were accompanied by screams so loud that there was a retreat to timidity. There was a considerable amount of jolting and jarring of the economy, but this came mainly from the Treasury's attempts to stabilize it. The various oscillating shocks the Treasury produced in the cause of stability were themselves among the factors inhibiting growth: even efficient businessmen found planning difficult under such constantly changing conditions, and on the more timid the effect was demoralizing.

There were constant export drives – the silliest of which had the advertising slogan 'Exporting is fun' – but they lacked strong economic impetus. The British rate of export growth was only about one half that of Britain's main competitors. One reason was the collapse in the 1950s of the controlled trading system of the sterling countries that was set up after the war and that discriminated strongly in Britain's favour. Some of these easy markets had been treated by the British exporters with the contempt of those who think they are on to a safe thing. Then, when the markets were freed, British exports often went down before competition. Prices of some British exports were too high; the design of some was poor; there were complaints about quality and delivery dates; salesmanship seemed uncompetitive. Perhaps what was most alarming was that Britain, compared with America, Japan, and Germany, was exporting most in those fields that were expanding slowest and exporting least in those fields in which markets were expanding most rapidly.

It is usually assumed that, somehow or other, this will all be fixed up. But is this necessarily so? One can take a more gloomy view. The burst of innovation that marked Britain's industrial revolution tended to peter out somewhere in the 1860s and 1870s, just at the time when other countries were affected by it. As both masters and workers looked not for further improvement but for stability, Britain's great revolution of coal and iron lost its momentum. It is likely that if they had been left to themselves, the British would have done no more. They were forced back into innovation by competition from the new industrializing countries, but they continue even now to be slow in their adjustments. Britain's first industrial revolution did not establish those strong new institutions that might have kept it going. The older order resisted the challenge with great resilience; the demands of Empire provided counter-attractions of enterprise; the public school system eroded much of the confidence and commonsense of businessmen; there was no systematic linking of science and technology. There was nothing to equal the growth of the American corporations or the German bureaucratization of inventiveness; after the Second World War there was nothing to equal the growth of the Japanese and French technocracies. Why is Britain likely to catch up with the rate of progress of these other countries when it has not even yet established lively technological and technocratic institutions or attitudes to business management? Estimates of economic development for the rest of the century place Britain behind the United States, Japan, Germany, France, Sweden, Canada. What sign is there that these forecasts are wrong?

Safe as the Bank

The sterling crisis began in 1919 and ever since then policies intended to maintain sterling as an international currency and to maintain Britain as an international investor have had continuing, debilitating effects on British industrial growth. When it is realized that the elusive hunt for a 'strong pound' has gone on – now this way, now that – for nearly fifty years it will be recognized what a depressing result it must have had on British business decisions.

In 1919 there was no awareness of a sterling crisis. There was simply a desire to return to what appeared to be the normalcy of a world in which sterling was as good as a book-keeper's gold. To get back to this situation the British government and the Bank of England tried to raise the value of sterling so that it would again be freely convertible into gold: to do this the government caused a domestic slump, with the result that in the 1920s, while most of the rest of the industrial world moved into prosperity, there was massive unemployment and non-growth in a British economy which became the most sluggish of the advanced industrial nations. After five years the slump that had been inspired by the government and the Bank had depressed everything so successfully that the government attempted a return to a modified gold standard. This did not work. Its main result was that when Britain moved into the world depression its financial policies had maintained such a steady state of self-generated depression in the 1920s that it did not have so far to fall.

In 1931 the attempt to keep a modified gold standard was abandoned. Sterling was devalued. As it turned out, this did not matter much. Of the currency blocs that formed in the 1930s the 'sterling bloc' was by far the biggest and the most important, including Japan and nations of Europe, the Middle East and Latin America, as well as the Empire countries. Sterling was still the single most favoured international currency and, probably at a cost to the total volume of world trade, the system of Empire Preference further helped to shore up its prestige.

But in every year in the 1930s except one Britain was faced with a more serious and longer balance of payments crisis than it has faced since the Second World War. Its general trading position was worse than it is now and there was no sign of improvement, or even of great concern. Sterling was safe and deficits in the balance of payments were met by selling up overseas assets. The old landlady was losing some of her absentee estates. This is worth remembering. Because Britain had to do a great deal more selling out of overseas assets to pay for the Second World War its subsequent problems are still sometimes hopefully traced back to this necessity. It should be remembered that Britain's export performance before the war was so bad that it would have had to go on selling out anyway.

In those days after the Second World War in which the dollar was still a hard currency, the form the sterling crisis took was that of the 'dollar gap'. A 'sterling area' had formed, consisting of those – mainly Empire – countries whom Britain owed £4,000 million; their conversion of these debts into money was rationed. Mainly at American insistence, although backed by an American loan, in 1947 Britain tried to make a break to sterling convertibility. Since sterling was the only 'soft currency' that became convertible, the result was a mess that could have led to a collapse of European economic activity. Convertibility lasted five weeks. Then, with most of the five-year dollar loan drained away, the pound became unconvertible again, and 'freedom' was postponed for another ten years.

The Attlee Government's policy of austerity was a primitive attempt to balance foreign payments. There was an attempt to support it in Sir Stafford Cripps's devaluation of 1949, when the value of the pound went down by 30 per cent. This didn't do much good – so many other countries also devalued that prices went up in Britain and in any case there was little surplus capacity to produce more exports. It may have done a great deal of harm, partly because it gave a certain false sustenance over the very period when Japan and Germany were recovering, but mainly because it may have dealt a lasting blow to the credibility of sterling as a reliable international currency. The following crises of 1951, 1955, 1957, 1961, 1964, 1966, and 1967 were initiated or accentuated by memories of 1949, particularly by the excessive size of the 1949 devaluation.

With the 1950s the stop-go policy seemed to become institutionalized. In 1951 inflation at home and lack of confidence abroad precipitated some currency speculation; whether it was sufficient to have necessitated the credit squeeze of 1952 is doubtful. All economic systems were 'go' again by 1954, and credit again flowed, but domestic inflation, combined with an excess of imports over exports in 1955 and gossip that the pound might go on to a flexible rate, caused a lot of selling of pounds. Perhaps over-reacting, the government again deflated, cutting down the capital investment that had begun to boom in 1954. By the time of the next crisis – in 1957 – the 'dollar gap' and balance of payments worries of the 1940s had gone. These worries were replaced by something more serious and mysterious, which was finally to affect the dollar as well as sterling: a free floating anxiety among international traders and financiers about the whole future of the use as international currencies of not only sterling but also the dollar, and the beginning of the uneasiness that led to the gold rush of March 1968 and the abandonment of the previous system. The first symptom of this change in disposition was a chronic nervousness about sterling that was no longer necessarily directly related to the British balance of payments. For instance, when in 1957 the franc devalued and there were rumours that sterling would do the same, although the

British reserves and balance of payments were good,
pounds poured out of London. The government announced a return to deflation. Unfortunately it announced
it at a time when unemployment was already high. In
other words, government policy increased an existing
tendency to recession. More expansionary policies followed in 1958, but in 1960 there was a disastrous trading year. However, the Bank rate went up, attracting a
lot of hot money, so that sterling again seemed safer. But
hot money is always a threat to a currency – when it
flows out again it tends to take other money with it – and
when a revaluation of the deutschmark in 1961 initiated
fresh rumours about the devaluation of sterling the
pounds began to flow out again. Treasury officials
panicked and, although Britain's current trading account
had improved, there was another credit squeeze and
Britain returned to being the stagnant society again for
more than a year.

As the 1960s progressed, the good results on current
trading accounts of the 1950s began to disappear. On top
of the new nervousness, reserves were being eroded
because Britain was increasing its imports of fully manufactured or semi-finished goods. Whereas expenditure
on these goods was once less than expenditure on raw
materials, it now draws level. Since some of these goods
were in the very fields in which British manufacturers
were supposed to be conducting export drives, this
seemed a significantly ominous sign. The Wilson government, which had campaigned against stop-go policies in
the 1964 election, felt unable to announce what would
have been the fifth deflation in ten years. However, the
novelty items it did announce were so unconvincing that
they caused the worst run on the pound since 1949. The
government ate its words and put up the Bank rate, but
this merely increased the run on the pound. The American Federal Reserve Bank and other central banks came
to the rescue, but, as one crisis passed into the next, by
1967 even their help was not enough, and Britain again

devalued, in circumstances that probably hastened the gold crisis of 1968.

More often than not, from the beginning of the 1950s, Britain's current balance of payments account recorded a surplus. During this period as a whole, Britain made more money by selling goods and services to the world than it spent in buying goods and services from the world. If Britain were a normal kind of trading country this would have been good enough. There might have been occasional difficulties, but they would not have been so frequent, or of such an order, that even the most incompetent government would not have needed to disrupt British economic growth as regularly as British governments did over that time.

But the use of sterling as an international currency meant that since Britain kept sterling going on a slender margin of reserves, the future of sterling tended to take priority over all other economic conditions. The British reserves of gold and foreign exchange were not big enough for sterling to play the role given to it. As each alarm sounded, a government was usually prepared to disrupt Britain's economy rather than damage the acceptability of its currency. Besides, an idea such as 'the pound' could be a more emotionally simple and politically effective concept than an idea such as 'growth', and the very drama of the deflationary measures taken could, with their familiar Puritan appeal and their calls to sacrifice and warnings of catastrophe, make them seem more familiar and easier to take than the innovations that might lead to faster economic growth. The sterling crises, periodically disrupting British life, provided a large part of British postwar political rhetoric, leading to that feeling of belonging to a country that could not finally do anything right.

But the sterling problem was not so easily got rid of as the last of the imperial commitments. The difficulties of pulling out of sterling compared with pulling out of the Persian Gulf can be realized only when one examines the reasons why sterling was so savagely defended. The first of these is its use as a reserve currency: most of the Commonwealth countries and several others 'lend' money to Britain by holding the better part of their international reserves in pounds in London. The second is the desire of all kinds of foreign business institutions to hold big working balances in pounds in London. Connected with both of these is the desire to maintain sterling as one of the world's important trading currencies in which overseas countries and firms can easily deal with each other. And connected with this is the desire to maintain the City of London as a world financial centre, earning foreign exchange out of its gold and foreign-exchange markets, its commodity markets, its broking houses, its insurance companies, and of course, its banks.

More is at stake than prestige. The insurance, merchanting, brokerage, and banking services of London may earn as much as £250 million a year in foreign exchange and the excess of British income from overseas investment over foreign investment in Britain can be as much as £450 million a year. But we don't know how necessary the use of sterling as an international currency is to the maintenance of London as a large financial centre. Big financial centres are maintained in Switzerland and Holland, for instance, without Swiss or Dutch currency being used internationally as sterling is used. There seems no reason why the City of London could not remain as some kind of entrepôt, maintaining its foreign-exchange, gold and commodity markets, and its banking and insurance services, even if sterling were just a currency like most others. What one cannot be sure of is the amount of business it would have left.

Many British people do not realize how well Britain does as an overseas investor or how this comes from money borrowed because sterling is an international currency. New post-war overseas assets – in loans or investment – now substantially exceed what was sold up during the war, so that Britain is second in overseas investment only to the United States. In its relation to the world,

Britain probably owns more overseas assets – in loans and investment – than it owes to overseas countries in sterling balances, but during a run on sterling Britain can't sell up these assets to meet the demands of the run, so it borrows from other countries as much as it can, hoping to see out the crisis until the pounds come back to London. Nevertheless, considered in itself, Britain does well out of being a world banker. As a bank it borrows short and lends long, paying low interest on the debts represented by sterling balances and getting a fairly high return on the overseas investment into which the borrowed money is put, with some capital appreciation as well.

However, the price paid has been high for the rest of the economy. Britain is not only a bank but an industrial nation, and from time to time, to defend its role as a bank, it may have lessened the possibility of its industrial growth. But was the ebullience characteristic of growth there in any case? There is the possibility that even if Britain ceased to be a bank, although this would mean in theory that economic growth could then be better sustained, in fact it might not be sustained or, if it were, it might not be sustained in the form of an increase in exports to equal the profit that would have been gained from overseas investment. Perhaps the British may be better as financiers than as exporters.

In any case they have been caught up in that continuing world problem of international liquidity to which no answer has yet been found. The future of sterling, in a fundamental sense, is no longer a matter within Britain's control. It is part of the unsettled business of finding an alternative international monetary system, a matter beyond even America's control, one to which answers are likely to be found only by a consensus of the major trading nations.

The cosiness of the Treasury

After the Second World War, economic decisions in Britain were usually reached as a result of interactions between the following conflicting groups of powerful Londoners:

The Bank of England. The Bank's business was to manage the markets for foreign exchange and government securities. Its over-riding interest was that foreigners should want to go on holding pounds. If foreigners were hesitant to do this the Bank would try to titillate their interest by using the gold and foreign reserves to make the pound look more confident; if that didn't work it would try to organize help from reserve banks in other countries to bid up the pound; if that didn't work it would recommend to the government that money should become dearer to borrow in London. Sometimes the idea of this last expedient was that this would attract foreign money to London, where it could be lent at a good rate, but more usually it was intended as a sign to the world that Britain, by making money dearer and deflating demand, was determined to make ends meet in a way that would cause its currency to look as if it were again worth holding. Sometimes the Bank would recommend other spartan measures that were intended to make Britain look a lean, tough nation, quick on its toes. The Bank's professional interest was entirely in the prestige of the pound in international finance and the state of Britain's gold and foreign-exchange reserves. It had no particular concern with the kind of policies that might increase exports, except certain invisible exports, nor were questions of general economic growth or of full employment its particular business: it was not in the expansion business, but in the business of maintaining a stable pound.

The Treasury had the most complex role of any such ministry in any big industrial nation. One half of it was concerned with the general running of the civil service – rates of pay, staffing methods, recruitment, promotions – functions that are themselves usually the business of a separate department of government but that helped to give the Treasury a special influence throughout the civil service and made the Treasury the élite of the élites. This high sense of influence was strengthened because the job of the biggest part of the other half of the Treasury was to control all government spending – itself also a power sometimes given in other nations to a separate department of government. In this role as the government's financial controller and general housekeeper, the Treasury was expected to concern itself indefatigably with the business of trying to cut down spending. In another section of this same part of the Treasury there was a responsibility for borrowing and lending, for overseas economic aid, and for the maintenance of the reserves. Men in both these sections – the Treasury as the controller of the government's household and the Treasury as keeper of the reserves – by the very way in which they filled in their day tended to be more concerned with stability than with growth. There was, however, another section of the Treasury which was expected to concern itself with economic growth and full employment, inflation and deflation, general questions of economic analysis and forecasts of what the economy was likely to do next. Such expansion as there was in the Treasury was usually found in this section.

The Department of Inland Revenue, although in theory merely an administrative body with the job of collecting taxes and expected to do what it was told, in fact could exercise strong influence towards sticking in the mud, resisting almost any tax proposal that was intended to divert resources.

The 'spending departments' were those that dealt directly with the outside world. In the nature of things, they often tended to see the world sectionally: the Ministry of Labour would tend to lobby within the government for trades unions, the Board of Trade for businessmen, and the Ministry of Agriculture for farmers; the Ministry of Housing would want more houses, the Board of Trade would want more exports; the Ministry of Town and Country planning would want more towns and country. If it was true that the Treasury saw things whole it was in the sense that it remained detached from these sectional views, although this could sometimes mean that its wholeness became a blank.

The politicians. Ministers of individual 'spending departments' would tend to sectionalize their vision according to the necessarily narrow vision of their departments. The general stance of the Prime Minister, the Chancellor of the Exchequer, and a few other leading ministers set the limits of overall approach to economic policy, but even when they were strong these approaches tended to be narrow; more often they were both narrow and weak. There was a remarkable ability for governments to philosophize about how the economy *might* be run, as if they were writing newspaper editorials. Since there was usually a crisis, the Chancellor was normally in a strong position to cut down other people's talk: here was another crisis; he must get on with the job; they could do some talking later.

At no stage did there appear to be among Cabinets a determined, coherent, and practical desire to change things decisively – or, as it can otherwise be put, to 'plan' them. Although Britain saw itself as a Welfare State it may have been the weakest of the major industrial nations in its efforts in economic planning. There was instead a concentration on 'butskellism', the policy, supported both by Labour's Hugh Gaitskell and the Conservative R. A. Butler when they were Chancellors, of basing almost all economic planning on the one factor – the level of demand. This humane and rational policy, with its use of fiscal and monetary measures to control purchasing power, to maintain the level of employment at times of threatened slump and to control inflation at times of boom, became the standard approach of the Treasury. It had two weaknesses. One was that its characteristically London concentration on the overwhelming efficacy of money alone ignored all the other factors that can affect an economy; the other was that, during the 1950s, despite butskellism, Britain had a higher ratio of unemployment than the other European industrial nations, except Italy.

By the 1960s people were looking around for something else. 'Growth' became a vogue word and Treasury officials went to Paris to see the planning. Planning seemed a pleasant kind of thing that could be carried out mainly by intellectual effort, without untoward disturbance; one simply had to be intelligent about it. Ideas came up for a board that would put up plans: some excellent papers were read at conferences. In 1961, showing that he had some new ideas, the Chancellor invited businessmen and unions to join a national planning council. In 1962 the resultant National Economic Development Council was formed. It was a foretaste of its ineffectiveness that it was at once christened 'Neddy': it was to be a lovable lion, without claws. Within a year it had produced a report on *Conditions Favourable to Growth*: it was agreed, for the sake of discussion, that the British economy should grow by 4 per cent per year, a figure that had already been suggested to Europe by President Kennedy. The N.E.D.C. was in no sense a planning body: it was nevertheless a useful pressure group. The steam it built up for the idea of growth blew in the right directions. But even in this task it was inhibited by lack of co-operation from the Treasury.

In his speeches in the 1964 election Mr Wilson seemed to put together every vogue word that had been generated in the last few years – growth, productivity, technological change, managerial revolution, retraining schemes, stopping the brain drain, a national plan – in short, Britain's second industrial revolution. As token of his seriousness, he established a Department of Economic Affairs and put his deputy in charge of it. In September 1965 the Department published *The National Plan*, 474 pages of it, and on 3 November 1965 the House of Commons resolved without a division 'That this House welcomes the National Plan.' Then the government forgot all about it and got back to the sterling crisis.

Although challenged by the setting up of the N.E.D.C. and of the Department of Economic Affairs, and by the extra functions given to the Board of Trade, the sterling crisis brought the Treasury back to its critical position in the making of economic policy. Yet there was doubt whether the Treasury people were the best for the job. For example, in the last period of the Conservative governments, after years of nagging that Britain's capital investment was so far behind Europe's, capital investment was encouraged to go up, but it went up in the wrong places. A lot of it went down the drain in public utilities like the railways, a lot of the rest of it went into housing and shops. Only one-tenth of it went into industrial equipment (compared with up to a half in other countries). But it looked all right as an item in the books. At times there seemed to be a nervousness at the controls when, in the name of stability, Treasury measures actually increased the kind of trends they were supposed to correct. In the 1950s the Treasury deflated when there was in fact a slump and inflated when in fact there was the beginning of a boom. This may have had something to do with the fact, now recognized for some years (and about which some action has been taken), that the Treasury was understaffed. There seemed to be little more than the whimsicality of the Southern Metaphor in the long determination to keep the Treasury so small and cosy. More than twenty years of economic crisis went on before the government department most centrally concerned began to take on adequate staff. The British economy became the gossip of the western world, but the group in the Treasury (the National Economy Group) that was supposed to worry about inflation, deflation, growth, employment, and economic forecasting consisted of only twenty people. Was it likely that Britain's economy would be fixed up if only twenty people were paid full time to think about it?

There continued to be the feeling that it was 'inequitable' that an old thing should go down and a new thing should go up: 'fairness' lay in keeping things the same. The level of unemployment in Britain remained higher than it should have been because of abnormally large unemployment in the depressed areas of the old industries (thought of as 'special areas' in 1934, they had become 'development districts' by 1960), but the Treasury's obsession with financial methods of dealing with unemployment, applied without discrimination, meant that it often tried to deal with local employment by raising the general level of demand. It was fairer that way, but it could mean that the unemployed living in the depressed areas remained unemployed, while there was inflation in the areas of full employment. Other ministries tried more positive local approaches, but again the desire to apply policies to *every* depressed area weakened their programmes, because it meant that some resources were wasted in areas that had no hope of revival. The effect of trying to keep growth fairly distributed all over the country was probably to slow the rate of growth down.

With a similar desire not to upset things too much, the subsidy scheme for farmers was so lavish that it provided 75 to 80 per cent of farmers' net incomes. (Since this was an average, it meant that some farmers drew 100 per cent of their net incomes from the government.) A Monopolies Commission was established, but it had only the power to report, not to act, and uninteresting industries were chosen for its investigations. After an extraordinary upheaval, legislation against resale price maintenance was passed, but reform was slow. One expects failures, but it seemed unusual that, by international standards of economic planning, there were no clear successes.

The task that the Treasury seemed able to take up quickly and promptly with the familiarity of the known was to put on its hair shirt and deflate the economy. The job of 'cutting out the surplus fat' was not only familiar to it in its role as the government's housekeeper; it seemed to fit in with a kind of general asceticism in the Treasury and the general view that what was really wrong with the British economy was the lack of a wage freeze. It was felt that if the manual workers and the lower-paid white-collar workers would just stay still for a while everything else would be fixed up.

There could be moral relief in the deflation that would follow an economic crisis: Britain could again draw strength from self-castigation. The ordinary people were getting less; growth could move backwards; things were back to normal. This ease with which each economic crisis could be turned into the pretence of a moral crisis was perhaps partly an unconscious social defence mechanism by which the élites were spared the contemplation of their own inadequacies. But it may also have been yearning left over from the old idea of 'moral leadership'. The gentle washing of so many Upper English brains with the belief that Britain's power was greater than that of other nations because of its moral greatness still left its impression as the greatness dissolved. For this reason economic crises could seem matters of morality. If Britain was not as prosperous as convention demanded there must be something morally wrong with it. If the ordinary people gave up H.P. and bingo Britain would become moral again and earn some new greatness.

What state of welfare?

The mere slogan 'the Welfare State' seemed to transfix the mind of Upper England. Because this phrase was a British invention there was belief that social welfare itself was a British invention and that Britain was uniquely concerned with the welfare of its ordinary people. Some boasted of this as another British first; others deplored it as another British first; either way it was another example of the desire for claiming a non-existent uniqueness that makes up a large part of the Upper English sickness.

Modern concepts of welfare were first put into practice by Bismarck. To suggest that, in the late 1940s, Britain provided the prototype of the modern Welfare State seems merely crazy. The Welfare State of the Attlee government in the 1940s was a belated attempt by Britain to reach levels of welfare that were already established in a number of other industrial nations. Even now, excluding family allowances, British spending on welfare is less than that of most of the advanced industrial nations of Western Europe; *with* family allowances it is at the bottom. And since an unusually high proportion of British welfare spending goes on medical benefits, if a comparison is made excluding medical benefits one discovers that, overall, the British are worse off in pensions and in sickness and unemployment benefits than people in comparable Western European nations. Furthermore, most of the European schemes, one way or another, allow for automatic or semi-automatic cost-of-living adjustments; in Britain special decisions are needed for adjustments. Apart from the greater amount of money devoted to medical benefits in Britain, there are, however, two British advantages – lower-paid workers do relatively better in Britain than higher-paid workers and the very poor are treated more generously than they are in Europe because of the supplementary benefits schemes. However, this does not seem a reason for describing Britain as the prototype Welfare State. The point is not so much that Britain is worse – welfare schemes in other countries have different emphases that make exact comparisons of 'total welfare' impossible – as that Britain is not so uniquely good (or extravagant) as it is said to be. It is simply part of modern industrial civilization.

It is in method rather than substance that the British welfare schemes differ from most others. Coming late into the business, Britain was able to set up a more 'logical' system; being older, most of the European schemes grew in a more higgledy-piggledy way, displaying all the confusions and whimsicalities of traditional British 'pragmatism'. In Europe welfare schemes are usually carried out by a muddle of semi-independent institutions; in Britain they are neatly and tightly directed by the state.

As in America, much of the pressure for welfare in Europe came from the trade unions. With such initiative from below, the responses tended to come in *ad hoc* arrangements. In Britain because of the unions' failure, the initiative for welfare schemes came from governments, and the organizations they set up were part of the general apparatus of government (with a thousand local offices). The British schemes also differ from most of the continental schemes because they are flat-rate schemes, based on a poll tax, whereas the European schemes are usually related to wages. One of the results of this is that, because of its possible effect on the lowest income groups, there is a natural political reluctance in Britain to put the rates up and this tends to keep down the overall level of welfare payments. The more obvious government control of welfare in Britain means that changes in welfare payments become more controversial than they are in Europe. It also means that the welfare institutions cannot, as they can in Europe, apply pressure on the government.

There is an enormous amount of controversy about the medical services. Questions as to how much people should pay for prescribed medicines, or whether they should pay for them at all, are matters that divide not only parties but governments. In these debates the inadequacies of the medical services themselves are often exaggerated. However, insofar as they can be measured, they are not quite as good as those of some other industrial nations. Taken in proportion to population, Britain ranks eighth in its provision of hospital beds, twelfth in its number of dentists, fourteenth in its number of nurses, and tenth in its number of doctors. There is a greater shortage of *locally* trained doctors in Britain than in almost all other similar countries. For the moment the British meet this deficiency by living on their luck. Sometimes half the junior medical staff of a hospital consists of immigrants, usually Indians and Pakistanis. In the poorest hospitals the proportion of immigrant doctors can reach two-thirds, or even four-fifths.

In housing there is also more reliance on public authorities than in any other Western European country, or in Europe Overseas. Elsewhere there is a greater reliance on cheap credit (private or public) or tax rebates or grants, or some mixture of these. In Britain there is more direct building, subsidized by public money. However, if these various forms of subsidy are costed out, the amount of public money that goes into subsidizing housing seems no larger in Britain than in Western Europe and, overall, new buildings go up at a lower rate in some industrial nations; in addition, the British scheme is particularly weak in provisions for lending money for repairs to older property, so that there is a greater tendency for houses to become slums.

It has already been indicated that unemployment in Britain has been worse than in most comparable Western European nations. There has, in fact, been a longer dedication to the ideal of full employment in America than there has been in Britain. And it is interesting to note that American policies have been partly a failure for the same reason that British policies have partly failed – that there is 'structural unemployment' in both countries; that is to say unemployment caused not by oscillations in the trade cycle but by special factors that are important even in a boom. In America this problem has been racial (the Negroes) and cultural (the hill-billies and the oakies, for example) as well as regional. In Britain it has been mainly regional. The slow-growth areas of Northern Ireland, Scotland, Wales, and Northern England (particularly North-East England) carry greater proportions of unemployed than most of the rest of Britain. When the overall British unemployment rate has been from less than 2 per cent to more than 3 per cent, the unemployment rate in Northern Ireland has been 8 to 9 per cent, in Scotland and Wales from 3 to 5 per cent, in Northern England from $2\frac{1}{2}$ to 6 per cent. There has been a continual improvement and refinement of government policy towards these areas, but results have been disappointing and probably a drag on general growth. It might have been less costly and easier to encourage labour to migrate to higher-growth areas. However, to make this criticism is not to suggest any special negligence or stupidity on the part of British governments – structural unemployment remains a problem in other countries – but to suggest that Britain has not been remarkable among the nations as a whizz-bang Welfare State.

Meanwhile, workers' average earnings doubled at a time when retail prices went up only by one half. Apart from the bigger share of the melon they now get in social services, the workers also get a bigger share of general income than they did before the war. And a considerable amount of this extra earning power has come from those 'irresponsible' wage claims that, although they continue to irritate the economic planners, may have got wage earners a bigger slice of 'welfare' than the planners might have provided for them. Perhaps meeting this wages bill also, in an unruly kind of way, provided businessmen with a greater stimulus for improvement than the plans would have achieved.

The posh papers

For intellectuals from Overseas Anglo-Saxondom – if they were Anglophiles as well as Anglo-Saxons – part of the immediate evidence of a higher culture in London was the 'quality press'. As news broke in the daily papers *The Times* and the *Guardian* gave it the gloss of a journalistic style that was both more mannered and more lucid than the visitors were used to in their own papers. Events were shaped with such sure and immediate significance that when the weeklies came out on Fridays the topics that it was fashionable to talk about that week could sometimes be treated allusively, like well-known bits of gossip; there was no need to restate them. One felt one was listening to an informed private conversation between members of an educated family in which, although there were differences of opinion, there were shared verbal inflections and family jokes. With the quality Sunday papers, the size of the family widened and the allusiveness was broadened, but there was the same sureness of touch about what to talk about that week, and the same civilized approach to events – somewhat sceptical, but backed by detail.

A Dominial visitor may have been so captured by these delights that when he returned to his own country he continued to read his favourite London weekly or Sunday paper so that he could continue to have the world presented to him by the London press even when he was back in Melbourne or Christchurch. If he couldn't afford an airmail subscription or didn't belong to a university common room or work in an enlightened bureaucracy he might, however, have had to decelerate his interest in the world with a seamail subscription, concentrating on the

significance of the events of several weeks before, like a
man running backwards after a bus he would never catch.

The more sensitive visitor might have noticed that the
sense of pleasure to be derived from reading the quality
press could have its crazy echo in the 'popular press'. He
would not have found in London the crude sensationalism
that he may have attacked in the 'popular press' of his
own country: instead he would have found what was
probably the most successful conversion of news into show
business in the history of daily journalism, in which
events were turned into variety acts with a smoothness
that presented a world of pantomime transformations,
staged at great expense, with even the scary bits obviously
make-believe, so that there was endless assurance that one
lived in a predictable world of passing English whimsy.
There has now been improvement as the popular papers
attempt to speak more seriously to a better-educated public. At the same time some of their sense of entertainment,
transformed by style, has now passed over into the
'quality press', lightening some of its previously more
serious approach.

A visiting Anglo-Saxon Anglophile sometimes does not
realize that what most attracts him in London journalism (as in other things) may be the extent to which
London is *European* – in this case showing a greater
acceptance of a large, vocal class of intellectuals and semi-
intellectuals in journalism. In parts of European quality
journalism, however, there is a greater seriousness, sometimes empty and ponderous, sometimes percipient. Nevertheless a light style can be as wise as a heavy one and it is
not necessarily superficial to throw up the significant
without going into details. The quality press in London
is of very high standard. Thousands of words come out of
it every week illuminating the condition of Britain and
the world, and prescribing remedies. The problem is that,
from any practical point of view, most of it need not have
been written. It has no significant effect on anything that
matters.

These newspapers and magazines have been produced in a society that responds quickly and with great intelligence and remarkable wit to slogans and concepts, but more in the mood of contemplation than of action, and with a final lack of concentration that prefers to turn to new slogans and concepts rather than do anything decisive. Since the 'real crisis' of so much of this society is not *What is to be done?* but *Who are we going to be?* it is not surprising that it can find so much sustenance in constantly changing hats. Perhaps the London journalistic style is not quite flexible enough. It can sometimes turn to amusing savagery, and get away with it, but bluntness is not usually within its scope. By bluntness I mean saying the unpardonable, *an honesty which makes things different*, compared with which mere savagery looks like the kind of domestic quarrel that can hold a marriage together.

The overriding tone and style in the quality papers represents in varying degrees the hopes and disappointments of the English liberal intellectual imagination, sometimes amusingly savage, sometimes sad, sometimes sceptical, but always entertaining. More than anything else, the virtues and faults of the quality press are the virtues and faults of this modern liberal approach.

The intellectual imagination

English intellectuals were not supposed to set themselves up as the judges of society and the guides to political action. According to the rules, unlike tricky continental European intellectuals, they were supposed to be fully integrated with their society, giving it helpful hints, preferably in private. But what is most significant about what now seems the traditional view of the role of British intellectuals in society is that, like some other traditions, it is merely a tradition of the day before yesterday. The influence of what we now call intellectuals shone brightly and confidently in Britain for most of the period of its great power. It was, after all, the reverence given to the aged President of the Royal Society, Isaac Newton, that made Voltaire see England as a country which, unlike his own, recognized the role of the thinkers, and it was the attention given to Charles Darwin in nineteenth century Britain that produced national debates far more serious in tone than the present trivialities. It is a signal both of the realities of British history and of the hollowness of present boasts that those who seek substance in the conceits of tradition do not do so by proclaiming their nation as the home of Newton and Darwin, Locke and Hume, Adam Smith, Bentham, and those others who helped set up a substantial number of the signposts of modern European civilization.

One of the characteristics of nineteenth century Britain that most distinguished it from Britain today was the influence of the political and economic theorists, the novelists, the biologists, and the others who threw up fresh patterns of what things might be. From all sides the strainings and pushings of the industrial revolution were projected by British intellectuals into new views of the world, and these were not only debated but turned into new forms of action, sometimes by the very crystallizers of the new thought. And as new action proceeded, it was not seen as neatly moving from empirical evidence towards necessary conclusions but as itself part of the mass of moral debate, still thrusting towards redefining the promptings of human action and of human society, even as it acted among them.

In the early twentieth century Bernard Shaw, H. G. Wells, and others, sure of their role as guides to society, if going about it in different ways, still expressed the seriousness and responsibility of the nineteenth century. But as the century progressed, there also developed a notion of the English intellectual as one apart from British society. The product of both the old world of power and the tremors of the decline of that power, a generation grew up that retreated to a greater interest in the individual or in the more personal relationships between individuals, attempting to construct theories of personality out of the flimsy mysteries that are left over when the character of a man as a social animal is denied. On the one hand there was still some of the optimism of the nineteenth century and a sense of inevitable progress, although the idea of progress had changed to a sureness that the inhibiting conventions of the nineteenth century would drop away and that things would become more clever and beautiful, more 'civilized'. On the other hand there was a cultishness and preciosity: the world would become better by becoming more like the devotees of the cult, pure in motive, rational, truthful, 'objective'.

Through this or alongside it there ran strains of 'right' and 'left'. At the most, rightism among intellectuals usually amounted not so much to the positive, sometimes fiendish assertions of Continental Europe as to a scepticism about solving problems, a lack of belief in theories of the natural goodness of man, a reverence for the past which confused the élitism of the excellence of the intellect with social élitism (which can often mean the exaltation of buffoons) and a contempt for the future. There was a kind of romanticized classicism, even an intellectualized royalism, and a strong anti-democratic fear that the tradition of civilization might be trampled into nothing by the mob. On the 'left' there was an idealization of the mob, which was seen as the regenerative proletariat that would cleanse society with its new vigour. However, since most of the articulate 'left' were public school chaps their contacts with the proletariat were often so remote that much of their discussion about the proletariat was concerned with their problem of lack of communication with the workers. There was considerable concern on the 'left' with both the workers at home and the natives abroad, but no sense of action, since the theory of regeneration meant that both the workers at home and the natives abroad should seize their own solution to their problems. Action consisted in opposing fascism

(although sometimes simultaneously supporting paci-
fism). In this the 'left' was joined by some of the 'right',
who saw fascism as the mob let loose.

During the Second World War the intellectuals re-
joined their fellow countrymen. In discussing the effects
of the Nazi conquest of Britain there seemed nothing
much to argue about. For some the war represented their
first meaningful sense of common purpose with their own
community and they came out of it more democratic than
they went into it, accepting, sometimes enthusiastically,
the subsequent plans for a Welfare State and for dis-
memberment of the Empire. In the early post-war years
it was the 'right' intellectuals who were most out of
joint with the times. Scepticism about solving problems
became a distrust of economic planning; scepticism about
the natural goodness of man became a fear of the Welfare
State as a destroyer of liberty; the belief in the traditional
nature of liberty became a hatred of democratic manners.
While scepticism or, at the most, sarcasm was the usual
style of criticism for their fellow countrymen, the intellectual 'right' projected their stronger passions outwards
against the ex-natives of the liberated colonies, for whose
failure in aping the British polity there was unconcealed
pleasure. As the Welfare State did not lead to immediate
cultural enlightenment at home and as the collapse of
Empire did not lead to instant parliamentary democracy
abroad, there was also a bitter nostalgia on the 'left',
although it could not be expressed as nostalgia. Some of
the 'left' abandoned its concern for its own countrymen
(except the sensationally poor); in terms that were almost
a kind of paraphrase of the criticisms of the 'right' it saw
the ordinary people as the demoralized creatures of
'admass'. (The 'right' blamed the 'left' for this condition while the 'left' blamed advertising.) On both sides
there was also a fear that society was about to be ter-
minally vulgarized. The 'left' began to look to Afro-Asia
for its new regenerative proletariat and then, since the
disappointments of independence in Asia preceded those

of Africa, it turned, for a while, mainly to Africa. Directly and openly frustrated by the loss of world prestige, the 'right' was increasingly angry and talked of 'toughness' – until the madhouse break of the Suez adventure. The 'left' was equally frustrated by the loss of world influence; the crusading spirit of the governess taking up the White Person's Burden was now inhibited; it was less satisfactory to criticize the President for running the world badly than it had been to criticize the Prime Minister. The announcement in 1968 of the accelerated British withdrawal from Singapore and Malaysia seemed to absolve the 'left', at least for a while, of any remaining pretence of interest in Asia (and Africa as well, for good measure) as, with relief, it rolled up the map of the world and unrolled the map of Europe, where Britain might yet some day be governess.

It would be inaccurate to see the attitudes of the more political intellectuals as necessarily typical of all intellectuals. The mildly self-satisfied mood of the mid-1950s was probably more like the state in which the majority of British intellectuals felt most at home; there was a gentle self-congratulation on what was seen as the decent honourable, and tolerant tone of British society. Rising 'affluence' at home and the liberation of colonies abroad were both accepted as aspects of this decency. The outrageous boasts of world power had gone and the outrageous claims for the moral leadership of the world were being toned down, but there was consolation for conceit in the thought that, after all, Britain was somewhat more 'decent' than the rest of European civilization, spared the gross materialism of Adenauer's Europe and the bigotries of Eisenhower's America. An acceptance of the provincial nature of so much of Britain was beginning to grow and there was the feeling that further progress lay in the fulfilment of small aims. There was nothing big that was left to be done. The lion was entirely lovable.

Then all anger was let loose. The moral self-importance that is part of the basic training of English élites could not be satisfied with the myth that British society was marginally more decent than all the rest of western civilization. The crisis that has existed since then has been partly false, insofar as it has been a crisis of expectations (moral leadership); it has also had in it, however, some elements of unfinished business that *can* be finished, principally that British people should find new and better ways of living with each other and of conducting their affairs. For instance, one part of the crisis has been a revolt by the provinces against Upper England, and in another part it is a general social crisis trying, in complex ways, not quite consciously realized, to break loose the whole hierarchical habit and bring it down. As an economic crisis it is the need for a new sense of values in practical affairs. Flickering its shadows over these shapes of 'true' crisis is the crisis in rhetoric: the lost sense of how to speak of Britain's role in events. And disguising the sense of impotence, of collapsed world power and changed economic order is the 'moral crisis', which can be described either as no crisis at all or as that most important of all crises, a crisis of self-importance. This also is a crisis of the élites. Their habits of mind still growing out of the habits of Empire, they see the present as disaster, when all that is really 'wrong' with Britain compared with a number of other democratic industrial nations is that it is now a bit more old-fashioned than they are.

All these crises are of a kind in which intellectuals with their ability to conceptualize, should play a part, and the crises of identity and morality are of a kind in which probably *only* intellectuals of some sort or other can play a decisive part. Yet the present English intellectual imagination may be too worn to meet such challenges. It has responded quickly and definitely to what might be described as the end games of domestic liberalism – the abolition of hanging, the dismantling of censorship, the liberalization of outmoded laws, the building of a society fit for consenting adults to live in. But it does not seem to respond vigorously (sometimes not at all) to the novelties of change, so that this field is left very largely to the merely angry.

Most of what might be described as the decent majority of British intellectuals are inhibited in their very virtues. Words such as 'decent', 'sincere', 'honourable', 'tolerant', and 'reasonable' point to both their strength and their weakness. For one thing these words are used far too often: there is a comforting vanity in them and some hypocrisy. But more to the point, they tend in their use, even if not explicitly, to be exclusive – not only of foreigners but of fellow countrymen. Decency, sincerity, honour, tolerance, and reasonableness are to be found throughout Britain not only, or even necessarily mainly, in intellectual groups, but there is little attempt to seek out these virtues in the ordinary people and, by speaking to them in their own language, to touch their imagination. To do so would require a mild social revolutionary approach. To speak honestly of decency, sincerity, and honour would be to speak bluntly of humbug in British institutions.

It seems likely that British intellectuals who want to change their society need a stronger commitment than belief in decency. Their very fastidiousness – admirable in some societies – inhibits the possibility of this. There are times when it is more practical to ignore the immediate practicabilities of politics and to raise general issues, practicable so far as a society generally is concerned, even if they do not fit into the habits of politicians as they stand that year. But the fastidiousness of some of the better intellectuals towards politics is matched by a fastidiousness towards generalization. They tend both to stand aside from the particularities of politics and also to abhor generalities, preferring little, lucid self-contained problems.

If intellectuals above all concern themselves with questions of *form* they abandon their sense of direction and their true intellectual intention. A concern with decency can be a self-congratulatory way of shutting one's eyes and stopping one's mouth. In trying to decide what the facts are one cannot act with a prior tolerance; an assumption of reasonableness does not allow for the grotesqueries of existence; sincerity is not a weapon of truth. Without the test of honesty, decency may become a mere matter of outward manners, while to speak frankly can be dismissed as bad taste or as exhibitionism.

A wash in the kitchen sink

According to the British cinema of most of the 1950s Britain was a pleasant little country with no great worries. Its people were almost entirely middle-class with a few aristocratic jesters and working-class clowns in the background. This meant that the middle-class virtues could shine all the better. The middle-class people who dominated these movies were decent, tolerant, and easy-going; they had a light sense of whimsy; they were kind, in a half-hearted and sometimes suspicious way; in their relations with each other they were unobtrusive. Although in the old wars that they insisted on re-fighting they would shout commands like 'Fire!' or 'Charge!', they could not be suspected of violence, or indeed of any particular emotion; they seemed very sure of themselves, rather stupid, and they lived almost entirely in the past.

In the theatre it was much the same. It was true that there were revivals of old plays, and that the work of Brecht, Beckett, and others was getting audiences, but native talent seemed to be most confidently expressed in slightly nostalgic musicals or in thrillers and light comedies. Fry's and Eliot's 'revival' of verse drama had not come off; Peter Ustinov had not lived up to his promise; Terence Rattigan was supreme. Novel-writing, although some of it was of high standard within its own confines, was mainly concerned with a narrow range within the middle-class, reflecting middle-class ironies. In painting, although an occasional face screamed, on the whole there was a kind of undemonstrative restraint; even violence was imitated coldly.

Then began a turning around of things. Younger writers of a different kind had success with plays of a quite different kind. Settings changed to working-class, or middle-class crumminess, or into a sense of contemporary doubt. Themes disintegrated into European and American questionings – disillusionments, savage bouts of pretence-stripping, quietist introversions, motiveless fury, illogicalities and absurdities, raging monologues, empty ambiguities and discontinuities, senses of mysterious defeat, unanswered questions, inexplicable terrors, confrontations of meaninglessness. These changes broke loose into television, and then into the cinema, and new voices began to speak among the novelists.

In the theatre and the cinema the new writers were mostly working-class, some of them not even grammar-school working-class; and while novel-writing still came from university-educated men, they had begun writing in a redbrick style. Into the art side of the entertainment industries there had come a new, vivid sense of speech, an unrefined wit, a peeling down to shared fundamentals. 'Outsiders' took the stage, thrusting aside bits of the old culture that were left over, seeking new forms and themes. The English imagination was being washed out in the kitchen sink. Some of this new work has scuffled in a blind alley, but it has nevertheless represented a return in British writing to the sense of artistic responsibility that tries to see humanity in its own age (the only age it can ever know), even if the effect is self-destructive.

One mould was being broken and new moulds were being cast of *the people art was supposed to be about*. An English middle-class ideal of what all people were, becoming increasingly stylized, narrow, and insipid, had almost obliterated the sympathetic consideration of the possibility that there might be other kinds of persons. When the revolt occurred the very misleadingness of the phrase 'angry young men' showed that something had happened, since it was also applied to novels that were not angry but comic, and even to novels that were conservative in

theme (but not in style). A liberation of the imagination
had occurred, in which it was to become possible to deal
with more kinds of persons in more kinds of styles.

These new movements gained their most public extension in the 'satire' boom. Although of no artistic interest,
and although almost at once commercialized into near-
harmlessness, the satire boom produced a new outspokenness that blew away a lot of rubbish. The mandarins of
decency and reasonableness were on the whole critical
and not always honestly so, since many of its targets
were those that the liberal intellectual imagination in
theory also opposed – if not so sharply. The criticisms
made of the satire boom – that it lacked the characteristics
of Juvenal or Swift – were, of course, true. Where it was
most savage it was confronting targets that were too
small; where it confronted bigger targets it became too
good-humoured. But in its liberal critics there was more
than a touch of snobbery: that the ordinary people could
share the laughter of the 'satirists' was supposed to show
that there was something wrong with the 'satirists'. What
it did show was that Average Britons could at last see on
their television a reflection of the irreverence towards
Upper England that some of them had for long shown in
private. It might be better not to regard this really as
'satire', but as an extension of the range of subject matter
for wit and humour so that it could include topics on
which for some time there had been taboos. There was
another side: some of it was mere petulance, hitting out
at everything from a concealed assumption that things
could easily become *perfect* rather than *better*. Nevertheless, with so much rubbish around, even this may have
helped to clean things up.

This does, however, bring up an interesting question
concerning the breakthroughs in the arts that began in
the late 1950s. In some of these the sense of inadequacy
or hollowness or despair was not, as it was in the European and American movements, a protest against the age,
or against life itself. In some of them there were elements

of a mere whingeing disappointment in the English condition, a rather second-rate matter for works of art, unless it is transfigured into a sense of being an example of something. The best of the international despair came out of the contemplation of that new knowledge which seemed to destroy almost all previous assumptions, and this was given extra bite in Europe by the catastrophes of war and in America by the apparent catastrophes of progress. But some of the British despair seemed to come from the artistically trivial questions of Britain's particular predicaments.

Making it new

How much of the nature of a society can be reflected in its art and philosophy is not a question with any particular answer. We can see 'reflections' of a society in its art and philosophy only if we already know something about the society. If we know nothing about the society, to speculate about it by examining its art and philosophy seems a waste of time, except insofar as individual works of description may be part of our evidence. But since we know a great deal about both British society and those 'modern' movements in the arts and philosophy that have seen the twentieth century as a time of uniqueness to which there had to be a reaction, there may be some point in comparing the arts and philosophy in Britain with British society. Before doing so, however, since the British have been only small innovators in these connexions, living only on the peripheries of most of the 'modern' movements, one should perhaps first summarize the present state of the discussion about what modernism has been.

One of its first forms, beginning in the late nineteenth century, was the fear that when confronted with modernity all conventional forms of the arts became merely archaic. The arts had to be made *new*, to express changes in the world. It suddenly seemed intolerable that conventional forms should be used in a world that no longer met the preconceptions that lay behind them. It was at first more the artist's vision or speech that was considered to be at fault rather than the world, and it was the artist's responsibility to change himself and his work to take on new tasks. Art had to be transformed, to regain validity. The changes took violent forms in painting; there were attempts at a new 'realization' of things; there was a fragmentation of perception and a reconstruction of forms; a cultivation of obscurity and diffuseness; a use of traditional forms in a kind of shocking parody; a passing into the precision of pure form, devoid of external reference; a use of pure form to express turbulence and incoherence; an employment of the sense of flatness and repose to be found in the artefacts of mass production. In writing, there was a sustained effort in verse to give new words that sense of value that belonged to the old and to accommodate the modern world as a possible subject for literary art; there were attempts to regain a sense of the colloquial and to capture what seemed to be the rhythms of modern life; on occasion there were attempts at greater 'realism', at getting 'closer to life'; to some the forms of writing of the immediate past seemed not only inadequate but false in tone, corrupting.

The great nineteenth century novelists were also, one way or another, concerned with change; the importance of their role as social interpreters was what gave them their recognition as prophets; but these novelists did not adopt towards change the view that it was a cataclysm: they saw the new and old together. The modernists, however, saw a new world confronting the past with its difference. In their approach the nineteenth century novelists were more *accurate* than the most global of the modernists: they saw a more complex picture; they did not feel the need to choose between violent hope and violent despair; they presented change as patchy; they did not seize on a crisis in vision of a number of European artists and project it out on to the whole world, as if it were a description of what was happening to it. But once the sense of crisis took hold of modern artists, once it was felt that mankind was passing over a dividing line in history, it became impossible for works to seem 'great' unless, in one way or another, they not only adopted modern styles and structures but also displayed a prophetic sense of crisis and, in one way or another, took as their theme the idea of decisive change for mankind.

In addition there were the uncertainties and perplexities developing in modern sciences and philosophy which destroyed the assuredness not only of the old theology but of the sense of rationality that had replaced it; the horrors of the First World War, the sense of cataclysm (and of either fear or hope) in the Russian Revolution, the disillusions of the Great Depression, the careful and detailed planning of monstrosity in the Second World War, the dissolution of the old colonial Empires and the challenges from Africa and Asia to the white man's self-esteem, the irritating blandness of the face of democracy in the new commercialist Welfare States – all of these created those crises of confidence in European civilization that stirred the anxiety and disillusion of artists and philosophers so that they not only saw their own preconceptions destroyed (as they were) but also imagined that everyone else shared their anguish (which they didn't).

While these movements were first developing, particularly in France, which more than any other country was their first true home, in Britain the principal new movement in painting and the applied arts came from a representation of the antique; verse was alternating between floridity and tepidity; and the novel was continuing more or less in its traditional form. When changes came to Britain the impulses towards them came almost entirely from France. British painters acquired something new, but more in the manner of variation than originality. In the new English verse the two most famous prophets were an Irishman and an émigré American (who began by stealing from the French); and of the two most famous experimenters in the novel, one was an Irishman, and one was born an Average Briton. The Upper English were not represented. Eliot was the only one of the four best-known modernists who lived in London and the longer he lived there the more his sense of lost tradition narrowed from the eclectic and bookish Europeanism of his early work to the purely Upper English sense of tradition in his later work.

The First World War, however, did produce from Upper Englishmen a literature and some paintings that were a reaction against the barbarity of their condition and had a cutting effect on the generation that followed them. Reactions to the Russian Revolution and the Depression, on the other hand, in retrospect seem mainly frivolous: the dissatisfied artists and intellectuals on the 'left' of a hierarchic society seemed to get a kick out of contemplating its decay and expressing a simple hope that everything that was rotten would soon peel off, revealing a clean new world underneath in which decency and honour would again shine. There was none of the struggle with Marxism that gave Trotskyism some significance in New York. Nor, except for Orwell, did the Great Depression bring out a radical and populist sense of feeling for the trials and character of the ordinary people, as it did among American intellectuals, some of whom, as a result of the nation's economic disasters, re-discovered or re-created a vision of America. The Depression of the British writers existed without people: it was a kind of serious technical hitch.

In the novel there was a significant narrowing of vision. While provincial life and the lower ranges of middle-class life and some aspects of the lives of manual workers still seemed natural subject matter for novelists writing in (roughly) the first third of the century, the view of British society given by novelists then narrowed so that while village or rural life became if anything more prominent, the life of people living in provincial cities or towns almost disappeared. The Britain of the novelist became a Britain that was usually either metropolitan or rural, with an occasional trip 'abroad', and its characters were not only mainly middle-class (as they had usually been) but were restricted to the polite middle-class of both birth and education – or, as I would put it, to those who had inherited their Upper Englishness and become most thoroughly trained in it. Even the sense of social mobility – so strong in earlier English novel-writing – was often reduced to snobbish caricature: even the more humane writers could not present sympathetically the man who had acquired his Upper Englishness rather than been born to it. The main modernist concern in this dead period was to produce a style which, at its best, acquired a simple, unpretentious elegance (and might be called 'modern mandarin'), but could sometimes become inhibited with the flatness of a country of small hills. This middle period of twentieth century English novel-writing was a period of a desperate illusionism and it has now ended, but it so narrowed the novel that most of the products of this age meant nothing in the rest of European culture – unless it was to Anglophiles, or through misunderstanding.

There were, however, continuing developments in verse-writing, at least in the 1930s. Since Yeats and Eliot were both up to the old tricks of poetry, in the linguistic sense more truly 'modern' verse was written by others, but with a flatness and lack of poetic tension. It was not perhaps until the 1930s that the technical problems of modernity in English verse were 'solved', in particular by Auden, who displayed the great talent of seeming to present a new literalness. But once this discovery was made, no one seemed to know quite what to do with it.

The British departure from what was international and 'modern' (without creating anything much of its own) showed itself just as startlingly in the complacency with which British artists and intellectuals regarded (and still regard) the Second World War. The British artistic and intellectual imagination was almost totally indifferent to the horrors of the 1940s. Reactions were almost entirely patriotic and chauvinist. It was not merely that their country was not overrun as were the countries of Western Europe, or that they were spared the destructions of Eastern Europe and Russia; the Americans were also spared in this way (and weren't bombed either), but the American intellectual vision of the war included the despair of Europe's self-strangulation and a horror at the scope and method of American military success. No significant work of art in Britain directly reflected the disasters of war, or its despairs, unless one includes those novels which saw the war as a distasteful time when the wrong kinds of chaps got into the officers' mess.

After the war, the sense of disastrous change that had marked so much of the 'modern' movements suddenly seemed to have real sense in it. But the movements of despair in the arts in continental Europe and America were not directly matched in Britain, and when they finally arrived, in painting and the theatre, they did not always have the fresh impact of common experience. In the same way, in the nonsense fringe, in the exaltation of sex or violence or hallucination, there was often in the British imitations – and this seems a matter for credit – too much of a sense of good clean fun for them to be altogether convincing. What became more convincing was regret at change, but this was not expressed with a comprehensive compassion.

The sense of the modern in Britain has been more concerned with the fear that culture will be destroyed not by its own impulses but by popularization and commercialization. But this fear has found a more convincing release in American literature and art: in Britain it becomes over-verbalized. It was difficult for most British writers to portray Britain as a confusing industrial society with no good causes left when so many writers had no direct experience of the industrial part of that society and could not create characters and situations from it. In this it was the Americans who had the advantage. It was also to their advantage that they could find it difficult to believe that there were no good causes left when they had their Negroes to remind them of the world's unfinished business. In fact it may be in America that the future of English as a language for writing in seems to lie. The Americans began their attempts at writing in a modern way with a manufactured primitivism – first an affected simplicity that produced a false tone when imitated, and then in self-conscious crudities. But in the best of the contemporary American novelists there is now a sense that English is moving along again in a sense that has not been known in British novel-writing for several decades. It is probably not irrelevant that this has been associated with more ambitious themes than are attempted in Britain together with a greater sense of release and new vision.

In painting it was out of America that there came new directions for Britain. But when international movements have been taken over, as in the theatre, they are sometimes adopted unconvincingly, at second hand, by people who do not seem to have had the same experiences as those they are imitating. One must note magnificent exceptions – Francis Bacon, for example, or Henry Moore. But the long period when British painters were devoted to a 'domestication' of influences from France, without seeming to be driven by the same impulses as the French painters, was replaced only by another period when they began to tame influences from New York (at a time when New York was perhaps itself drifting). Some of this painting seemed too bland for its aims, somewhat squeamish. If, as is now suggested, this is no longer true, then it might be because more British painters are now motivated more by their own experience.

Can there be a way in which one can still express some form of hope in art? This has been the problem with which so much of the 'modern' movements have been concerned. Not hope in a simple sense, but in the sense that there can be some kind of acceptance of change and also that, among the uncertainties of science and other intellectual speculation, there can be found some workable pattern, perhaps modest, perhaps making a certainty of uncertainty, but something to go on with anyway. That there has been more concern with these matters in continental European literature than in British may have some relation to the quite different intellectual role of philosophy in Britain, compared with continental Europe and to the fact that America, though once entirely Anglo-Saxon in philosophy, now has it both ways.

Although the distinctively British approach to philosophy and the distinctively European approach may nevertheless be concerned fundamentally with much the same things, the two approaches *feel* different and the sense of intellectual role is certainly different. Philosophy has become more specialist in Britain than in Europe. English philosophy (or, as it is sometimes put, Oxford philosophy) is now a matter which most British artists and intellectuals simply do not take into account, whereas in Europe not only do writers take philosophy into account in contemplating the puzzles of life, but some European philosophy has been developed as much in literary works as in more technical forms.

In both Britain and Europe the old certainties of systematized rationality were destroyed by philosophers, but the European philosophers seemed to care about this, and the English philosophers did not. For a time the most extreme form of destruction in Britain was one that destroyed philosophy itself: *What is, is – and that's that: everything that even philosophers themselves say is meaningless.* When the noise of this explosion subsided philosophers crept out of the debris and offered at least this hope: that while language was not capable of logical exactitude it could, in certain ways, perform tasks of communication; language in general could not be analysed by logical and reductionist methods, but the language of everyday life was of great scope and flexibility; if the circumstances of particular cases were taken into account, language could be *clarified*; in this pursuit philosophers could not start from logic, but they could accept the facts of experience and, from what they knew of experience in particular cases, attempt to make clear the ways in which people of some particular common experience could communicate. With no anguish that so much human expectation had proved insupportable, and no interest in giving their findings wider communication, the specialist philosophers in England got on with their game, with considerable coolness and pedantry.

Although as robbed of certainty as the English, continental philosophers have not been so light-hearted about it and they seem to have shown more sense of responsibility to the general world of the intellect and of the arts. Some seem to see a total inability for humans to communicate; some, though seeing countless complexities, nevertheless see communication as possible where there is a community of feeling and experience. For some a life without salvation is one of despair; for others it is only human expectation that gives rise to despair and they suggest that humans change their expectations. They raise the real problems of 'modernity' for the artist or the intellectual: is communication possible at all? Given what we now know of existence and the previous traditions of European culture, in what sense can life still seem worth living? The novels of men like Sartre or Camus or Robbe-Grillet are fundamentally concerned with such problems.

The relation of the arts in Britain to modernism has been uneasy. At first there was a confident and original participation, strongest in writing (usually the strongest of the arts in Britain), led mainly by men who were either not of British birth or who, if they were British, were not Upper English. Then Britain seemed to drift away from direct and original participation in the modern movements, avoiding not only the nonsense but also those general concerns with cultural diagnosis that made up the greatest strength of the modern movements. This was not accompanied, however, by the kind of inspired parochialism that sometimes produces the greatest art: in writing, at its best, this period produced 'minor poets' and good second-rate novels, shorter than nineteenth century novels, smaller in scope, without the same prophetic sense of social range and with a narrowing of class observation, and written in modern mandarin, with both its virtues and limitations; in painting and sculpture at their best, it produced sports such as Henry Moore and Francis Bacon (whose sense of horror was modern enough, and a thing of his own); in the theatre it produced almost nothing. It was in the theatre, however, that Britain made its re-connexion with the new modern movements. In fact two things happened at once in the theatre: there was a return to the international concern with cultural diagnosis and at the same time a breakthrough in native social observation, up till then apparently almost impossible in the mandarin novel. At the same time in painting the switch of influence from Paris to New York seemed to provide a new stimulus.

Setting all this beside what one already knows of British society one might risk the guess that the caution with which the arts in Britain have reacted to international movements in modernism tended to increase as Britain's confidence in its power declined; at the same time this caution was not associated with the kind of strenuous local concern that sometimes produces the greatest art, but with a protective narrowing of scope and flexibility. It seems good that at the end of this period there was a widening of local concern and some return to the international discussion of the general conditions of human existence.

GOD IS AN ENGLISHMAN

A bit of a giggle

Why do things *have* to change in Britain? After all it is a comparatively prosperous country and many or perhaps most of its people find it comfortable enough to live in. Its ways are their ways and many of its inhabitants would be happier with things as they are, instead of fussing themselves with change. Britain may not matter much any more in the world, but what's wrong with decaying quietly, surrounded by the things one loves?

What is wrong with decaying quietly is that it cannot be done. Britain *has* been decaying, but so much fuss has already been kicked up about the process that there does not seem any possibility of a quiet, pleasant, ruminative retreat into a well-earned retirement. In any case a quiet retirement requires a pension – and nobody else is going to pay Britain's pension. Britain is not a hermit kingdom. Like Japan, it is insular; like Japan's, its former imperialism was in some ways both a projection of insularity and a protection of it; but, like Japan, Britain must remain global in its economy, and, like Japan, as part of the liberal democratic industrial world, it remains open to the influences of that world. In any case Britain is even less free of the infections of this world than Japan because its insularity is of a special kind; despite the envies and snobbishness of some of the Upper English, the insularity of Average Britain is potentially that of Anglo-Saxondom, not only of Average Britain. Unlike the Japanese, the British have been one of the world's great emigrant races; if things don't seem right at home they can go and live in one of the other nations their predecessors founded. There is also the problem that most of Average Britain is not going to admire the picturesqueness of decay (except in its own overmanning of machines or in its other restrictive practices); it wants decent houses and things to put in them, more leisure and ways to spend it, something more than the Puritanism of successive deflations, however acceptable these gloomy expedients have been to the sense of high morality among the élites. Average Britons are also likely to want something better in their relations with their fellow countrymen than the enervating stickiness of the two-nation system. And there are signs of a coming revolt of the provinces.

One cannot any longer say optimistically of the British that they will muddle through as they have in the past. One of the whimsies of the Southern Metaphor, the idea of 'muddling through', grew up in the period when Britain had strength and confidence of such magnitude that it could afford mistakes, muddles, and compromises. Britain now works on a much narrower margin of potential. Either changes will occur, in which case Upper England begins to fall, or changes will be postponed, thereby causing a decay that cannot be sustained and might later force changes more violent than would otherwise have happened.

The British Empire collapsed in a way that did not have immediately catastrophic effects on the heartland, yet the fact that its end was a dream safely enacted 'abroad' provided a hidden disaster: the old habits that had sustained its rise were not destroyed by its fall. What once worked well began to work badly. Strengths became enervating trivialities. Change was confronted with supercilious whimsy.

It is not just a matter of there being things wrong with Britain. All kinds of things are wrong with any country and you have to be patient about some of them: countries are not immediately perfectible, like works of art. Nor is it a matter of being cautious about unpredictabilities of change; Britain's immunity from the general demolition work of history has left it with styles and attitudes that we now *know* modern industrial liberal nations can do without. What can be most irritating about Britain is the importance still given to causes that now seem to be so trivial.

In the 'quality' press, in books, in general discussion, in political debate there are enough good ideas going around Britain to run a dozen countries. But what is the point of putting up policies when people won't really carry them out? It was wisely suggested by John Mander, in an article in the American *New Leader*, that when, on his way up to power, Mr Wilson was ticking off his shopping lists of reform, British electors both enjoyed the abrasive talk of dynamism, because they knew that this was now the vogue, and also felt comfortable with Mr Wilson, because they somehow felt they were safe – he wouldn't really carry out his reforms. In a society in which there is not sufficient determination to change things from what they were before, policies become mere matters of fashion. It is not policy that keeps Britain gummed up but the style that comes from its ingrained wisdom and from its concepts of how situations are best approached.

Given this, those policies are best that will change *style* – not by mere proclamation but by the enactment of drama or, in some cases, by simple destruction. The demonstration needed is that *new things can work*, that beyond the shadowy changes of fashion permanent change is possible; and that worthless old things can disappear without any damage to Britain as a liberal, democratic industrial nation. Merely dismantling antique ceremonies and abolishing old names could significantly change the look of Britain so that the Educated Moderns could feel that they belonged to their own country and followed their own styles. If that happened, the frustrated creative vigours of the nation could find channels that might relieve their frustration.

That the two-nation system was disastrous earlier on humane and liberal grounds did not guarantee its downfall; what will bring it down is that the future will not tolerate it. All kinds of approaches and beliefs that later seem absurd can be tolerated by a society so long as they still have apparent function and apparent meaning, but it becomes intolerable in a society that it should see itself as merely silly. Part of the disjunction of life in Britain now comes from the feeling that the nation is nothing much more than a bit of a giggle. Things are eroded by derision which might more healthily have been destroyed by definite action. The two-nation system now divides society on matters of mere whimsy. An enormous creative effort goes into the preservation of quaint, shabby frivolities and jokes that fall flat. Things will really change in Britain to the extent that the two-nation system disintegrates into a more diverse society, with a multiplicity of conflicting values and snobberies in which diverse groups of people can follow their diverse purposes with sustaining belief and the ability to support their diverse images of society and of social values.

This cannot happen merely by universal acclamation. When countries are run down it sometimes needs a considerable disaster to change them – a military conquest, a revolution, a union, a separation. Without shocks of some kind a run-down society may simply continue to run down until its decrepitude provides some catastrophe. Examples of the kind of shocks needed in Britain are easy enough to give – but it may be more profitable to guess at what is likely to happen. Some of it is already clear. In the society of the giggle, insisting that the Monarch continues to play an outmoded role does not preserve the old attitudes to the Monarchy; it turns the Monarch into a TV joke. Maintaining lordships, knighthoods, and so forth does not maintain old attitudes to the state: it prompts young people to see their flag as something they can sew into the backsides of their trousers. Continuing to respect hierarchy and antiquity when they are emptied of meaning leads to dressing up in old uniforms as a joke. Maintaining a Commonwealth when it will not work leads to an aggrieved, self-pitying, claustro-phobic revulsion against all sense of responsibility to the outside world. Keeping up the public school system means that children are still being trained as performing animals for a circus that has been shut down. In societies in which old things are losing their apparent function and mean-ing, it is inevitable that those who are aware of this should see the past as senseless. But in Britain derision itself becomes a form of nostalgia.

The people themselves may finally create new issues (such as Scottish nationalism) that to those who carry on the old wisdom may seem merely crackpot interruptions to the natural course of events. But if life, as traditionally projected, also seems absurd, everything may become folly. In such a state things will change, but perhaps disas-trously. Britain may now be too small to be a lion; but it is too big to be a pussycat. Part of Britain's problem is still to get a feeling of its real size.

God is an Englishman

Believing that just as God had once used Moses to reveal his purposes, he was now using England as his instrument of revelation, John Milton wrote: 'God is decreeing to begin some new and great period in His Church, even to the reforming of Reformation itself. What does He then but reveal Himself to His servants, and as His manner is, first to *His Englishmen*?' Preaching in St Margaret's Westminster to the Parliament of 1640, Cornelius Borges, recalling that he was preaching on the anniversary of Elizabeth's accession, said: 'Remember and consider that this very day ... eighty-two years sithence began a new resurrection of this Kingdom from the dead.' Matthew Parker, Elizabeth's Archbishop of Canterbury, had already said: '*When Almighty God is so much English as He is*, should we not requite His mercy with some earnesty to prefer His honour and true religion?' And John Aylmer, Elizabeth's Bishop of London, had proclaimed that it was God's wish that out of England's womb came John Wyclif, 'who begat Huss, who begat Luther, who begat the truth'. He then summarized his conclusions by saying that in His second birth, Christ had been born of England. In a final summary he became even more succinct, writing: 'God is English.' God was an Englishman and His nation was to be the New Jerusalem.

English conceit was born in the anxious but exhilarating nationalism of the founding of the English Church. It was by the act of founding its Church that England declared its uniqueness. It was not only that England broke off from the Papacy and the old concept of Christendom; it declared its independence from all Europe. It had become the kingdom God had chosen for his new purposes. The other Protestant national churches of Europe saw themselves as Lutheran, or Calvinist (as did the Church of Scotland): they belonged to something that was characteristic of other European countries. The Church of England was a thing in itself. God had chosen not the Church of Rome, or the Eastern Church, or the Lutheran or Calvinist faiths: he had chosen England. England was the only nation to produce a form of faith it shared with no one: alone in feeling both Catholic and Protestant, it was the nation of revelation.

The English attitude has, for four centuries, been a special form of vanity, both unique and revelatory, spreading from its justification in religion to a belief in the unique excellence of the English polity and then to the concept that it was England's responsibility, and England's alone, that the world should become a proper (which is to say an English) place to live, a place in which, because England was humanity's principal policeman and governess, what served England served humanity. Rewarded not for what they did but for what they were, it was the morality of the English that was said to be their final strength. If humanity suffered because England was temporarily in decline, then this was because the morality of England had declined.

In the imperial stage of English conceit, there developed a sense not only of uniqueness but of *bigness*. Although this had to be made a cosy kind of bigness to accommodate itself to the other vanities of smallness it nevertheless stretched the imagination of English vanity so that, despite its resilience, it was strained and part of it lost its tone and became floppy. It was not the moral *goodness* of England on which humanity was believed to rest, but its moral *greatness*; there developed a necessary relation between self-regard and power. In its foundation, English conceit rested on a vanity that did not require success to justify it. To begin with, England was satisfied with feeling superior: later it also required others to recognize its superiority.

It was the imperial equation between the conceit of the Upper English and the power of Great Britain that caused the present crisis in Upper England. Debauched by the habits of the imperial imagination, the self-importance of the élites as they now stand must remain frustrated. Power and influence of the old magnitude have gone and nothing will replace them. The English cannot play Greeks to the Romans; they are not going to inspire the Commonwealth; they are not even going to be the governess of New Zealand. They must now look to the Scottish and worry about maintaining the Union. The crisis of Upper England is that its prevailing expectations cannot be fulfilled, except in make-believe, but its élites cannot yet contemplate other kinds of roles because of the basically false conjunction in the Upper English imagination between success and morality. There is no consolation for this fallen pride, except the destruction of pride itself, or, more realistically, its mutation into new aspirations which would admit some sense of fulfilment.

If the Upper English want to go on being superior, if the mere *feeling* of superiority does not satisfy them, they must find new aspirations that have a chance of coming off. If they had wished to be morally superior to America they could have made realistic plans for racial integration in Britain. If they had wished to be superior in the arts and the intellect all they had to do was to write better, paint better, and think better than other people. If they had wished to be better than the Japanese in growth in world trade, they could have pinched some ideas from the Japanese and improved on them. If they had wished to appear morally superior to continental Europe they could have given Europe a lead by being the country that was best at providing economic assistance to the poor nations. As it is, of the European colonial powers, Britain has been the *least* generous in economic assistance: on a per capita G.N.P. basis its spending ranks only sixth, after the colonial powers of France, Portugal, Belgium, and the Netherlands, and after non-colonial Switzerland as well. How greatly are the role-players of London interested in the world they have argued about so much except to plunder it for symbols of their own importance? Yet the world does not owe Britain a feeling of self-importance. If it wants to demonstrate its excellence, there are many fields in which nothing now stops Upper England from displaying its talents except the slowness of its own creative energies or its inhibition of the creative energies of others.

Even if English vanity is to remain, if it is to be more than an expression of nostalgia or resentment, it must at least be cleared of its imperial extensions, the craving for influence without earning it, and the need to justify vanity by power. Otherwise the habits of imperial self-importance are likely to live on, without Empire and without importance, as an unsatisfied expectation, taking increasingly enervating forms. In this process it is not enough merely to say 'We haven't got an Empire now' and it is not enough – in fact it is repressive and illusory – to suggest that the Empire did not matter much. Imperialism cannot simply be dismissed as a quaint kind of habit that Britain once engaged in for a few years and that wasn't really very important: it must be acknowledged as a force of great corruption within British life, the effects of which continue in new forms. These effects may not be removed until there is an honest recognition of the guilt of Britain's history. Only this might set English conceit free for new action. To deny this is to suggest that the present state of Britain can be understood without examining its past. To believe that Britain can forget its history is to believe that Russians should not discuss the crimes of Stalin nor Germans the crimes of Nazism. There is not yet in Britain any institutional reminder of the guilts of Empire: the builders of the Empire are still the great men of the history texts, and monuments still stand to them in London – but where is the monument to the 'natives' out of whom they constructed their pride? For that matter, where is even the recognition that Scottish, Welsh, and Irish history are part of the history of Great Britain?

There is a need for a re-writing of history, for a purging of some guilt by its contemplation. But English conceit is so much part of British history that it seems more likely that at best it could only be purified, not destroyed. Not only because a nation, like an individual, is likely to fall to bits if its only attitude to itself is one of contempt; and not only because English conceit may be indestructible; but also because there is so much in their history in which the British can still take pride – if they are prepared to be satisfied with goodness rather than uniqueness, with excellence rather than superiority.

A new history and a new rhetoric

Even when a general history of a nation is more or less accurate in its facts, the arrangement of those facts tends to tell lies. Faced with the meaninglessness of unrelated details, a general historian fits them into a narrative that seems to lead up to the point of an imagined present which is imagined not only by concern for those recent events that make it up but also by theories, or hopes, or despairs about the future. When there is a change in the nature of an imagined present – because theories, hopes, or despairs about the future are changing – a history may have to be re-written: the pattern it has given to the past now seems wrong; the old history no longer leads up to an imagined present.

Until recently, British history was that of a rising nation. It was usually patterned into a sense of inevitable progress, particularly in the development of political and social institutions and of British world power. This kind of history now usually phuts out in the 1940s. Attlee's falsely promoted 'Welfare State' becomes the last development in domestic politics and Churchill's earlier Battle of Britain the last development in foreign politics, although some turn the disbandment of Empire into an aspiration for a new kind of world influence. Images of the future cease to sustain the old pattern of history. There seems no future that could be an extension of the story so far. At the same time general historians do not seem inclined to re-write British history as a story of decline, although they could do so. British general history now simply stands still. The curve rises. There is a disconnexion. Then ahead there stretches an infinite dotted straight line.

It is one of the main tasks of British intellectuals to provide their countrymen with a new sense of history – both more accurate, in that where the old boasts are fake they should be eradicated, and more relevant, in that it should show whatever connexion it can with Britain's imaginable future.

If we are to destroy the false sense of the historic uniqueness of the English within the British Isles, such a national history should begin broadly and diffusely, giving equal weight to the various kingdoms and principalities set up from one period to the next in the British Isles, so that what was going on in what later became Ireland, Scotland, and Wales can seem of an importance equal to what was going on in what was later to become England.

To destroy a false sense of uniqueness and a false sense

of continuity, when we approach the feudal period in the British Isles we should see those councils that were the formal nexus in the king's struggles with his great men as merely an example of a type of institution that was also associated with feudalism in other parts of Europe, just as the primitive and brutal institutions of justice should be seen as part of Europe's brutality. These institutions were not necessarily going to lead anywhere. If a time-machine could throw a man with modern political concepts back into the feudal period he would not find that England was advancing towards a future of liberal and democratic forms in a way that distinguished it from other kingdoms.

Even in recognizing that at least in the post-feudal period of absolutism the Puritan revolution started something, there is modesty to be gained in looking at some other parts of Europe as well. There should be particular study of the history of Holland – of the foundation of the Dutch Republic in the sixteenth century, and of Holland's golden age in the seventeenth century. But there is not only the sense of shared experience to learn from this: there are also puzzles shared with the oligarchic period of English liberty. Whose liberty was it? What was it liberty to do? Is a system of privileged liberty freedom? Can freedom destroy liberty?

In a new history there should be less concern with Saxon kings or Norman councils and a greater sense of significance in the true rise of England, which lay in the nationalism that developed during the Reformation and turned a client state of Spain, with a population of three million or so, into a nation of which it was possible to believe that God was its principal national. It is from this point onwards that England assumes a special significance in the history of the British Isles. What happened before then might be dismissed in a couple of general chapters, hopping from one area of the islands to another with a care to give no false emphasis. But Chapter Three should be headed 'The Rise of England'. It was at this time that England developed its sense of itself as the elect nation.

English conceit has not yet been seriously studied by English intellectuals. But if it is recognized that the history of modern Britain begins with the birth of English conceit, much of the rest of British history must be concerned with a study of that conceit – the beginning of global arrogance in the eighteenth century, and the high moralism of the new industrial and financial power and the new imperial power in the nineteenth century, with the oppressive aftermath of the long make-believe of the twentieth century. As part of this the rise and fall of the British Empire should be presented without humbug, but with balance. There might be some congratulations, for instance, on the greater tolerance shown by the British in India, where they allowed a considerable Indianization of the Indian Civil Service and a considerable, if restricted, political life. Compared with the conduct of the French in Indo-China and the Dutch in the East Indies this British approach now appears liberal. But against it should be set the greater racial bigotry towards the 'natives' shown by the British compared with the French and the Dutch.

The insular forms of conceit should also be studied historically – the belief in the superior and antique nature of English political institutions, the contempt for the fringe lands and the provinces. It might be instructive to give the better part of a chapter to the long brutal relationship with Ireland, which manifested a cruelty in the English élites that preceded the corruptions of later Empire but did not diminish with them. It would be inevitable in dealing with the arrogance of Upper Englishmen in the British Isles that Southern England would be given some of the role that British historians gave to Prussia in the manufacture of modern Germany, although 'Prussian dominance' was not so great in Germany as Upper English dominance in Britain. Nor was the power of London similar to that of metropolitanism in France. Paris spoke in the name of Paris or of France: London brought to itself the arrogance of speaking not in its own name, nor that of Britain, but of England, only a part of Britain. In such an approach to British history it would be necessary to speculate about how 'English' the forms of British power were, and how much they were provincial. How 'English' was the industrial revolution? What elements other than Englishry were there in the Empire? To what extent did Upper England, although growing rich on the industrial revolution, inhibit it? Or was Upper England in its modern form something thrown up by the industrial revolution?

The two-nation system may be a more modern invention than it looks, perhaps stronger and now more pervasive in its silliness than at any earlier time. The oligarchic pride and sense of adventure of the eighteenth century and the sense of experiment and the multiple clashes between many social classes in the nineteenth century contrast so strongly with the muffled tone of twentieth century British society that the latter society may not simply have evolved from the former: some of its characteristics may be due to a critical discontinuity. The tone of twentieth century Upper England is almost that of a *mutant* society. Does British history really belong to these people? Or are they impostors? Is the real task to return Britain's history to its true heirs?

A critical examination of the very bases of British power in the world and Upper English power in Britain is directly relevant to Britain's imaginable future; it could destroy the enervating contemplation of decline. It is true that in the future it is unimaginable that Britain or England can enjoy power of the kind it has exercised in the past. But if that power is revealed as the product not of unique excellence but of more humdrum matters – greed, force, accident, vanity, and so forth – the imaginable future need no longer seem disappointing when compared with the past. If the past is relieved of the grotesque belief that success came from virtue and virtue from success, the period of imperial magnificence can be seen merely as a construction thrown up by a special period of history, a construction that was bound to collapse because its size exceeded Britain's ability to sustain it when Britain's bluff was called. One also hopes that such a history would reveal sufficient that was bad in the British world role for some sense of responsibility to the world to remain, and sufficient that was good for a sense of responsibility to be sustained by a practical sense of confidence.

A reduced Britain cannot, as happened with a fallen Spain, simply wrap itself up in its pride. English conceit is less self-sustaining than Spanish pride: it requires more external demonstrations of affection. And as an advanced industrial power Britain is still too caught up in the world for a full retreat to be physically possible, without such a disturbance to its equanimity that the effects of retreat would push it out into the world again. As a materialist society it cannot, like fallen Spain, be too proud to feel poor and, in any case, as a major power of the second order, Great Britain is too big to squeeze back into Little England. But there is still enough to be found in British history to sustain self-belief and to see a relevance of the past to the future. What is wrong with Upper England's sense of the past is not that it seeks sustenance for the future from tradition but that it seeks escape from the future in tradition – much of it false tradition. The impostors of the mutant society became not traditionalists but dealers in fake antiques.

To hold up the glass of British history as a reflection of Britain's future produces some of that sense of reassurance with which this book began, but without its ironies. I shall now speak optimistically, without qualifications, and therefore not so much rationally as rhetorically. In speaking of Britain's future there is no certainty that things will go well or that they will go badly, since Britain is not a divine but a human institution. (I am assuming that God is *not* an Englishman.) Optimism is as likely to be as good a guide in guessing about the future as pessimism.

The optimism of many of its élites was for so long a characteristic of Britain that it provides the prototype of the restless modern nation. If there is to be a search in British history for something that approaches uniqueness it can be found in the convulsions of the agrarian revolution and the industrial revolution that, starting in Britain, still transform the world. But the optimism of Britain is to be found even before this decisive break in continuity: its impulses can be traced back two centuries before, pushing vulgarly against old things and knocking them down.

However, if British history were to be written as an account of British optimism, instead of as an account of the rise of British world power, a conjunction between the two might be shown to have been temporarily disastrous to one of them. The melancholy of Empire seemed to subdue the optimism of industrialism: the imperial necessity to believe in stability frustrated the industrialist necessity to believe in change. A system of indoctrination that was developed to create imperialists also drenched the innovators: a society that was becoming parvenu suddenly developed a protective fustiness. Yet the sense of optimism, even if restricted in application, still sought expression. If optimism, as something more serious than ebullient looniness, is the ability to concentrate on the good things that are possible and not to be unnerved by the possibly bad, it accounts for the apparently insane agreement among the British that they would continue the war after Dunkirk. I produce such a platitudinous example because its very platitudinous character – the way they go on about it, over and over again – gives it significance. It was not an expression of arrogance, but of optimism, which is to say that it came from a narrow interest in continuing to explore the possibility of success, a kind of concentration on a task. The sense of British history reasserted itself.

At times in the nineteenth century it was not at all obvious that imperialism was going to win, and thereby create a new sense of the antique and stiffen what was until then a decline in the sense of hierarchy. It sometimes seemed equally obvious that native democratic radicalism would win. It was a bluff type of radicalism, 'typically British', in the now discarded sense of Britain as John Bull. This native radicalism was determined to clear away some of the litter of humbug in human relations, prepared to be more open and direct, even a bit disorderly. It was almost an expression in democratic terms of the straightforward outspokenness of the eighteenth century oligarchs. Really the expression of the desire to extend the benefits of commonsense to the ordinary people of Britain, native radicalism may have had more to do with British history than the subsequent whimsy.

Even George Orwell repeated that dreary self-congratulation on stupidity that marks one of the normal and most misleading methods of trying to distinguish Britain from continental Europe. He spoke of the 'lack of philosophical faculty, the absence in nearly all Englishmen of any need for an ordered system of thought or even for the use of logic'. This is an example of how part of a national rhetoric can be the exact opposite of the truth. For while it is true that in the intuitive arts the British have contributed less than their share to European civilization, it has been in those speculative arts that try to give order to events that they have contributed so much. Britain, one of the very sources of the modern sciences and of philosophic speculation, might even be considered as the greatest single initiator of distinctively modern thought. Newton laid the foundations of physics; Harvey laid the foundations of physiology; Darwin laid the foundations of biology; Adam Smith laid the foundations of economics; Hume and other British philosophers laid the foundations of both positivism in science and scepticism in philosophy; and Locke, Mill, and others laid the foundations of what we think of as liberalism. If you put together physics, biology, physiology, economics, positivism, scepticism, and liberalism you have described a large part of what is distinctively 'modern' in world thought. The fields of speculation begun by these great British thinkers are still strenuously alive in Britain. In fact one of the clearest examples of continuity in modern British history has been the strong intellectual impulse towards ordered speculation and inventiveness. And although the companion of this impulse – a high degree of serious intellectual concern on the part of writers with the nature of society – is at present in decline, for most of modern British history their influence has been strong.

At a certain level this vigorous and illuminating intellectual tradition is part of what is meant by the 'Anglo-Saxon' element in European civilization. The Upper English may prefer to believe that one day Newton sat under an apple tree and capriciously established modern physics: but Newton devoted a lifetime to ordered and strenuous speculation about the nature of material things. It has been a concern with the *material* – with what *is* – that has marked the Anglo-Saxon, even in his scepticism. And while his 'empiricism', from Bacon onwards, was sometimes over-philosophized so that it became unreal, it has been the seeking for systems that has nevertheless marked Anglo-Saxon speculation, as it has marked other kinds of European speculation. Where, as in logic, the systems finally could not be found, it was not accepted arbitrarily but because the desire to systematize had been pursued so vigorously and honestly that its failure could be convincingly established: only those who have hunted for certainty have the right to claim it does not exist. Anglo-Saxon scepticism provided a shield against the continental habit of developing systems out of the head and imposing them on reality: but this does not mean that Anglo-Saxon thinking was not itself searching for systems, merely that it was more honest about it. And where the search failed Anglo-Saxon optimism was usually ready to make what it could out of the mess.

It is partly in the hard-headed Anglo-Saxonness of their history that the British can still contemplate a meaningful future, if their élites can overcome the envies and boredom that come from the necessity of sharing this history with America and the rest of Europe Overseas. Innovation, optimism, native radicalism, intellectual modernity, scepticism, liberalism – these are among the characteristics of modern British history that originally most distinguished it from most of continental Europe. As a hierarchic and antique society Britain was a fraud. It was one of the first of the parvenu societies, but from its own dislocation it created a mutant pseudo-aristocratic system. It developed a new strain that seemed strong in an environment of imperialism but that, in a changed environment, is now a variant that circumstances must make extinct. British 'commonsense' was not a pseudo-aristocratic and whimsical refusal to think straight: it was a straightforward attempt to sort things out.

These are the forces in British history that seem most relevant to an imaginable future. Apart from native radicalism – which has been almost starved to death – these forces still exist vigorously in Britain. But they exist in exile within their own society. The grotesque shapes of the impostors still cast dominating shadows. If the shadows could be cast away the conceit of England would still be there, arrogant, sometimes apprehensive, sometimes absurd, but it need no longer be expressed in the nostalgic vanities of Empire and antiquity: it could be expressed in the determination to make British society a light to the world; if the old spirit of showing off did not altogether die, Britain, so far as its strength allowed, could return to some of that globalism that has been a central part of its imagination since the English took seriously the idea that their new Church was Christ reborn.

A new rhetoric could take from British history what was relevant to the future, providing a framework of belief to prompt new action. But such a rhetoric would be as illusory as all the other failed slogans if it came from the mouths of the present performers. All that can be expected of those who are now prominent performers in British life is that they might be prompted to dismantle, bit by bit, and not always for reasons they understand, the accumulated rubbish that was not blown away by disaster. By this means social value could be given again to those creative continuities in British history that are relevant to its future.

If the spirit of native radicalism does not recover from its present emaciation this is not likely to happen. It is this spirit that is the only alternative to disaster as the true remover of the rubbish of history. And if it does recover its vigour it may sometimes take weird shapes, growing outside existing social institutions, of necessity threatening some of them, and taking up what might appear to be strange causes. But the causes it will take up are old enough: it is simply that they were frustrated some decades ago. They are part of the very substance of British history and it will not be until the unfinished business that they represent is settled that British history will be returned into the possession of its rightful heirs.

INDEX

*Some more Australian Penguins
are described on the
following pages*

The Lucky Country

Donald Horne

Not before time, a book that honestly analyses
Australia today, both in her home life and in
her relations with other countries. Donald
Horne's provocative discussion of old attitudes and
new responsibilities is conducted with an open
mind; the findings may be startling, but the
thought is constructive. Australia in the sixties is
indeed a lucky country, but she may not stay that
way unless she takes stock of her institutions
and policies, and examines her attitudes to politics,
business, the arts, the cities and the country.
Donald Horne's book does just this; moreover, it
does it with wit and style.

'*The Lucky Country* will stir up more saloon-bar
argument than any other book in a decade. . . . It
reveals a new and unexpected Donald Horne,
mellow, studiously aware of his own prejudices,
and with a deadly eye for the faults and foibles of
the Australian way of life . . . a full-scale
Dobellian national portrait' – Max Harris in the
Australian

Three Cheers for the Paraclete

Thomas Keneally

'Keneally's novel about a doubting priest is rich in unexpected visions and sudden epiphanies. He writes like an angel.'
New York Times Book Review

'The writing gleams with quiet, graceful clarity. The characterizations are memorable – and critical. An admirably sustained novel.' *Book Week*

'His book is infused with a pawky clerical awareness that human life, though sometimes capable of holiness, is often merely funny.' *Time*

'I've read it with great pleasure. I found it very funny indeed: the rather awful comedy inherent in a priest's life, especially a post-conciliar priest's life.'
Graham Greene

The Solid Mandala

Patrick White

This is the story of two people living one life. Arthur and Waldo Brown were born twins and destined never to grow away from each other.

They spent their childhood together. Their youth together. Middle-age together. Retirement together. They even shared the same girl.

They shared everything – except their view of things.

Waldo, with his intelligence, saw everything and understood little. Arthur was the fool who didn't bother to look. He understood.

Riders in the Chariot

Patrick White

In *The Tree of Man* Patrick White re-created the Garden of Eden in Australia: *Riders in the Chariot*, his story of four outcast mystics, powerfully re-enacts the story of the crucifixion in a like setting.

'Stands out among contemporary novels like a cathedral surrounded by booths. Its form, its impulse and its dedication to what is eternal all excite a comparison with religious architecture. Mr White's characters . . . have the symbolism of statues and spires' – Maurice Edelman in the *Sunday Times*

'He seems to me an unmistakably major writer who commands a scope, power and sheer technical skill which put even our more ambitious novelists in the shade' – A. Alvarez in the *New Statesman*

'This is a book which really defies review: for its analysable qualities are overwhelmed by those imponderables which make a work "great" in the untouchable sense. It must be read because, like Everest, "it is there"' – Jeremy Brooks in the *Guardian*

Also available

The Aunt's Story

Not for sale in the U.S.A. or Canada

Voss

Patrick White

The plot of this novel is of epic simplicity: in 1845 Voss
sets out with a small band to cross the Australian
continent for the first time. The tragic story of their
terrible journey and its inevitable end is told with
imaginative understanding.
The figure of Voss takes on superhuman proportions,
until he appears to those around him as both deliverer and
destroyer. His relationship with Laura Trevelyan is the
central personal theme of the story.
The true record of Ludwig Leichhardt, who died in the
Australian desert in 1848, suggested Voss to the author.

'. . . by far the most impressive new novel I have read
this year' – Walter Allen in the *New Statesman*

'A work of genius . . . Voss has an epic quality, the ageless
sense of the power and pride of man battling with his
condition' – John Davenport in the *Observer*

The Tree of Man

Patrick White

This great novel could eventually claim to stand as the
Australian Book of Genesis. The young man at the turn
of the century, takes a wife and carves out a home
in the wilderness near one of the growing cities of
Australia. Stan Parker becomes a small farmer: he accepts
life as he finds it. To him Amy bears children and time
brings a procession of ordinary events – achievements,
disappointments, sorrows, dreams.

'Something of the pathos, the enormous panoramic
dignity and compassion we find in Tolstoy' – Peter Green
in the *Daily Telegraph*

'A greatly simple novel that stands out above most
contemporary fiction with the fine, clean lines of a beech
against scrub' – John Davenport in the *Observer*

Not for sale in the U.S.A. or Canada